Storytelling in the M

Exploring a Contemporary Verbal Art

STORYTELLING IN THE MOMENT

EXPLORING A CONTEMPORARY VERBAL ART IN BRITAIN AND IRELAND

৩০০৪

MICHAEL HOWES

ACADEMIA PRESS

© Academia Press
Eekhout 2
9000 Gent
T. (+32) (0)9 233 80 88   F. (+32) (0)9 233 14 09
info@academiapress.be   www.academiapress.be

The publications of Academia Press are distributed by:

UPNE, Lebanon, New Hampshire, USA (www.upne.com)

Michael Howes
Storytelling in the Moment – Exploring a Contemporary Verbal Art in Britain and Ireland

Gent, Academia Press, 2014, xviii + 169 pp.

ISBN 978 90 382 2199 1
D/2014/4804/4
U2063

Layout: proxessmaes.be

Cover: Studio Eyal & Myrthe

For my Lover

Contents

ഇറെ

FOREWORD

ℰℭ

T his is a joy and very likely unique. Apart from some magnificent ethno-graphically-based works like those in the new World Oral Literature series, almost all accounts of stories and story-telling are either works of high theory, ethnically blind accounts, text-only focused or glimpses from some remote height. This is different. The author can truly claim to have been there, done that – and it shows.

It is beautifully written too, with none of the high jargon apparently de rigueur in much contemporary academic work or the PhD-focused, reference-obsessed obscurity only too often found today. Like the stories Mike Howes so engagingly presents, this is for everyone. And without his close and meticulous description, who would have believed that, not in some far-off forest or in the recesses of bygone ages, but here and now, here in the Britain and Ireland of today, the rich creativity of story and story-telling would be flourishing in full glory. This is a book all should read.

Ruth Finnegan
Visiting Emeritus Professor
Faculty of Social Sciences
The Open University

PREFACE
JOURNEY PLANNING

ഗൗ

Our journey begins, as many journeys do, with a chance encounter. A print flyer for a performance of traditional storytelling catches our attention at London's Barbican Centre studio theatre. What can this be? The tumultuous development of Britain's performing arts in recent decades is very familiar to us, but this is something wholly unfamiliar, an elemental and ancient art form flourishing in our digital age but largely hidden from wider public awareness. 27 October 2006: Daniel Morden stands before us on a bare stage to tell us traditional Welsh Roma stories, Oliver Wilson-Dickson on fiddle evokes the inner demon in us all, staging is by the Crick Crack Club.

An internet search at the latter's website reveals more and includes a list of recommended books and essays. Further searches using key words 'storytelling' and 'anthropology' signpost a profusion of leads: anthologies, anthropologies, human communication, cultural history, ethnography, ethnopoetics, essays, practical guides, linguistics, literacy, mythtellers, narrative forms, orality, politics, revivals, sources, theology. From here the search becomes hopelessly diffuse. Yet strangely there is nothing to be found about the practices of today's storytelling, its wider applications in our society, its component parts and how they are connected. There is nothing on the human story of storytelling as a creative enterprise, here, now, in the moment.

Never one to resist a challenge that catches my attention, I sign up for a Beginners Storytelling Workshop led by performance storyteller Ben Haggarty, two days of practical exercises to develop compositional and performance techniques. Attendance at further storytelling events follow at the Barbican Centre, then at a children's storytelling festival, a children's literary festival and a site-specific performance in deepest rural England. A chance meeting with a director of the Society for Storytelling leads to my own membership, and in turn, to still broader vistas: specialist storytelling in schools, the social sciences, organisations, the criminal justice system, for environmental awareness, at museums, galleries, visitor attractions and increasingly the subject of academic conferences and research degrees. It seems that storytelling clubs abound nationwide and attendance at some of their monthly meetings reveals a rich human geography. Advance notices of storytelling festivals in almost every region of Britain and Ireland start arriving in my inbox so plans are laid to be there whenever and wherever possible.

I start to strike up conversations with almost any and every storyteller I meet. What drives them? What is storymaking? What role does storytelling play in society? How come so few people have heard of storytelling? What are its recent precursors? By and large the storytellers I meet warm to the idea of a wide-ranging, grassroots study of contemporary oral storytelling. Most offer their enthusiastic support. Others however introduce a note of caution, as one said, 'It would be like a study of, say, singing, it's a whole world of human experience. It can't all be encapsulated.' Sometimes if I dropped the word 'anthropology' into the conversation a certain chill would ruffle the surface of these conversations. But at least these sincere reservations were expressed with the greatest good humour.

> April 2007, Beyond the Border International Storytelling Festival in Leeds and I am interrogating anyone who can spare me a few minutes – audience members, performers, front-of-house staff, management, anyone. In backrooms questions are being asked. 'Who is this guy with note book and intrusive questioning?' 'Oh', says one storyteller I'd met earlier, 'some sort of anthropologist wants to investigate us.' Morning brings us a morality tale, The Kingfisher and the Otter, for a family audience, told by a Native American storyteller. What's going on? There's a human on the river bank with a notebook and pen. 'Who's he?' asks Otter. Kingfisher looks up, 'Oh him, an anthropologist come to investigate us.' There's sniggering in the audience. 'And nobody likes anthropologists do they?' cries the storyteller. The children roar their agreement. Suddenly, it seems, my shoe laces call for urgent attention.

But these gentle warnings were rare and storytellers' encouragement mostly heartening. By early summer there were 53 entries in my diary/log of storytelling-related events – an enchanted and capricious spring indeed.

Research planning

These rather headlong experiences had brought me to a fork in the path, and to a dilemma. I had reached retirement age that January, and after an exacting and varied working life of over forty five years, retirement beckoned and the pursuit of more familiar interests and aspirations presented an inviting prospect. Yet, and yet, the lure of the unknown and of other-worldliness is a wicked temptress and an immersive exploration of this little-known world was hard to resist. Then again, if this was the path to be taken, it would have to be trodden surefootedly, well-grounded on professional experience.

My credentials for undertaking such a study lie far from academe and are centred on extended, parallel careers as a documentary filmmaker and screenmedia consultant. The fifty-or-so productions that carry my personal credits as writer, director and/or producer have brought experience of hands-on creative practices and processes that are also familiar to storytellers. The music, arts and the humanities programmes I have made for broadcast television have required insights into a broad range of performance, staging and presentational skills which lie close to storytellers' core competences. Many specialist forms of oral storytelling and storymaking share similar platforms with my own productions in support of the public service, education, vocational skills training, charity campaigns, organisational communications, healthcare and welfare. My science and technology films have called for a familiarity with the methodologies of both the physical and the social sciences. Commissions for the thirty-or-so screenmedia consulting projects on which I have been engaged have brought insights into how the media of film and television are developed in support of the public service and how they apply in very diverse cultures across four continents. Of particular value to the conduct of this study has been insights into the way that national broadcasters, international agencies and worldwide governments interact and engage with emergent creative and cultural phenomena in a highly politicised world.

For the progress of these twin careers I should acknowledge my deep gratitude to the late G. 'Buck' Buckland-Smith, one of the last working members of the British Documentary Film Movement, an innovator of audio-visual aids in education, winner of three British Academy Awards and a pioneer of applying the mass media as essential tools for building civil society. His advice was widely sought by governments and international agencies in four continents. From the period I worked with him at British Films his quiet sagacity is evident everywhere on these pages. Three other brief vocations, as chartered surveyor, army officer and environmentalist, have also greatly informed Chapter Three and have added extra dimensions to other parts of this unconventional study. All these varied walks of life have called for exacting standards of research and analysis, collaborative practices with academics and professionals in a broad range of disciplines, and the leadership of large creative and/or professional teams at a strategic level of policy-making.

The music documentaries I made in the 1980s and 1990s were greatly inspired by *The Hidden Musicians: Music-making in an English town* by Ruth Finnegan,[1] at that time Professor of Comparative Social Institutions at the Open University and an authority on the anthropology of human communication and performance. Re-reading this again in 2007 it struck me that its approach and structure might provide a powerful research model on which to base a grassroots study of contemporary oral storytelling. This exhaustive study directs its empirically-based research methodology towards the working practices of local musicians, both amateur and professional, and the multifaceted social roles that music-making plays locally, and by inference, nationally. It reveals the hidden and often unacknowledged efforts of ordinary people and the important role they play in local music-making. It directly challenges many mass society theories, shows how ubiquitous music-making is in our society, how it is an intensely collaborative community-based activity, and it blows away many of the assumptions made in text- or theory-based monographs about how music-making is studied.

I renewed my acquaintance with Ruth in July 2007 and she immediately greeted with enthusiasm my proposals for a study of contemporary oral storytelling. A robust discussion followed on the ways and means of realising such a broadly-based work and before we parted she had made an overwhelmingly generous offer: to guide the development of a research plan, to mentor the research methodology employed for this study and to peer review draft manuscripts on a chapter-by-chapter basis – all informally and most definitely not as part of a research degree. Words cannot adequately describe the extent of my gratitude. Only her robust approach to subject matter, her infectious delight at the foibles of the human condition, her penetrating scrutiny of my shortcomings in theory and method and her enlightened counsel, have made the completion of this study possible at all. The challenge of pursuing a wide-ranging study of contemporary oral storytelling had become irresistible.

Research methods

As early as our first meeting Ruth had identified an obvious weakness in these plans: I am not a professional anthropologist. For this reason her advice was to 'play to your personal strengths' when adopting research methods, to structure the study as a personal journey through an unfamiliar human landscape, and to set the descriptions of storytelling phenomena in the widest possible social and cultural contexts.

In the first of many departures from academic convention the research methods adopted for this study are outlined here in the body of the text, rather than banished to some never-to-be-read appendix. There are several reasons for doing this. First, a number of practising storytellers who have generously peer-reviewed early draft chapters have thought I was expressing personal opinions in the text rather than the product of hard-won evidence and systematic analysis. Second, by outlining the methodology employed here in the Preface, I hope that any shortcomings in theory or method may be laid bare for all to see so that future researchers who carry out more focused studies may proceed more surefootedly to their own conclusions. Third, I am particularly fond of the introductory chapters of travelogues from the heroic age of exploration that describe the trials of expedition planning and thereby foretell of disasters yet to come – the thieving muleteers, the humiliating rituals before the river gods, the discovery of faint lettering on a decaying map that reads 'cannibals?' In this respect I quote my own godfather, Freddy Spencer Chapman who led an expedition to the Himalayas in the late 1930s.

> Earlier in this book, I quoted a remark of the great explorer Stefansson to the effect that the story of a successful expedition makes dull reading, because, if all goes according to plan, there should be no adventures to relate. If this is true, then our descent of Chomolhari would make an epic of incompetence, for one mishap followed hard upon another.[2]

Most evidence for this study has been drawn from extended face-to-face interviews of between one and four hours duration. This research method has been employed with 48 career storytellers, the leadership of 8 local storytelling groups, 4 festival directors, 3 academics, 3 PhD students of storytelling, 10 undergraduates of creative writing, 5 venue managers who host storytelling events, 6 representatives of public and membership organisations, 6 prominent figures in the performing arts and 2 professionals in the fields of branding and corporate sponsorship. All these interviews shared common lines of questioning, all contained questions relating to their own individual experience and all were conducted through linked 'open questions' that allow interviewees to talk freely, and at any length, about what is most important to them. By these means discussions ranged widely across subject matters relevant to oral storytelling and often explored ideas that had not previously occurred to me.

Brief face-to-face interviews of between five and ten minute's duration were used with 134 audience members at 13 widely varied storytelling events across Britain and Ireland. These interviews sought to answer 10 questions that were so structured as to elicit responses of only a few words each, although more detailed discussions often followed when time permitted. Significant numbers of these interviews could not be completed and/or responses not fully elucidated because of the challenging circumstances of the interviews themselves.

'Participant observation' as a research tool forms the foundation of much cultural anthropology and much social science for which the researcher becomes both active participant in the events studied and dispassionate observer and recorder of those events. The greatest strength of this research method lies in the opportunity for a researcher to share the subjective feelings of their co-participants. The greatest weaknesses lie in the risk of the researcher's presence adversely impacting on the events being studied and/or the risk of the researcher becoming so absorbed in the events studied that they lose objectivity in what they observe and record. Standard protocols have been developed to bring out the best qualities of this research method which I have employed to research public storytelling events, local storytelling groups, festivals, conferences and training workshops. Perhaps unconventionally I have included under this research method the retrospective participant observation of several of the documentary films and screen-media consultancies I have undertaken over the last three decades.

Several other standard research methods have also been employed. The internet has been particularly useful for monitoring the changing fortunes of storytelling groups and organisations over the four-year research period. It has also been useful for revealing inconsistencies between what storytellers say in interview, what they say in their websites and what is self-evident from their storytelling. A literature search has, as always, been as much value for what it does not reveal as for what it does reveal. Over 90 literary and other creative works have been consulted and evidence for this study is supported by over 80 direct quotations listed in the Notes and References. To gain insights into the full spectrum of communications media used by storytellers I asked three to keep diary/logs of all contacts they made in any medium over a three month period. Perhaps not surprisingly, this research method was abandoned when one diary/log was returned empty; a second was comprehensive but irrelevant because it covered the final three months of the storyteller's pregnancy; and the third, although detailed, could be mistaken for a rap libretto to an edgy atonal opera. And Chapter Seven takes the form of a thought-experiment, a common research method in many branches of the physical and social sciences.

In addition to these standard social science research methods this study has also looked beyond the closely focused methodology of academe, has cast its research net more broadly and called on evidence and methodologies more commonly found in multidisciplinary research and implementation projects. Anyone who makes documentary films for the public service will be familiar with the experience of embracing specialist evidence and methodology from at least five very varied professional and academic disciplines. A feasibility study I worked on for a multi-stage film production centre in Nigeria called on research evidence and methodology of about twenty varied professional disciplines, and this being Africa, all were heavily qualified by political considerations. In this respect, and to create a well-rounded profile of contemporary oral storytelling, it has been necessary to call on research evidence from some forty-five distinct professional and academic disciplines.

Another method commonly employed in real-world research and reporting projects is to engage the clients themselves – storytellers in this study – in every step of planning and realisation. By this means they become collaborative stakeholders in the eventual outcome of the project. So from my earliest conversations with storytellers I would ask them what topics they would like included in this study. If time permitted during interviews I would invite respondents, especially those with professional qualifications, to comment on the conduct of the interview itself (and highly pertinent many of their responses were). Copies of the research plan, synopses, early draft chapters and the completed manuscript have been widely distributed amongst storyteller practitioners and their comments, corrections and criticisms have been openly invited. I am particularly grateful to the following for their sustained support for this study: Dr Donald Smith, storyteller and Director of the Scottish Storytelling Centre; Dr Simon Heywood, storyteller, folklorist and lecturer on storytelling and creative writing at the University of Derby UK; Ben Haggarty, performance storyteller (called 'platform storyteller' in the USA) and Honorary Professor of Storytelling at UDK Berlin, Germany; and for his insights into American academia, Austin Quigley, Brander Mathews Professor of Dramatic Literature and Dean Emeritus, Columbia University, New York, USA.

Another research technique employed, now commonplace in anthropology, but still rare in other academic disciplines, is to embed descriptions of my own experiences as a researcher into the completed text. This, Ruth Finnegan assures me, 'definitely adds to the convincing effect and is in fact quite fashionable amongst researchers under the label of "reflexivity".' Finally on the subject of methodology, I know of no more reliable way of corroborating real-world evidence than by seeking a consistency of findings between all disciplines and all research methods.

Recurrent themes

Research has revealed many storytelling words and terms that carry widely varying definitions. (Many admonitory fingers have tapped kitchen tables for my apparent word-abuse.) There are also regional variations to the meanings of some storytelling words and phrases. Unsurprisingly, each storytelling specialisation tends to create its own vocabulary. And for these reasons peer reviews have sometimes been returned to me annotated with **<wrong word>** inserted in the text. This is no special pleading on my part but merely to mention that I have tried to use dictionary definitions wherever possible and otherwise have added some qualifying note to reduce ambiguity.

For example, there is little consensus on the precise meaning of the word 'storytelling', although in storytelling circles it refers exclusively to stories spoken from memory as a verbal art, with the word 'oral' sometimes added to reinforce this meaning. The term 'storymaking' was coined to describe a specialist tool in therapeutic practices, but now often refers to any form of reciprocal storytelling, as in 'story-swapping', and to any intensely active or creative participation by those involved. The term 'career storyteller' is used in this study to describe those who tell stories to paying and/or community audiences and those who use storytelling as a tool in their professional practices, for example, as teachers or social workers. The many and varied forms of specialised storytelling are here named collectively (and perhaps arbitrarily) as storytelling 'genres'. Definitions of the term 'performance storytelling' are diffuse but mainly refer to storytelling at public venues, often to paying audiences and principally as staged entertainment. This term is widely used synonymously with the term 'platform storytelling' as it is known in the USA and I have heard this latter term used also in Ireland. The term 'applied storytelling' also needs clarification. In the sense used in other of the performing arts, it refers to outreach activities in the community, as distinct from their core activity of staging public performances. The use of this term in the world of storytelling is confusing because there is little consensus as to what a core activity is and what an outreach activity is. The most common use of this term refers to storytelling genres practiced by social science professionals, teachers and those engaged in community storytelling, as distinct from performance storytelling, as defined above. I have struggled to find a collective word to describe what are generally called 'storytelling clubs' but which are seldom constituted as such, so I have settled on the generic term 'local storytelling groups' or 'local groups' in this study. Since this study casts its research net widely over several social sciences and several performing arts it is clear that some terms have slightly different meanings in different disciplines. And finally I use the dictionary definition of the term 'performing arts' (any art or creativity performed for an audience) whereas this term is often confused with 'performance art' (combines visual art with dramatic performance often with a reduced role for spoken text).

Still with word-use, many of those I have interviewed have described storytelling practices in terms of being part of a 'continuum' in the sense of a continuous sequence of elements on some conceptual scale of values. Research shows this to be an over-simplification of relationships between storytelling phenomena. For example, the words 'amateur' and 'professional' are virtually meaningless as a measure of effective storytelling. Attempts to create hierarchies of story types or storytelling genres tend to break down under closer scrutiny. The qualities that audience members appreciate most about storytelling events tend to be more diffuse than is assumed by many storytellers. No priority can be afforded to any particular organisational structure in the world of storytelling; each tends to adapt to its own stakeholders' needs, wishes and aspirations. And there is little evidence to suggest the storyteller's core skills can be arranged in order of priority along a scale of values. Instead I am suggesting the word 'mosaic', in both the pictorial and the ecological senses of the word, as a more fitting metaphor for the relationships between storytelling practices and phenomena.

Many of those I have interviewed are familiar with the concept of 'emergence'. This is not a subject I bring any degree of expertise in but is perhaps worth a brief mention here. It describes the processes in which many simple actions by, and interactions between, independent entities or agents, can display self-organising collective behaviours, properties and characteristics, without apparent external influence or centralised controlling stimuli. It is prevalent in nature, in living and non-living systems from ecology to crystallography. It is commonplace in all human society, culture, organisations, economics, even traffic jams and stock markets. The scholarship of the performing arts confirms that all live performances are to some degree an emergent process and the phenomenon is a primary driver of many functions, processes and practices of storytelling today. A good example in nature is flocking birds which appear to co-ordinate their motion and create complex manoeuvres when there is obviously no tree-top choreographer to direct them. And since they are by nature, er, bird-brained, individual birds cannot possibly be aware of their personal role in the collective movement of the flock as a whole. In a marvellous computer simulation of this effect Craig Reynolds has shown how his 'boids', as he calls them, self-organise into complex flocks when programmed with only three simple steering capabilities – well within the innate ability of all bird species. Best of all, in one run of the programme a boid collided with a virtual pole, fluttered randomly around the screen as if dazed, then darted forward to join its flock-mates as they wheeled by again.[3]

Network theory is another scientific discipline that has developed greatly over recent decades and has been found to bring insights into such diverse subjects as airline routes, economics, earthquakes, neurology, meeting people at parties, the food web, population movements and synchronized insect chirps. Again, I claim no expertise on this subject but have read widely around the work of theoretical biologists, witnessed the phenomenon in many of the screenmedia consulting projects I have been involved in, and for this study have referred extensively to Richard Koch and Greg Lockwood's *Superconnect: The Power of Networks and the Strength of Weak Links*.[4]

We are all familiar with the idea of hubs as individuals, groups, organisations and even governments that generate relationships and provide forums for inter-action. Network theorists also identify two different types of connecting link between hubs which can take the form of any combination of communications media – spoken dialogue, train journey, advertising slogan, Mayday distress signal or the worldwide web. 'Strong links' are identified as relationships we have with friends, family, work colleagues and organisations we are closely associated with; however, these links tend to be self-reinforcing and offer few or reduced oppor-tunities for developing the network as a whole. 'Weak links' are identified as rela-tionships we have with more casual acquaintances, yet paradoxically, they offer increased opportunities for developing the network as a whole.[5] These ideas are highly relevant to change, development and growth in oral storytelling because much evidence in this study shows how strong links tend to be more prevalent than weak links amongst individuals, communities and organisations. The generic term 'complex network interaction' is used throughout this study to refer to all these phenomena associated with network theory as they apply to oral sto-rytelling.

At the time of writing the Society for Storytelling has recently appointed an 'experienced web editor, digital strategist, journalist and writer, who believes the web can offer many more possibilities for the arts in general and the SfS in par-ticular'.[6] There has, however, been a tendency throughout the history of human communication media to attribute the greatest merit to the newly fashionable and currently pre-eminent medium of its age, often affording it a specious authority. Meanwhile, the continuing merits of traditional media are often overlooked, just as radio and television are now losing credibility to internet-based social network-ing media. What is notable from research evidence for this study is how almost every known medium of human communication is potentially available to indi-vidual storytellers – something that cannot be claimed for other performing arts. These include rhetorical skills created by the ancient Greeks, the printed word developed in the European renaissance, a personal theatre of the body that has evolved as a skill in personal presentation and stagecraft, and of course today's electronic media without which oral storytelling would remain an exclusively local phenomenon. From personal experience I have seen how screen media consulting projects can go horribly wrong when they fail to utilise the fullest spectrum of available media, in particular when they ignore traditional, more intuitive, modes of human communication. The most sublime example of this phenomenon came during one screenmedia consulting project I was engaged in during the early 1980s.

> In a pre-internet age I am working with colleagues from the Somali Film Agency in a hi-tech post-production facility in central London. A phone call brings family news to one technician from a remote region of the country. Knowing there is no telephone or postal service there I ask him how the news has travelled. 'In the usual way with us nomads, I don't know precisely', he replies with a straight face (many Somalis have a delightfully ironic sense of humour). He only knows he has passed a verbal message to several London-based acquaintances from his own Isaaq tribe. All of them will have passed the message on to several other Isaaq acquaintances. Sooner or later one of them will have been flying to Somalia where he will have passed the message to several more Isaaqs of their acquaintance. Of these, at least one will have been visiting his home village by bus and will have delivered the message, probably to his uncle. The family news will have then been returned by the same method, reaching the hi-tech post-production facility in central London by digital telephone.

Perhaps as many as thirty hubs connected mainly by weak links, utilising multiple word-of-mouth media, telephone, intercontinental flights, bus journeys and traditional ritual greetings, all transmitted with complete fidelity within a few weeks. There is more to complex network interaction than the worldwide web.

Scope and aims

The scope of this study is precisely described by one storyteller, PhD holder and published author on the subject in their peer review of early draft chapters: 'Your contents plan sounds wonderful! It is ambitious in scope but then this is the first time, as far as I am aware, that anyone has attempted such an overview so it has to be wide-ranging and suggestive of future lines of enquiry rather than exhaustively narrow. Your approach is also evocative at times and I can imagine that the academics may grumble a little!'

This study shifts the focus of many existing dissertations, monographs and other literary works away from history, theory, practical guides, politico-ideology, text-based studies and even the nature of stories themselves. Nor does it take a narrowly-focused monistic view of storytelling as seen through the disciplines of, say, folklore, anthropology, theatre studies, psychology or specifically as a tool for effecting behavioural change in society. It is however an empirically-based study that seeks to reflect on the pluralistic nature of contemporary oral storytelling, to share the personal experiences of the many, not just the elite few, and to seek out unfamiliar territories that other researchers have not so far explored. As planning progressed through the autumn it became clear that new knowledge should be created by directing research methodology mainly towards three particular aspects of this subject area: the practices – the doing and making – of storytelling by today's storytellers and other participants; the social roles that oral storytelling now plays in our society; and the complex network interactions that link all its component parts.

This form of more open, interactive research plan has brought other benefits: Evidence can be interrogated in alternative ways to answer questions that the research plan had not anticipated. Errors, omissions and observations can be corrected before they become embedded into the bigger structures of this study. Conjectural observations can be tested, sometimes to destruction, in a loquacious and critical environment, often in the moment of their realisation. And as the reviewer above says, wide-ranging research can suggest some wholly unexpected future lines of enquiry beyond the scope of the present study. But there are also penalties to be paid for such an open-ended research plan: I readily acknowledge that by extending the geographical scope of this study to include all of Britain and Ireland it now contains strong evidential biases towards my own home territory of London and southeast England. When methodology is pushed to its inherent limits then it is inevitable that statistical evidence will lose clarity to general approximations; this is unavoidable. Different research methodologies applied to different elements of a study tend to diminish the value of comparative observations. And for all these reasons, what had been planned as a three year study resulting in a 20,000 word text has inevitably become a five year study resulting in a 76,000 word text.

Mention was made in the opening paragraph above to the sometimes hidden qualities of oral storytelling and, just as Ruth Finnegan found with local music-making, two kinds of hiddenness can be identified in contemporary oral storytelling. First, it is commonplace for such community-based cultural movements to evade the attentions of a wider public, even though they are ubiquitous in our society. This situation is often compounded by the lack of systematic research in this form of micro-sociology. Second, many of the social and cultural attributes of oral storytelling are hidden even from participants themselves. This is not as paradoxical as it seems. Most of us take part in creative and cultural events for the value and enjoyment they bring to our own lives and/or bring to the lives of others. We remain unaware of the emergent properties, rituals, cultural norms and social roles we are playing in the event we are engaged with. The following chapters reveal numerous examples of how the attributes of storytelling events can pass unnoticed in the rich fabric of everyday life.

There is one aspect of this wide-ranging research plan that has given rise to an exhaustively narrow objective. Throughout the planning phase and during many of my early storyteller interviews three topics often arose spontaneously in our conversations. With some on-going refinements they became the three research questions posed by this study and which the final chapter attempts to answer.

> What are the principal drivers of change, development and growth in oral story-telling today?
>
> How is oral storytelling adding social value in our society?
>
> Can and/or should ways be found to raise public awareness and attract greater rec-ognition to oral storytelling?

By late 2007 an outline contents plan was emerging. By means of extended inter-views with a broad range of practicing storytellers Chapter One would yield evi-dence to answer the all-important question: Who are the storytellers? For Chap-ter Two large numbers of audience members would be interviewed at widely varied events in the hope of revealing what role they play as co-creators of a sto-rytelling. Divergent pathways taken in Chapter Three would explore the many ways the storytellers' art is applied in our society, as a tool in education, leader-ship, therapy, counselling, welfare, cultural awareness and as entertainment. Chapter Four would attempt to discover the beating heart of the oral storytelling movement by studying the informal groups, organisations and representative bodies that support and sustain oral storytelling today. From Edinburgh north, to Exeter south, Cambridge east and Dublin west, Chapter Five would join the celebration of oral storytelling at festivals, conferences and competitions to ana-lyse their organisational models, their practices and the roles they play in our wider society. Chapter Six would call on evidence from academic and profes-sional disciplines as varied as folklore, anthropology, human communication and performance disciplines to reveal the common values they share with the prac-tices of oral storytelling. By conducting a form of thought experiment Chapter Seven would hope to discover whether, for the storyteller, all the world really is a stage and all men and women merely players. Chapter Eight would take a lengthy detour through a landscape of diverse arts and other creative enterprises to reflect back and reveal extra dimensions and perspectives on the condition of storytelling today. And Chapter Nine would bring us homeward bound with evi-dence collected from all the preceding chapters in an attempt to answer this study's three research questions.

The first days of January 2008, the first storyteller interview is now less than a week away. There are now 83 entries in my diary/log of storytelling-related events. All would be researched, analysed and written into this manuscript over the coming months and years. Ruth Finnegan's early advice that this study should be conducted as a personal journey, a wide-ranging exploration of an unfamiliar human geography, has now been endorsed by other storyteller-social scientists. Personal accounts of epic journeys jostle on the threshold of the subconscious mind.

On a jagged path, high on the granite massive of California's Yosemite National Park, we come upon a young man alone with worn boots and dark unfocused eyes photographing himself beneath the drifting spray of a waterfall. 'How far have those boots come?' I ask. 'These? Dunno, five hundred miles, my second pair.' 'Where next?' I enquire. 'Every mountain chain in North America, 'bout eight thousand miles, twelve months, nine, ten pairs of boots.' I hesitate, but then venture, 'Have you discovered the secret of life yet?' 'Hope not, might have to stop hiking.' His eyelids droop for a moment. 'Sorry, gotta go; post office closes in an hour.' And he's gone. Just a wisp of dust hangs over an empty boot print.

Notes & References

1. Ruth Finnegan, *The Hidden Musicians: Music-making in an English Town* (Cambridge UK: Cambridge University Press, 1989).

2. F. Spencer Chapman, *Memoirs of a Mountaineer* (London UK: The Reprint Society, 1940), pp. 158-159).

3. Boids: visit www.red3d.com/cwr/boids for a demonstration and update on this topic.

4. Richard Koch and Greg Lockwood, *Superconnect: The Power of Networks and the Strength of Weak Links* (London UK: Little Brown, 2010).

5. For an ingenious table-top experiment involving buttons and string that demonstrates this phenomenon, see John Gribbin, *Deep Simplicity: Chaos, Complexity and the Emergence of Life* (London UK: Penguin Books, 2004), pp. 163-165.

6. 'Greetings From the Board', *Storylines*, Society for Storytelling UK, Summer 2011, p. 3.

ONE

TRAVELLING COMPANIONS

෨෬

January 2008: Planning and preparation are complete, the journey begun; it is time to meet the storytellers, our constant travelling companions throughout the progress of this study. Through extended open-question interviews with 48 eight storytellers and attendance at many of their public tellings, this chapter endeavours to answer the question: Who are the storytellers?

Those approached for interview were selected mainly for the diversity of their formative experience, the spread of their storytelling-related activities and their geographical and cultural diversity. Almost all were interviewed individually, two were interviewed together; however, interviewing four simultaneously is not an experience I would wish to repeat or recommend to others. Most are career storytellers, a term used in this study to include those who tell to paying and/or community audiences or who use storytelling as a tool of their professional practices, for example as teachers, therapists or social workers. All of those interviewed are over twenty five, in equal proportion women and men, although this compares with a proportion of about two-thirds women and one-third men amongst today's adult career storytellers.

Their age profile more or less matches that of all storytellers and their audiences, with 3 in their twenties, 9 in their thirties, 15 in their forties, 15 in their fifties, 5 in their sixties and 1 in their seventies. 16 are based in London, 23 are scattered widely across the English regions, 6 in Wales, 2 in Scotland and 1 in Ireland, and while this geographical bias towards London and south east England is evident in many of the observations and reflections made in this study, most storytellers work throughout Britain and Ireland and some internationally. They represent the widest possible range of specialist storytelling disciplines which are referred to throughout this study as genres. They represent very varied levels of experience and competence, and to bring an outsider's view of storytelling, they include one who describes themselves as a performance poet and another as a dramatherapist. Two are British minority ethnic and one mixed race, and two, following a cultural tradition that predates the Homeric epics, are blind.

Nearly all those approached for interview gladly agreed, many embracing this project more as willing participants than as interviewees. One refused outright for reasons unconnected directly with this study. One was hostile to such a study, saying, 'I want to be my own voice, not someone else's.' And two raised very interesting objections before agreeing to meet me which proved most helpful in shaping all future interviews.

> Hi Mike. I'd be interested to meet when I have some spare time, though partially because I feel a little wary of the work you are doing. [...] Your message gives me the impression that you seem to want to intellectualise, sanitise and organise a folk art. I'm not sure that folk arts should be forced upwards and publicised in the method that popular art is. Why do we need to analyse whether it's delivering public good? It's not an NHS Hospital. It's art! [...] Much respect and curiosity, [signed]

> Dear Mike. I'm always wary of this sort of conversation – when I talk about storytelling to academics I feel like a tightrope walker who makes the mistake of looking down! Plus, I don't know that I have anything particularly insightful to say. But for what it's worth, if you're in the area we could chat. [...] [Signed].

All these interviews have been a delight to conduct and it is of great regret that the agreed terms make all quotations unattributable and preclude individual acknowledgements and my sincere thanks on these pages. All the lines of questioning followed a more or less similar form but were adapted for the specialised practices and experience of individual tellers. Some came to interview with very clear ideas of what they wanted me to know and it was often difficult to bring them back into Earth orbit, as it were, in one case only after an unstoppable seventy two minutes. Several, in their habitual role as lords of misrule, subverted all reasoned methodology and managed to turn their interviews into some sort of joshing session. Oh, and one insisted on referring to me as 'loathsome anthropologist' and himself as 'loveable storyteller'; although I must have acquitted myself satisfactorily because on my departure I was granted a little manly hug. So, setting on one side these early rites of passage this chapter proceeds to explore our storytellers' formative experiences.

The making of a storyteller

Following the usual interview protocols most interviews opened with the question: What formative experiences led you to becoming a storyteller? Forty four of the forty eight interviewed recalled very varied experiences which can be loosely grouped under about ten overlapping headings. Most referred to some prior exposure to, or participation in, the performing arts, community and/or folk arts, or community theatre, as a professional, semi-professional or recreational participant. This response was unexpected because many storytellers have a natural resistance to the influence of other performing arts. Most also recounted their own early exposure to a public storytelling event, a storytelling festival or a local storytelling group (commonly referred to as a 'club'). Some navigated improbable pathways to a storytelling career.

> A successful retail manager, having resisted for years his wife's blandishments to attend the local storytelling club she co-founded, one day saves her from extreme embarrassment by agreeing to stand in at short notice as master of ceremonies. To his own great surprise, he catches the spirit of the occasion, holds the audience spellbound, gives up the day job and in no time at all becomes a prominent and popular career storyteller.

Nearly half our respondents cited prior careers amongst their formative experiences: some as school drama teachers or teachers of core curriculum subjects, or with backgrounds in community theatre and a few others have come from acting, library service, business management, psychiatric social work, dramatherapy and church ministry. Some described their love of literature, poetry or other arts as a significant formative experience. Others of all ages spoke of childhood storytelling in their own families, perhaps indicating a greater continuity of this genre of storytelling than some commentators have assumed. A few respondents referred to their religious faith and two cited dreams as a formative experience.

More significantly, about a quarter of these respondents recounted various forms of epiphany, cathartic moments or single enlightening events that had occurred during public storytellings, or through chance encounters, or during earlier careers. The widely-held sense of what storytelling is can be summarised by one who described their own epiphany as a realisation that storytelling is 'a form of naked communication'. Seven respondents recounted cathartic experiences unrelated to storytelling that involved their own physical or mental ill-health, disability, personal loss or some form of social trauma in their lives. All seven went on to discuss the value of storytelling as a form of self-therapy that enabled them to come to terms with their changed circumstances and helped them create a new personal identity as a storyteller. Reflecting on all these form-

3

ative experiences it seems that storytellers are very much their own people, individualists, meeting challenges alone, 'ploughing my own furrow' as one described it.

Only one respondent, from a family of storytellers, has pursued this career from early adulthood, the remainder having come from very varied career backgrounds. This raises the question: What academic qualifications, specialised knowledge and work experience is feeding into, and therefore enriching, the world of storytelling today? Three quarters of those interviewed have degree-level qualifications and a third have either multiple or higher-level academic qualifications, although it seems unlikely these proportions are representative of all career storytellers. The favoured degree subject amongst storytellers is English, followed by other arts and humanities and degree-level qualifications in health and welfare-related subjects, including psychology, psychotherapy and sociology. Just over a third of this sample has recognised qualifications as teachers, workshop leaders or coaches in education, the folk arts or music. A similar number has recognised qualifications in drama or theatre studies. And one each has vocational qualifications as a musician, librarian, public service manager and church minister.

In his publication *The New Storytelling*[1] Simon Heywood identifies eight cultural and historical precursors of the storytelling revival that began about three decades ago. For this study thirty storytellers were asked: Who or what has most inspired your storytelling career? By comparing our storytellers' responses with Heywood's historical precursors it is hoped we may gain some insight into how the driving forces of storytelling have evolved over time. I am aware that comparing 'historical precursors' with factors that 'inspire' a storytelling career are leading us into a methodological morass, but this is the only plausible way I have found to measure driving forces over historical time.

The literature and scholarship of traditional stories and folklore remain valuable sources of traditional stories for those specialising in this genre, however only a few respondents made reference to literature and scholarship as an inspiration for their careers.

By contrast, the application of storytellers' skills in analytical psychology and psychotherapy and their associated disciplines of counselling, reconciliation and personal development have grown exponentially in recent decades and is now the subject of a growing literature and frequent academic conferences.

While Heywood includes the 1960s' counter-cultures and alternative spiritualities amongst his historical precursors, no respondent even alluded to such an influence on their careers (this may of course be a generational thing, important to those of my generation, but a bygone era to be disassociated with, by those younger than I).

Professional and semi-professional theatre traditions remain powerful influences on some storytellers' careers. First, 'poor theatre', which evolved in the 1950s and 60s and later fused with alternative, community, street and political theatre movements, is evident in much public storytelling today. However, whether we are witnessing direct descent from these movements or the reinvention of necessity is difficult to judge. Second, a storytelling movement that developed in the early 1980s and is based on a distinctly theatrical style of storytelling, has come to be known as 'performance storytelling' ('platform storytelling' in the USA) and may be considered a distinct genre. This movement is associated with the names Ben Haggarty, Hugh Lupton and Sally Pomme Clayton who formed the Company of Storytellers in 1985 and later attracted a wider circle of followers with a successor group, the Crick Crack Club. Significant numbers of respondents cited these names as having inspired their careers and it is notable that some of their performance skills have been adopted by storytellers more associated with other, non-performance, genres.

The cultural traditions of informal minority communities with historic lineages continue to influence storytelling today. Communities defined by faith are the most obvious example, along with traveller and some immigrant communities, and I am informed that bardic storytelling traditions endure in Wales. How much these cultural traditions run true to historical precedence, how much they have been adapted by each successive generation and how much is being reinvented to satisfy an appetite for populist nostalgia is a debate beyond the scope of this study. For example, it would be hard to categorise a personal story told recently by a prominent Jewish storyteller that recounts how they came to be confronted by their rabbi wandering the streets carrying a sizzling pan of pork chops. Heywood, who peer reviewed an early draft of this chapter, affirmed that in his experience of the Jewish communities he was familiar with, these observations undervalue established minority traditions, where 'literally everyone [...] takes a basic level of familiarity and expertise with storytelling for granted [and where] audiences are less forgiving [and] standards higher'. On my part I was happy to concede that my research had not specifically addressed this point. On his part our on-going e-debate prompted him to undertake 'some training with a traditional Jewish storyteller so [as to] (re)discover some links between traditional and contemporary storytelling'.

Better attested are the traditions of storytelling in schools and libraries, both having origins early in the last century.

The influence of folk revivals since the middle of the last century has fed into the recent storytelling revival and is strongly evident in the folk-style storytelling festivals that are now popular throughout Britain and Ireland.

The final historical precursor identified by Heywood is the mass media, and although no storyteller referred during interview to its influence on their careers, there is substantive evidence that this factor now plays an influential role as a driver of change, development and growth of storytelling today.

Beyond Heywood's historical precursors of the storytelling revival many cited their more experienced peers as a prime inspiration for their own careers. Some referred to storytellers with a very personal style of stagecraft, or to individual traveller-storytellers, or to those with certain pedagogical skills, or even one who tells with 'quiet radicalism'. Only a few cited the social roles played by their peers, including those who have 'gone their own way' or 'done their own thing' rather than following a more conventional career path. And one disabled storyteller admired those who are similarly 'on the margins of society' but who nonetheless managed 'to connect with mainstream society through their storytelling'. Several cited the high standards of teaching practice during storytelling workshops they had attended, in particular those who had attended Emerson International Storytelling College, a Steiner Waldorf school that puts storytelling at the centre of its holistic educational methods. Some respondents identified cultural phenomena from beyond the realm of storytelling, including stand-up comedy, pioneering theatre companies, specialist publishers, cinema, pantomime, music hall and one identified 'the landscape' where they lived. Others cited named individuals who had inspired their careers, including their scout leader, a playwright, a professor of folklore, musician, singer, a music teacher and their parents or other family members.

Reflecting more generally on the experiences and influences that go into the making of a storyteller, a very complex mosaic emerges. No bigger picture and few patterns are identifiable, except of course, the manifest diversity of formative experiences, professional and academic qualifications and sources of inspiration embraced by the wider storytelling movement. At the level of the individual storyteller this speaks of a strong sense of self-motivation. While at the collective level it speaks of a self-organising and rapidly emergent social and cultural phenomenon with a future that is open, driven largely by the initiatives of individuals. Any student of sociology or anthropology, or even theories of what makes organisations and movements thrive, will recognise this diverse heritage as one of the greatest strengths of contemporary oral storytelling.

Working lives

From the earliest stages of this study there has never been any doubt that career storytellers undertake a wide range of activities. Just how wide was brought home to me when I found myself trying to conduct an extended interview with one prominent storyteller as we sat side by side at the reception desk of an international storytelling festival. While they sold tickets to the public, directed the distribution of chairs amongst festival venues and organised their own role at another forthcoming festival, I sat dumbstruck beneath a notice that read INFORMATION, handed out festival programmes and yet was incompetent even to direct visitors to the café or the public toilets. Hard evidence for this provisional observation came only once I had analysed the responses of all my storyteller interviews and in particular their responses to the question: What is the full extent of your current storytelling-related activities?

All respondents outlined multiple activities but the full extent of these still came as a surprise. About three quarters of this sample are teacher-storytellers or freelancers engaged for schools storytelling, or for children's out-of-school activities. Add to these some engagement with storytelling in tertiary education, as part of academic duties, or in some advisory capacity, and these numbers add some weight to anecdotal evidence that more than three quarters of all storytelling in Britain and Ireland takes place within the broader scope of education. Just under half of storytellers interviewed also tell to audiences at public libraries and about a third at museums, galleries and other visitor attractions, and about a quarter tell at arts centres. Taken together it seems that well over half of all career storytellers may be making contributions to life-long learning and cultural development.

About three quarters are also regularly engaged in community storytelling. The definition of this term varies widely but is used in this study to describe any form of storytelling that relates directly to the common interests or purposes of any bounded social group. This includes, for example, residents in a care home, senior Royal Marine Commando officers, delegates to a trade show and those attending social clubs, refugee centres or camp fire storytelling.

About two thirds also report they are engaged for the entertainment of paying audiences. Included here are those who describe themselves as 'performance storytellers' and those who tell at public auditoriums, theatres, in public community centres and at festivals, fairs and conferences. Although some respondents are occasional and/or aspirational public storytellers this high percentage is notable given how many storytellers seek to distance their telling style from any form of theatrical performance. This observation also breaks down any clear distinction that some maintain between 'performance storytellers' and what are sometimes referred to as 'fireside' or 'intimate' storytellers. An example of this is the respondent who described themselves as 'mainly a fireside storyteller' but who the very next week was booked to tell to a paying audience of conference delegates numbering two thousand five hundred.

About two thirds of those interviewed are involved in storytelling in support of organisational, managerial and leadership functions, for businesses, the public service, charities and other organisations. Here the role of the storyteller varies widely, from those who provide light relief for stressed-out middle-managers, to the partner in a global management consultancy who coaches senior executives in storytelling for management change.

Significant numbers of respondents are health and welfare practitioners who bring varied levels of competence, from the unqualified volunteer at a care home who leads reminiscence storytelling for the elderly, to the professional psychotherapist who uses storytelling as a tool for ameliorative treatment of their clients.

Some also tell stories to promote environmental awareness and a greater understanding of the landscape. Some storytellers apply their art within the criminal justice system, in prisons or as justice coordinators in Youth Offending Teams. Some speak of their storytelling as a bridge between minority communities and mainstream society, or at private parties, for group mediation, pastoral care, bereavement and family counselling.

But it would be wrong to leave an impression that storytellers just tell stories. Although not representative of all storytellers, many respondents are also engaged as coaches and leaders of skills workshops. The range of contexts in which storytelling workshops are held varies widely, from the hired-in coach at a local storytelling group, to storytelling festival workshops, to full-time staff at dedicated schools of storytelling. Mentoring of the less experienced by the more experienced storyteller is another form of such coaching. All the workshops I have attended as participant observer have been fully subscribed and this adds weight to anecdotal evidence that there is a large un-met demand for storytelling skills, even though the standard of coaching remains variable.

> At one voice development workshop I attended the coach exhibited clear symptoms of emphysema, and sure enough, in the coffee break I discovered them on the pavement outside drawing heavily on a cigarette. I am ashamed to admit my researcher's duty of detachment was overwhelmed by rising irritation, and sputtering something about role models, I reminded them their fees were paid mainly by students and the modestly waged. Their only reaction was to hold out the back of their free hand as if expecting a sharp blow from some starchy Victorian-age schoolmistress.

Still on the subject of skills, many respondents incorporate song, music, puppetry, movement/dance or multimedia arts in their performances. And even though an uneasy relationship persists between storytelling and the mass media – the phrase 'Disneyfication of storytelling' is often heard – significant numbers of storytellers have been featured on national or regional radio and/or network television channels. Others again are published authors of magazine articles, booklets, fiction, treatises, histories, children's stories, story collections and academic dissertations. And some produce and market CDs of their own storytelling.

Many of those interviewed (but again not representative of all storytellers) perform leadership and/or organisational roles for local storytelling groups, festivals, conferences and competitions, National Storytelling Week, the Society for Storytelling and other representative and membership bodies, and some perform advisory functions with client organisations and state bodies. The contribution these activities make to change, development and growth of storytelling as a whole cannot be overestimated, especially as most perform these duties without financial remuneration and in time that could be spent more profitably – and more enjoyably – as storytellers. Finally, significant numbers undertake storytelling commissions abroad, an activity beyond the scope of this present study.

Reflecting on these interview responses it can be seen how storytelling-related activities are undertaken without any centralised co-ordination or organisation, yet is clearly not a random or spontaneous process. This observation compels the next question I put to twenty five storytellers: How do you get storytelling work? Many expressed an active distaste for any sort of personal marketing and most make little effort to promote themselves, as one said, 'I don't have to sit by the phone long.' Work comes in by word of mouth recommendation and most are satisfied with the amount and type of commissions they receive. As a former independent television producer who had to fight dirty for every primetime commission I was sceptical of this response till follow-up questions revealed that only a few had to work hard to win jobs or would welcome more opportunities for storytelling commissions.

Some reported they improve their chances of getting work by keeping in touch with clients by phone or by mailing promotional flyers. Some receive enquiries via their website (although few seemed aware of where these enquiries had originated). A few keep in touch by email. Others answer 'Storyteller Wanted' adverts or seek work by internet searches. Some organise their own work as part of the leadership role they play. By any interpretation of these responses storytelling is at present a seller's market, where the demand for storytelling exceeds the supply of willing and able tellers. Only three challenged this observation and most of those interviewed seem indifferent to competition from rising numbers taking up storytelling as a career. In terms of network theory, discussed in the Preface, most storytellers seem to rely on a small number of loyal client relationships – strong links – and feel no need to develop an enlarged circle of casual acquaintances – weak links – that often open up new and unexpected opportunities.

To explore what potential complex network interactions exists beyond the one-to-one relationship of storytellers and their clients, twenty nine of those interviewed were asked: What other communications networks are you an active part of? One academic loftily opined that 'individuals and storytelling communities are hermetically sealed against all outside influence'. No research evidence for this study supports that view in a literal sense; however, compared with many cultural vocations, professions and walks of life I am familiar with, the interconnectedness of individuals and associated groups and organisations is very limited. Career storytellers do take part in small discussion groups, workshops and bonding sessions, while many attend their colleagues' performances and in turn are asked for constructive feedback. Those who are members of representative bodies do take advantage of the resources offered, including participation in Special Interest Group meetings, annual gatherings, on-line discussion forums and social networking sites, while others have 'no interest in being part of the storytelling mafia'.

It was also surprising that some specialist storytellers are unfamiliar with the literature of other genres and a few are unfamiliar with the literature of even their own storytelling genre. Responses to this question also revealed how storytellers' network interactions with organisations beyond the world of storytelling is very limited indeed, the common exception here being storyteller members of professional bodies representing health, welfare, the caring professions and teachers. For example:

> I ask one prominent performance storyteller and academic, who had already described their own performance style as 'tentative', whether they had ever made contact with their own university's drama department. 'No', they replied, waving a hand towards the window, 'they used to be over there in the trees, but the last time I looked, they seem to have disappeared.'

When time allowed I asked our storytellers whether there were matters that were important to them that my formal lines of questioning had not touched on. Some wanted to talk about spiritual aspects of their storytelling in the broadest sense of the word, as the non-physical part of their being, the seat of their emotions, beliefs and character. Sadly, in most cases I had to say this was beyond the scope of the present study and I preferred not to rummage about in this very private aspect of their working lives. However, three questions, slipped into the formal business almost as asides, came close to illuminating the nature of the private person behind the public persona.

The question that prompted the strongest reaction was: How has your storytelling career impacted on your private life? Selected, near-verbatim responses speak for themselves: 'Storytelling is my life'; 'storytelling is rooted in my whole life'; 'I have little time for anything else'; 'storytelling permeates everything'; 'home life merges into my work'; 'all storytelling experience impacts on life'; 'I live, breathe and eat storytelling'; 'storytelling is my social life, its impact on life is total – it imbues all life'. Others referred to 'improving family relations'; 'becoming a calmer person with broader interests and values'; 'a way of navigating an uncertain future'; 'being more relaxed'; 'it helps emotional and home life, creates a comfort zone and I enjoy the status it affords me'; 'it's a holistic experience, physical, intellectual, emotional'; 'my story-based faith is important to the exploration of life'; 'it gives me a sense of my own identity'; 'it impacts enormously, makes me more human'.

> During an interview with one of our more voluble storytellers this question rendered him improbably speechless. A moment of frozen silence descended on the house, only to be shattered by the disembodied voice of his wife calling out from an adjoining room, 'I'll tell you what. He's a nicer man to live with and a better father to our children.'

Something of this all-consuming nature of a storytelling career is illuminated by those who responded to the question: What's the most extreme storytelling experience you've had? Of those who offered examples, all recounted moments of other-worldliness or of greatly heightened emotion: the moment a client undergoing long-term therapeutic counselling realises they can change their own personal story; answering a knock on the front door reveals a young Marine Commando seeking an afternoon of sanity before operational service in Iraq; telling a Greek myth in a cave when the narrative seems to take on a life of its own; a fifteen-year-old in a Pupil Referral Unit suddenly envisions a future of his own emotional maturity; an abusive and resentful prisoner asked by a storyteller, 'What stories will you tell your children when you have your own family?' becomes calm and begins to tell his own personal story.

Little of significance arose from the twelve who answered the question: What other interests and experiences have brought benefits to your storytelling career? Except that nearly all responses referred to deep attachments to their families, to leisure activities and cultural interests that reflect broadly liberal views.

Core skills

Thirty three of those interviewed were asked: What are the core skills of the storyteller? Setting on one side for a moment one who said, 'in storytelling, there are no recognised skills or practices', it seemed at first that most responses had little to do with skills and techniques as I understand the term to mean and more often described what I would call aptitudes and approaches to their storytelling. Only repeated reading of my contemporaneous interview notes has enabled me to draw their responses together for analysis under three general headings: those that relate to the story itself, those that relate to personal communication and/or presentation skills, and those that relate to something that I could not quite encapsulate. More than three-quarters of respondents referred to skills under each of these headings and it became clear, as one prominent teacher of storytelling confirmed, that 'core skills are personal to the individual'.

First, are those responses that can be associated with the story itself. Identifying appropriate stories was commonly referred to, as was the need to build a large repertoire. Several identified the need for scholarship and the researcher's skills, while one offered forthright advice to 'select the stories the audience wants to hear and keep the stories you want to tell for the psychiatrist's couch'. Several identified the need to understand the 'essence', 'concept', 'bones' or 'central message' of the story 'below the level of words'. The 'development' or 'composition' of the story and its 'narrative structure' were cited often. The 'use of language', 'a love of language', 'creating word pictures', 'telling economically', and developing a 'language that creates tensions between story and performance' were all referred to. One cited their use of 'a seven-part story structure', others alluded to the need for a 'respect', 'love', or 'trust' for the story itself, and several claimed they 'allowed the story to tell itself', or that 'a story tells itself' and even that 'I let the story do most of the work'.

Second, are those responses that can be associated with personal communication and/or presentation skills. 'Voice' was commonly mentioned in two senses: the acoustic qualities of speech and the opinion, attitude or point of view from which a story is told. Body language was alluded to, but often obliquely, in terms of 'gesture and movement', 'telling with the whole person' or was described as 'stillness, physical, grounded, intuitive things'. A few cited 'improvisation' as a core skill, one affirming that 'impro is king'. A few looked to the skills of stand-up comedy as an inspiration, while others referred to 'living in the moment', 'thinking ahead of the moment', 'experiencing the moment' or being 'present' and several alluded to the 'emergent qualities' of storytelling. One mentioned forum theatre (anyone can interrupt the performance and demand plot changes) as an influence on their storytelling. Some expressed an awareness of the creative opportunities of the performing space itself, for example, by 'adjusting the size of the performance to the venue'; 'expanding the self to include the audience'; 'creating a magic place with candles'; 'moving the furniture' to enhance the audience's experience; favouring 'site specific performances'; and 'creating a sense of place and space'. A few mentioned costume choices and the use of artefacts as a core skill (see also Chapter Six).

For the third category of response I must confess to several failed attempts at finding an apt heading that would embrace the remaining, highly pertinent, responses. The idea of the storyteller's relationship with their audience came close, but it was only when I trawled through my interview notes yet again that I noticed several prominent storytellers had referred to storytelling as a 'social art' or a 'social skill'. A further review of my 134 audience interviews (see Chapter Two) also revealed how the storyteller's social skills played an important role in the listener's appreciation of a public storytelling. A summary of storytellers' responses speak for themselves: Storytelling is a 'relationship [with the audience] based on dialogue', 'a shared experience', 'a complicity between storyteller and audience', 'a unique relationship', 'based on trust', 'personal to each audience member' and requiring their 'active participation'. Storytelling is 'visceral, frightening, a war to make the audience love you', with 'the storyteller as member and leader of a social group', 'leading the audience out into another world, then bringing them back safely'. 'It is more about the audience than about me', 'a social art'. 'Play is a vital [teaching] method, [as is] a social atmosphere for fostering relationships', while storytelling can also 'teach children social skills'. It calls for the storyteller's 'capacity to make friends', 'an ability to listen', 'with empathy', 'an understanding of the audience and their aspirations'. Storytelling aims 'to raise emotions, provoke reactions, connect with the listener and the story', 'put the story at the service of the audience', or as 'an act of love', 'a love of [...] the audience and emerging relationships', by 'speaking from the heart, with generosity, tolerance and integrity', with 'imagination and a delight in humanity'.

This very provisional outline of three types of core skill prompts an immediate follow-up question: How have these skills been acquired? Of the thirty asked this question, six reported they had attended a single workshop of one day's duration or less; ten had attended several workshops of up to a week's duration; one had attended six workshops of one day's duration; one had attended a single workshop of two weeks duration; three had attended the three-month course at Emerson International Storytelling College; and the remaining nine had received no formal coaching in the storyteller's core skills, relying instead on their experience of prior careers or learning by observation and intuition.

Since many storytellers use terms for their core skills that are common to other performing arts, it seemed relevant to test the extent of their familiarity with these by asking them: How aware are you of the core skills of other performing arts? Of the thirty six who responded, seven reported they incorporate puppetry or acting techniques in their storytelling; six have attended voice workshops and one is a professional voice coach; six have received tuition in music or singing; four have attended physical theatre or dance workshops; one is a drama school graduate; and one a published author on theatre arts. Otherwise all these respondents have acquired their awareness by observation and intuition.

Asked whether they would be interested in adding to their present skills base, four had firm plans to attend further workshops, two wanted others to be better trained but not themselves, one pointed out that time spent attending workshops was time lost to storytelling, and the remainder expressed only a generalised interest in acquiring further skills. As someone who spent ten years acquiring the technical skills of the filmmaker before applying for my first employment in the industry, I must confess to some confusion at these responses, that is, until I extracted from my interview notes, these respondents' more general comments: Core skills are 'all intuitive, I have an increasing resistance to formal training'. They are 'innate human skills [that] rely on instinct, not an acquired technique'. They are 'acquired by observation [and] self-directed apprenticeships [and by] listening and doing', 'by doing the telling', by 'listening [...] understanding and having empathy, [...] trial and error, experimentally, being fully present'. 'Storytelling is a gift'; the storyteller must have an 'aptitude for storytelling'; 'performance and staging skills are no concern of the applied storyteller' (referring to storytelling genres other than those mainly for entertainment).

Yet there is also a strong counter-current running through some responses about the storyteller's core skills, for example:

> I believe passionately that there is a skills gap amongst storytellers; that relying on natural talent and instinct is not good enough if storytelling is to survive in today's media-hungry world. We need a new theatrical form for our own narrative heritage, even though the roots of its performance techniques must remain planted in storytelling's unique traditions. We have to embrace the skills of others, invent a new artistry, go beyond intuition and observation. We have to push at the boundaries of the storyteller's core skill. Discipline is needed even for improvisation skills. The future lies in experimentation, so long as it supports the story. Resistance to the skills of others is down to storytellers' insecurities. Storytellers have to be as professional with their techniques as actors are with theirs. Most storytellers have too limited a range of performance and staging techniques. All skills need rigorous training and practise. I'm aware of the benefits [to storytelling] of having a theatre background, but while theatre companies now engage storytellers, so storytelling ought to reciprocate. Resistance to engage with other performing arts results from a lack confidence, a fear that storytelling will be swallowed up, taken over by theatre. It's a real shame that most storytellers have a natural resistance to rigour. The standard of storytellers' skills is not good enough. Storytelling is also bound by too narrow a definition of what storytelling is; [it] needs to be more open to outside influence and inspiration. Storytelling is an adolescent art form and we should look at other art forms and learn from them. We must create a new form of British storytelling for the twenty first century.

Unweaving the skills rainbow in this way has revealed some widely varying and strongly held views of what the storytellers' core skills actually are, how they can be acquired and how they are applied to the many genres of storytelling found today. Part of this complex situation, I would tentatively suggest, results from there being no common vocabulary, or even a shared language, amongst storytellers for describing their core skills (although storytellers are no builders of Babel and no evidence suggests God's displeasure with storytellers). The comment quoted above, 'in storytelling, there are no recognised skills or practices', which comes from a storyteller and workshop leader, may say more about the lack of a shared language to describe storytelling practices, than about its core skills. In my own creative discipline, the practices of filmmaking rely heavily on very precise and widely understood techno-creative languages to describe any mood of lighting design, any emotion-inducing camera movement and any syntax of shots in a narrative film sequence. Similar techno-creative languages are also found in all the performing arts. At one recent post-show discussion, when an audience member suggested that dance skills could develop through instinct and innate gifts, the acclaimed American choreographer, Mark Morris, rebuked the questioner with the words, 'No way, but some kids still think they can just impro their way into a dance career.' It would be a brave, if not foolhardy, amateur anthropologist that attempted an unambiguous definition of the storyteller's core skills, however Chapter Six, does attempt to reconcile the divergent views and divisive language that storytellers use to describe their own core skills.

Self-reflection

It is widely held that a storytelling event often affirms an identity – individual, community, cultural or national – and audiences as we shall see in the next chapter often experience a story through the individual persona of the teller. Here we attempt to gain insights into how storytellers see themselves. Twenty nine responded to the question: How do you define yourself as a storyteller? Clearly, many had never asked themselves this question, so if they hesitated, I would add: What kind of storyteller do you see reflected in the bathroom mirror each morning? Predictably their responses varied widely: 'Just a storyteller' captures the spirit of many responses, while some added such phrases as '… and musician and workshop leader', '… and entertainer and living oral tradition'. Others were more specific, answering, 'performance storyteller' but adding phrases like '… engaged in the essence of the performance itself', '… of well-crafted stories', '… as a theatrical artist' and '… in the role of priest, creating psychological alchemy'. Others added 'I call even my applied storytelling "shows"' and 'I pick stories that concern myself but my telling persona is me, but with more clarity'.

Other common self-identities include 'community storyteller', 'social storyteller', one adding '… and intimate storyteller'. Only two identified themselves as a 'fireside teller', a term sometimes used to indicate intimate or small-scale story-telling. Only two used the term 'revival storyteller', referring to the re/emergence of storytelling since the 1980s and several used the term 'applied storyteller'. Others identified themselves by the nature of the stories they told, affirming some 'cultural tradition', 'cultural identity' or 'ethnicity' they associate themselves with, or as 'a bridge between cultures'. Others reflected on their personal style of story-telling as 'expressive', 'compelling an audience reaction', 'responsive to the audience, conversational', 'it depends on the audience', 'tentative', 'not showy, quiet', 'neutral', 'natural' and 'I am the storyteller my client or audience asks me to be'. Responses also included 'a proficient storyteller', 'a good one', one 'who inculcates people into the art of storytelling' and one identified themselves as 'a story-telling institution'. One referred to their entrepreneurial role as 'an artistic producer', another to their leadership role as 'an animateur'. And inevitably one dissenting voice considered that 'most storytellers are self-regarding'.

These responses reveal, not only a very diverse range of storytellers' personas, but also contrasting views of what storytelling actually is. As one academic commented during interview, 'Storytellers too often claim ownership to the *true* story-telling and make few concessions to other forms.' With such insightful self-reflections it seemed to me that storytellers would have some sort of forward-looking vision of how their careers might develop in the future, so thirty two were asked: Do you have a personal vision of what you'll be doing in, say, five years' time? To my surprise many responses were either negative or reflected a polite indifference to the question. Most are happy and settled in their careers and none has undertaken either 'forward planning' or has developed a 'planned career path'. Most foresee a future of doing slightly more of what they currently do: developing their repertoire (curiously, many with similar stories); expanding the range of genres practiced and/or the type of audience they tell to; introducing dance, music, art and puppetry into multi-skill shows; writing a book and/or undertaking research; selling themselves more or doing administration less. For one, their vision is a secret, while another's sounds suspiciously like audio-pornography, and all will be guided by personal choice and a powerful sense of enquiry. It was only later that I realised what a methodological morass I had blundered into.

> I am talking to a young woman anthropologist – very French – in the coffee break at a storytelling conference. I ask her why, apparently, storytellers take such a casual approach to their own future development. 'I think', she says, all pursed lips and pointy shoulders, 'your question is probably not one that storytellers would ask of themselves, but more likely be asked by an ambitious anthropologist.' Ouch!

It may seem perverse, in view of the inherent diversity found amongst storytellers and their storytelling-related activities, to try and categorise storytellers further, so please forgive me for a brief detour on our journey. Howard Gardner, holder of professorships of education at Harvard and neurology at Boston universities in the USA, has developed a widely acclaimed theory of what he calls Multiple Intelligences. It proposes we all possess latent 'human capacities' or 'talents' in varying proportions, and in his *Multiple Intelligences – The Theory in Practice*, he identifies two intelligences that seem to fit well with the personal characteristics revealed by storytellers in this chapter. The first, 'interpersonal intelligence', he describes as 'the ability to understand other people: what motivates them, how they work, how to work cooperatively with them. Successful salespeople, politicians, teachers, clinicians, and religious leaders are all likely to be individuals with high degrees of interpersonal intelligence'. The second, 'intrapersonal intelligence', he describes as 'a correlative ability, turned inward. It is a capacity to form an accurate, veridical model of oneself and to be able to use that model to operate effectively in life.'[2] For those who follow Gardner's reasoning it may be that combined interpersonal and intrapersonal intelligences are the defining characteristics that distinguish the storyteller from practitioners in other vocations.

Social roles

It has frequently struck me as curious that we seem to have a clearer image of the social role of the storyteller in ancient societies, say Greece, the so-called age of chivalry or in traditional pre-literate societies, than we have of the role of the storyteller in our own culture today. Some attempt to explore this theme was made by asking twenty storytellers from widely varying backgrounds: Can you identify a collective role of the storyteller in our own society? One respondent can probably speak for many when they said, 'Storytelling is the ultimate act of shared humanity. It gives a shape to what it is to be human.' Others responded that being a storyteller is 'its own social role', 'a storyteller may develop an individual role' or 'a self-appointed role' but collectively storytellers have 'no exclusive role in society'.

Two respondents likened the storyteller's role to that of a shaman. Mentioning this in subsequent interviews brought out divergent comments, ranging from a certain recognition of this role to 'a horror of the shaman image' and an insistence that 'storytelling has no privileged position in relation to shamanism [...] though historically both shamans and storytellers are separated from mainstream society'. Two referred to an 'ecumenical role' in both religious and secular senses of embracing broadly varying views, and another described how the purpose of storytelling was 'to bring people together [to] create an ethos as a balance to [the current ubiquity of] technology'. Some respondents associated their social role with the cultural identity of a particular community – religious, regional, racial, cultural or even an historic era. And while one referred to such storytellers as 'tradition bearers' another suggested they were often 'feeding a spurious sense of public nostalgia'.

Many agree that community storytelling, as opposed to performance storytelling, 'is the core storytelling function, at its best in prisons, classrooms and as a pastoral skill, where applied storytellers tend to bring greater competences to their art'. Other comments in this vein included 'Storytelling and storymaking change people's lives – they gain power and identity [and] share values'; and the aim is 'to change people's personal stories in order to change their real lives'. The social role of some genres is described as 'a powerful tool in varied applications'. So 'springboard storytelling' is a tool for effecting management change in organisations, 'transformative storytelling' is a tool for ameliorative treatment in therapeutic practices, and 'restorative storytelling' is a tool for re-integrating criminal offenders into mainstream society. Some of those identifying themselves as performance storytellers referred to their role as mainly for entertainment, one describing it 'as an alternative night out, but less aggressive than stand-up comedy' and another referred to their role as 'muddy' and regretted that 'storytelling is not much more than a form of light family entertainment'. One pointed out how 'the role of storytelling as a term hasn't displayed itself well, [its definition] has become diffuse. [The public knows] what the role of a doctor is, but not a storyteller. We don't share a vocabulary with society generally'. And another added, 'There is a [...] gap between the reality of storytelling and its public perception – it can be a bore's charter.'

The sense that emerges here, perhaps like music, is that storytelling can be nearly all things to nearly all people – a virtue in its many and varied applications but a curse when trying to identify its collective role in society. One further step was taken in our quest to track down the social roles played by storytelling, to ask twenty eight of our storytellers: Have you identified any current trends that might show us the way forward for storytelling? Most responses were subjective impressions: storytelling is growing and the public is increasingly aware of it; there is greater collaboration between storytelling disciplines; there is more musical accompaniment; more young people taking up careers in storytelling; and there is an expanded range of tools being developed for applied storytelling. Other comments amounted to lists of hopes and fears: more of this, less of that. One regular refrain comprised barbed comments about 'the storytelling mafia', storytelling being 'too incestuous, too cultish' and a deep regret for 'factional spats'. A few reflected on how 'storytelling is too precious for its own good', or as one put it, in danger of 'being up its own arse'.

But it would be quite misleading to end this chapter on a negative note. There is a palpable sense of pioneering adventure amongst today's storytellers and a huge body of experience and skill pressing forward towards an unknown and perhaps unknowable future. One storyteller did however express a clear vision for the future of storytelling: a sincere hope 'for storytelling to be carried to the heart of every community'. Others too have referred, in more general terms, to similar aspirations. I find this idea inspiring because much evidence for this study reveals steady progress towards this goal, and the storytelling movement as a whole has already acquired many of the qualities needed to realise this dream. The future development of oral storytelling is not constrained by a lack of centralising organisations, diversity of its practitioners' formative experiences, or the skills and aptitudes described above. All are emergent qualities that commonly drive change, development and growth in socio-cultural movements.

Notes & References

1. Simon Heywood, *The New Storytelling: A History of the Storytelling Movement in England and Wales* (Society for Storytelling UK, Daylight Press, 1998), pp. 7-17.

2. Howard Gardner, *Multiple Intelligences: The Theory in Practice* (New York USA: Basic Books, Harper Collins, 1993), p. 9.

TWO

THE STORY OF A STORYTELLING

୫ଓ୯୫

T he previous chapter explores the idea of storytelling as a social art, even suggesting this quality as perhaps the most significant factor that distinguishes storytelling from other performing arts. The anthropologists also bring a wealth of scholarship to this debate when they describe the relationship of teller and listener as an act of co-creation. This chapter traces the course of a public storytelling from both the tellers' and listeners' points of view to reveal some of the qualities of this co-creation process. Evidence has been gathered from three principal sources: the extended interviews with storytellers from the last chapter, my own attendance as participant observer at some 35 public storytelling events and brief interviews with 134 audience members at 15 very varied public storytelling events. But the story of our storytelling begins weeks, sometimes months before the event itself. Our storyteller has just received a commission by telephone from a regular client. It is for a public telling, for a paying audience, of mixed ages and unknown background, it is scheduled for early evening but the venue has yet to be decided. The storyteller hangs up and pauses to think.

Planning and preparation

Twenty career storytellers, mostly associated with performance storytelling, were asked: How do you plan and prepare for a storytelling? Just over half start by developing the story, a quarter by considering the demographic profile of their audience, a few treat the story and the performance as a unified whole and two start by settling the contract terms and administrative details of the event. The development of these elements takes very varied forms. Researching the story, whether from their existing repertoire or from source books, generally leads to a shortlist of 'stories on a suitable theme'. Some tellers follow their own 'current obsessions' or 'preoccupations' while one identifies 'the stories the audience wants to hear'.

Some proceed by repeat-reading of the story from source books, others develop a story 'all in their heads', by 'waking dreams', 'haphazardly' or 'with no formal plan, no formula'. For one the story is developed by 'going nuts ... wild ... off at a tangent ... being away with the fairies' and for another their stories are born out of 'blind terror'. Some report they 'feel their way into a story', 'get the power of the story in mind' or complete a 'story breakdown', think till they 'inhabit the story' and then develop a 'story structure' or 'compose a narrative line, language and voice'. Some 'storyboard key words' on cards. One develops their stories by drawing patterns, symbols, numbered sections and shapes, and one writes their stories in full then edits them on paper.

Many rehearse their stories on 'thinking walks' as one calls them. Some rehearse by recording and playback, or from written notes, or in front of the mirror, while one seldom has time for rehearsals at all. Some try out newly developed stories on friends, colleagues or at a local storytelling group and then invite constructive feedback from this sympathetic audience. One aspiring career teller allows three hours preparation and planning for each fifteen minutes of telling. Most develop their performance only in the late stages of story's composition. The selection of planned performance techniques, 'storytelling tools' as some call them, may involve ways of 'meeting and greeting' or 'connecting with their audience'. Techniques for the telling itself may involve 'audience participation' or planning 'the emotional journey' they will lead their audience on. A few refer to 'the structure and stagecraft of the performance', while others speak of developing 'movement', 'voice' and 'an awareness of the physical performance'.

Administrative planning for the telling may include 'a bespoke briefing' from the venue management, research into the 'nature of the gig', the 'profile' and 'social context' of their audience and the 'the physical space' they will share with them. A few refer to modifying the telling venue, sound amplification, seating, props and lighting. And only two prioritise the administrative formalities – booking form, contract, payment methods, venue facilities, timetable, check lists, publicity – and one manages all this on standardised computer forms and formats.

The evening of the telling has arrived. Audience members are assembling at the venue ready to take their seats. But this is not a real audience but a composite of all 134 audience members interviewed for this study: 22 at three theatre tellings, 2 at a site-specific telling, 15 at a rural folk-style festival, 39 at city festivals,

10 BA students of creative writing, 10 conference delegates and 36 at seven varied local storytelling groups. Many of these brief interviews were conducted under challenging circumstances and fell far short of the standards normally required of more formal, systematic studies. Some were conducted individually while others were group interviews of up to six audience members where they were attending together. Some interviews were curtailed or interrupted by the storytelling events themselves or some unforeseen circumstance. I should also mention a serious sampling bias amongst audience members at one folk-style storytelling festival where, owning to the geography of the venue, a significant proportion had attended for reasons other than the storytelling, and of these, several were only there for the speciality beer. Another point worth noting for readers unfamiliar with social science research methods is how some people interviewed on a subject they are enthusiastic about are often eager to please their interrogator, their responses speaking more of their personal enthusiasms than considered answers to the interviewer's questions. By contrast, six rather wild-eyed women, apparently still under the influence of some sort of Mexican storytelling encounter, brought a decidedly anthropologist-baiting agenda to their group interview.

Who's here tonight?

About 65 per cent of our audience here are women, a figure that approximates those for all storytelling audiences across Britain and Ireland. Significant variations to this figure do occur across the different types of storytelling event and even the nature of the stories told. For example, women represented an estimated 80 per cent of the audience at a London theatre telling of Tales of Lakota Women (a Native American tribe). I have also been granted access to two large-scale audience evaluations: the first from the 2008 Scottish International Storytelling Festival which noted that about 65 per cent of audience members were women[1] and the second from the Traditional Arts Team's 2005 report on their Storytelling Café's five venues across the English Midlands which noted that nearly 75 per cent of their regular audience members were women.[2]

The estimated age profile of those attending here tonight shows about 1 per cent are under twenty years old, about 10 per cent are in their twenties, 40 per cent in their thirties, 25 per cent in their forties, 20 per cent in their fifties, 2 per cent in their sixties and 2 per cent are over seventy years old. Again, these figures correlate quite well with the Scottish Storytelling Festival where just under 50 per cent are forty or over and the Storytelling Café's evaluation where more than 50 per cent are forty or over.

As a rough and ready measure of whether storytelling is seen by attenders as a social event, this study estimates that nearly 45 per cent of our composite audience is attending alone, about 30 per cent is here with one companion, about 15 per cent in groups of three and less than 10 per cent in groups of four or more. This contrasts with figures from the Storytelling Café's evaluation where more than 50 per cent attend in groups of three or more.

Insights into the evolving relationship between teller and listener have been sought by asking 122 audience members: What is the extent of your storytelling experience to date? This deliberately very open question did however attract some highly ambiguous responses, in turn requiring some fairly brutal interpretations. Only formal storytelling events have been included and only those attending in the capacity of teller, audience member or administrative supporter of the event have been included and analysed; while storytelling in families and water-cooler and pub-type anecdotes have been excluded from these findings. For about 35 per cent of our respondents this is their first and only experience of a storytelling event. Another 35 per cent have participated in ten or more storytelling events, some of these being storytellers themselves, although with very varied levels of experience. About 25 per cent have experienced between one and five storytelling events and less that 5 per cent between six and ten events. The figure for first-timers correlates well with those attending the Scottish Festival referred to above but otherwise comparisons become difficult. As usual there is a danger of over-interpreting such figures, however evidence from other parts of this study suggests there is a long-standing core following for storytelling in Britain and Ireland and a surge of interest in recent years.

Turning to the complex network interactions that bind storytelling communities together, 87 audience members were asked: How did you hear about this event? Nearly 50 per cent were attracted by word of mouth recommendation; about 30 per cent through membership of representative bodies such as the Society for Storytelling or by e-notices as regular attenders at similar events; about 15 per cent learned about this event through publicity and promotion; about 5 per cent by web searches; and a few by other means. These figures cannot be reliably analysed by type of storytelling event; however, there are some indications of a higher percentage for word of mouth recommendations at the theatre tellings and a higher percentage for publicity and promotion at city festivals. The Storytelling Café's evaluation notes that over 40 per cent of attenders hear about their events by word of mouth and a further 25 per cent by local advertising.

Still with network interaction, 90 audience members across all five types of storytelling event were asked: What other storytelling events do you know about anywhere in the country? Over 60 per cent have no knowledge of any other storytelling events; about 30 per cent know of between one and three other events;

and less than 10 per cent have an extensive knowledge. It seems that the range of network links that trigger audiences' attendance at storytelling events are quite limited in variety and scope.

To complete this demographic profile of tonight's audience this study sought insights into the cultural hinterland of our audience members and to this end 109 were asked: What other interests and skills inform your experience of events like this? Only a few reported they have no relevant interests and skills while nearly 90 per cent referred to a complex mosaic of experiences that might be grouped under three headings. First are popular entertainments that included theatre, music, cinema and other performing arts, and while one referred to internet games, none mentioned television. Second, many referred to active participation in cultural leisure activities that included singing or choir membership, music-making, 'the folk scene', festival-going, handicrafts, amateur dramatics, reading, museum and gallery visits, dance and several mentioned Druidism. And third, many reported that their own occupations and vocations strongly informed their storytelling experience. Amongst these, many have careers as teachers, mostly in mainstream education, but also as vocational coaches in the arts, business, public service, the professions and one in international relations. Other vocations that inform our audiences' storytelling experience include tourist guiding, psychology, psychotherapy, dramatherapy, pastoral care, counselling, social work, sales and marketing, human resources, public relations and communications, anthropology, therapeutic storytelling, the priesthood and speech therapy. Other individual respondents also referred to their experience as a lay-preacher, social scientist, architect, engineer, illustrator, aspiring storyteller, conference manager, artist, art student, sculptor, actor, poet, playwright, author, theatre student, digital artist and performer, craftsperson, dance student, filmmaker and screen media creative. It would be hard to imagine a more diverse cultural hinterland that our audience members have brought with them here tonight.

To step back for a moment from the inner world of our audience members and to observe their collective behaviour as they assemble here tonight, it is striking how their social conduct differs markedly from audiences at other, more formal performing arts events. As a participant observer here, who habitually attends well over a hundred theatre, music, opera, dance and other live performances annually, it is noticeable how the babble of conversation is more constant here. Attenders are greeting strangers, chatting with their neighbours, sharing food and drink and it is common for the evening's host/ess, or master of ceremonies, and sometimes the storytellers themselves, to be engaged in informal conversation with audience members. However, this notable characteristic of storytelling events is less evident when it takes place in a formal theatre setting where audience members tend to conform to the social norms of theatre-going rather than an informal storytelling. This kind of formality can also extend to the performance itself where the storyteller is often introduced to the audience by a host/ess or MC and the storyteller makes their entrance from the wings to the audience's welcoming applause.

But enough of audience studies, we are here to share an evening of traditional storytelling. Tonight's storyteller stands before us. Their eyes sweep across our expectant faces and there is an imperceptible intake of breath. But before their first spoken word is uttered they must be very clear as to how they are going to establish an emergent relationship with their audience.

Meeting of minds

28 career storytellers, mostly those who tell to larger and paying audiences were asked in interview: How do you develop a relationship with your audience? All have developed individual ways of 'saying hello', or ways of 'introducing myself and stating why I am here'. Some like to meet and greet before the show, 'have a cup of tea with them' or just 'share the telling space'. Others start their story by engaging the audience in casual conversation; or by engaging an individual in personal conversation; or in other matters of mutual interest; and if possible, by getting 'halfway through the first story before they realise it has started'. But above all a storyteller aspires to demonstrate a 'capacity to make friends'. Techniques to 'establish a dialogue with their audience' can include jokes, riddles, magic, chanting, humour, short anecdotes, question-and-answer sessions, song, music, 'a silly game', call-and-response, rhythm-clapping, informal chat and eye contact, and each of these techniques can be adapted to work with all ages and backgrounds of those attending.

Sometimes an audience's listening skills may need to be re-tuned. Children from story-poor communities may need to learn story-listening skills. Adults from any social background may need to be reminded how to listen, or coaxed into overcoming social inhibitions so they can 'surrender themselves to a well-told tale'. Some storytellers use the word 'complicity' to describe how they 'signpost routes' through a story so that audience members can navigate their own way through it as proactive co-creators. As the last chapter reveals, this 'shared experience' creates an appropriate 'social atmosphere for fostering relationships'. It is a relationship 'based on trust' with the 'storyteller as member and leader of a social group' guiding 'the audience out into another world, then bringing them back safely'. These techniques aim to put 'the story at the service of the audience' as 'an act of love', 'a love of [...] the audience and emerging relationships'.

By now our storyteller is well into their tale and the broader range of core skills outlined in the last chapter is now in play. It is time to take a closer look at this emerging relationship between teller and listener and probe deeper into this much heralded co-creation process.

Audience experiences

We have already witnessed something of our audience's prior experiences of storytelling and the cultural hinterland they bring with them here tonight, and now they are to be asked to describe some of their most personal thoughts and feelings about this event. Most of us are unprepared for such an ordeal and lack the necessary vocabulary to put these experiences into words. So it came as an unexpected surprise that most respondents displayed an uncanny ability to answer my searching questions with concision and notable self-insight. Often I had to seek clarification of ambiguous answers; sometimes I felt the need to transpose common word-use from some other medium, art form or cultural convention; and occasionally I had to call on personal experience of twenty five years as a documentary filmmaker to interpret the full meaning of responses given.

95 audience members at sixteen varied storytelling events expressed 130 diverse responses to the question: What do you enjoy most or least about this kind of event? Unsurprisingly, nobody expressed their general disapproval, although some added significant reservations. A crude breakdown of these 130 responses can be treated under six headings: About 30 per cent can be associated with the social atmosphere of a storytelling event; about 25 per cent with some aspect of the stories told; another 25 per cent with qualities of the teller's performance; about 10 per cent with some cultural or heritage aspect of the telling; about 5 per cent with storytelling primarily as entertainment; another 5 per cent with the physical environment of the telling; and a few enjoyed attending workshops and other qualities of a telling event.

These global figures need some serious qualification. The term 'social atmosphere' is used here to include responses such as 'relaxed', 'friendly', 'sociable', 'socially inclusive', 'meeting others' and 'a good feel'. The term 'the stories told' is used here to include responses such as a story's 'moral lessons', 'narrative structure', 'stories that connect with people', 'accessibility of the stories' and 'the story's shape'. I anticipate the term 'the teller's performance' will cause controversy in some quarters since some storytellers make little distinction between the story and its physical and vocal realisation. However, audience members do make such distinctions when they say they enjoy 'the storyteller's performance', 'entering into the performance', 'the quality of the performance' and an 'energetic performance', while other responses refer explicitly to identifiable performance skills like 'humour', 'magic', 'music', 'song' and 'ad-libbing'. References to 'cultural or heritage' aspects of a telling embrace responses such as 'connectedness to our own cultural roots', or 'a growing respect for' unfamiliar cultural traditions, or enjoyment of the 'heritage dimension' of the teller and/or their performance. References to storytelling as 'entertainment' reflect audience members' own use of this word. And the term 'physical environment' refers mainly to attractive surroundings, mostly rural, parkland or site-specific storytelling venues.

It is always problematic to compare figures across different types of event when overall numbers of respondents are low and interview conditions vary between events. However there are some indications that audiences' enjoyment of the 'social atmosphere' scores higher at local storytelling groups and at rural folk-style festivals and lower at theatre tellings where, as discussed above, audiences tend to adopt the more formal social conventions of theatre-going. There are also some indications that the enjoyment of the 'stories told' and 'the teller's performance' score higher at the theatre tellings, although this might also reflect more on the demographic of the audience than on qualities of the performance itself. And enjoyment of the 'cultural and heritage' factors seem to score higher at the theatre tellings and the city festivals – again an observation to be treated with extreme caution. Perhaps a more reliable comparison comes from the Storytelling Café's evaluation report in which 'sociable atmosphere' and 'quality of the performers' are reported to be dominant factors in audience members' enjoyment.

Attempts were also made to see if audience members make a distinction between the qualities of an actualised performance of a story and the personal qualities of a performer. To this end 59 were additionally asked: What qualities do you most admire in a storyteller? Some referred to aspects associated with performance skills that included phrases like 'an expressive body', 'vocal and physical performance', 'rhythms of telling', 'acting and facial expression', 'movement', 'stage presence', being 'comfortable in themselves', 'an energy to support the story', a 'dynamic' performance, 'passion and enthusiasm', 'improvisation', 'use of space', 'self-belief' and 'connecting the story with the audience'. Others also referred a storyteller's ability to conjure up imagined worlds or paint what are commonly called 'word pictures' using phrases like 'a vivid picture of the landscape', 'creating environments across space', 'vivid descriptions', 'creates a mythical space', 'being taken out of day-to-day thinking', 'transports you to an imagined world', 'awakens the audience's visualisation of the story' and 'creates images'.

Some respondents referred to the teller's relationship with their audience, using phrases like 'able to hold an audience', 'human contact', 'warmth and emotional connection', 'relationship with the audience', 'tailoring the story to the particular audience' and 'addressing individual audience members'. The personality of the teller was also mentioned by significant numbers of respondents, calling on phrases like 'telling out of their own personality', 'expression of personality', 'charisma', 'personality of the teller', 'revealing their own cultural roots', 'improvising as social outsiders or lords of misrule' and 'the persona of the teller'.

To focus more clearly on just one defining characteristic of co-creation, 41 audience members across four types of storytelling event were asked: What do you think about active audience participation in storytelling? An overwhelming majority enjoyed it; a tiny minority disliked it; the few remaining respondents either approved of it with qualifications, or disapproved of it with exceptions; none elaborated on their response.

While our respondents have shown remarkable self-awareness and an ability to articulate some deeply felt personal experiences, it seems important here, by way of comparison, to gain some external point of view of audience members' experience. To this end 86, from across all common types of storytelling event, were asked: How does your experience here differ from other performing arts you attend? Over 75 per cent of responses alluded to storytelling being more intimate and more personal. Selected near-verbatim responses speak for themselves: 'It's personal, not elitist', 'less formal', 'a personal and immersive experience', 'a shared experience', and 'a one-to-one relationship'. It 'affects me more, it's closer, I feel it in my heart', with the 'the teller sharing herself with the listener' and calling for 'greater human contact', 'greater audience concentration', it is 'more interactive', 'a personal dialogue with the audience'. 'The storyteller is there for you', there is 'an intimate involvement', a 'stronger energy exchange with the teller', 'a closer relationship of teller and audience, like childhood storytelling', it 'engages the listener individually'. It is 'like stand-up [comedy] but closer', requiring 'more active listening, stronger visualisation [and an] individual interpretation of the story'. 'It touches you like music does', 'it feels as if I'm amongst friends', 'being more part of it [with] active participation' and a greater 'interplay with the audience'. 'I like the closeness of storytelling', there is 'a greater personal connection with the story'.

Other responses that made clear distinctions between storytelling and other performing arts included, 'artists in other performing arts can be too full of themselves' and 'storytelling is more interactive, on equal terms with the storyteller'. It is 'like theatre, but a storyteller is not like an actor' and it is 'a modest art form'. 'Plays are between actors, storytelling [is] between teller and audience.' 'I like joining in, unlike theatre where it's all done for you', 'the best storytelling *is* theatre', 'theatre has more energy but even storytelling can have some theatrical elements'. And 'theatre is more artistic and creative'.

One perennial issue that arises from such interviews is judging whether audience members' responses are a true reflection of personal experience or whether they are reporting imaginative interpretations of those experiences. Some clues emerged when I approached a group of three friends for interview at the Scottish Storytelling Festival. They declined on the grounds they had only met here for its convivial café, none had ever attended a storytelling event, nor had any intention of doing so in the future. This presented me with an opportunity to exploit a deeply paradoxical situation, and they an opportunity to join in a ten-minute psychological parlour game. With this mutual understanding they agreed to submit themselves to my standard line of questioning. To my great surprise their responses matched closely those of veteran audience members. How did they know? Further questioning revealed they were extrapolating their responses from unconnected personal experiences: from 'hearing the Hindu epics as a child' or from 'children's comics' or from 'pub storytelling on holiday', 'water cooler chat at work', 'blogging' or 'stand-up comedy'. They even managed to speculate about qualities of the storytelling performance itself, offering comments like 'it's not quite acting', but a 'stylised performance', 'physically closer', the audience 'putting themselves into the story more', 'less passive listening', 'visualising the story more' and even that storytelling happens 'between the storyteller and the audience'.

Listening and experiencing

This minor detour from our story of a storytelling seems to have brought us dangerously close to matters of the mind and in particular to the psychology of human perception. This is not a subject I know anything about but is one that I can recount a personal story about.

In the early 1990s Channel 4 Television commissioned from me a one-hour, primetime documentary programme on the psychology of listening to music, called simply, *The Listening*.[3] It sought to answer such questions as: What is the role of the listener in music? What does music do to us physically and mentally? We took our cameras into a wide range of performance situations, turned audience members into experimental test subjects and conducted psychological experiments on them as a form of 'live science on television'. The intrusive nature of television production obviously compromised any claim to laboratory-grade experimental methods but the tests were supervised and the results more or less validated by experimental psychologists recruited to the programme. This innovative approach inspired a feature article in *New Scientist*[4] that outlined the methodology we had used for making the programme and was written by the programme's chief consultant, John Davies, professor of psychology at the University of Strathclyde, Scotland.

From a creative point of view the programme was a complete nightmare. Just checking details in the postproduction script to write these few paragraphs has made my palms clammy – more than twenty years later. There were the aggressively competitive 'theatre mums'; teenagers emoting to music by face-pulling alone; choral scholars rendered hysterical by trying to sing atonal (12-tone) music from memory; a posse of fourteen-year-olds caught breaking into a night club gaming machine – No more! No more! Space does not permit even brief descriptions of the fourteen experiments we conducted for our cameras but the conclusions drawn are probably still more or less valid today. Some may suggest future lines of enquiry, others may strike a chord with storytellers, or indeed anyone engaged in public speaking, the performing arts and any kind of human communication.

Within a shared culture our emotional responses to music show remarkable similarities, even if expressed in artistic media as different as dance and painting.

We can detect emotional expressiveness through both sight and hearing. When these are mutually matched the emotional experience of the listener is greatly enhanced. However, when we detect a mismatch between sight and hearing, human psychology tends to afford greater priority to our sight.

Within a shared culture we all tend to experience heightened emotional responses at the same moments in a piece of music. This suggests that certain combinations of notes, rhythms and harmonies evoke more or less predictable emotional responses in us all, sometimes called 'hot spots'.

In music, as with all human perception, our emotional experiences are shaped by cultural conventions, acquired skills, familiarity, preconceptions, age and social context of the listening experience.

Complex music we tend to appreciate only gradually after a large number of hearings and our appreciation of it declines only very slowly with subsequent hearings. Un-complex music, like pop music, we tend to appreciate after only a few hearings and our appreciation of it declines rapidly with subsequent hearings.

In the short term we tend to favour the kind of music we find middling-complex, but over longer periods we tend to enrich our music listening experience by favouring progressively more complex music.

And absolutely my favourite experiment involved the Alegri String Quartet, one of the world's best, who were invited to play a Joseph Haydn string quartet badly to a judging panel of total non-musicians. These musical know-nothings then had to direct the world-class professionals on how to improve their musical performance. This experiment confirmed that even an audience of intelligent but unlearned people is very much more discerning in their judgements than is generally believed.

The concluding voice-over commentary of *The Listening* proposed a rough and ready template for the co-creation process in music, and based on evidence provided by tonight's storytelling audience, may also suggest pathways for exploring the co-creation process in storytelling.

> Music can be understood as some sort of coded instruction to get us doing something. And if we should demand from music some social function, then this cannot be a passive process, not like just feeling wet when we're caught in the rain. Far from sitting under a shower of notes, we construct music in our minds, responding to it, using it for some purpose, however abstract. That's surely what music does to us, what the listener's role in music is.

Afterwards

Our storytelling has spun to its ingenious denouement and has rushed towards a satisfying resolution. At more informal storytelling events the teller gently leads their audience back to a more familiar everyday world. Generous applause breaks out and is acknowledged with a self-deprecating dip of the head. Socialising with and between audience members may continue before teller and audience head for home. But the storytelling event itself will journey on in the minds and lives of those who have experienced it. The teller will have already begun a process of self-analysis. They may phone colleagues they have spotted in the audience to discuss possible changes to the narrative, the use of language or some technique of audience participation. But whatever path they take for their onward journey, the process of planning and preparation for their next public storytelling will have already begun.

Our audience members' experience will lead them in a rather different direction. My brief interviews with them concluded with the question: What will you take away with you from this experience? If respondents hesitated in their replies I would follow on with a prompt such as '… perhaps some experience you might apply in your working or social life'. Methodological purists will rightly worry about this prompting which is indeed a leading question, and while I make no excuses for this lapse, I mention it so that readers can judge for themselves the validity of responses offered. 76 interviewees offered 82 distinct responses to this question. Just over a third of these treat such a storytelling event as a learning experience which they will then apply in their careers or in some vocational pursuit. The careers specifically mentioned included teacher, conciliation counsellor, wildlife warden, psychiatric social worker, healthcare professional, humanities professor, rescue service radio operator, business professional, tourist guide, IT manager, career storyteller, social scientist, academic, vocational coach, painter, sculptor, museum curator, political lobbyist and one student architect uses narrative structures learnt at events like this to explore the aesthetic spaces he designs. Just over a third of responses suggest little will be taken away except for the enjoyment and/or entertainment value of the storytelling event itself. And a little over a quarter of responses suggest a new or continuing interest in storytelling as a recreational activity and their experience will therefore be applied in some relevant social context in the future.

Although any more detailed analysis of these figures should be treated with the utmost caution, it may be worth mentioning that at the theatre and site-specific storytelling venues the 'learning experience' response recorded the highest proportion, while the 'enjoyment/entertainment' response recorded amongst the lowest proportions. And at the festival and local group venues these proportions were reversed.

Reflections

True to many of the best stories, this story of a storytelling reveals its narrative structure only with hindsight and inevitably raises further pressing questions. Is it not remarkable that so many of the audience members who have little or no experience of storytelling can account precisely for the nature of their enjoyment of such events, the qualities they admire most in a storyteller and how their storytelling experience differs from that of other performing arts? Perhaps, like the three friends interviewed at the Scottish Storytelling Festival their responses involve a far more imaginative extrapolation of unconnected personal experience than is generally assumed. The storyteller interviews in the last chapter reveal how storytelling plays very diverse social roles in society, while in this chapter our audience members reveal how they instinctively apply their experiences of a storytelling event in multiform contexts in their vocational and social lives. Are we witnessing here some universal quality of oral storytelling? Do we all share some common response to a well-told story? Is there something about our innate abilities that enables our judging panel of non-musicians to direct the Alegri String Quartet to a more musical performance?

Another intriguing phenomenon to arise here concerns the storytelling event as an effective transmitter of practical skills. In the last chapter we find how few career storytellers have much formal training and few are aware of the core skills of other performing arts. In this chapter we find how audience members are using their innate powers of observation and intuition, and without any apparent form of interpretation, adaptation or formal learning process, are applying these new found skills in a broad range of vocational and social contexts. Are there any other performing arts and emergent cultural phenomena that can make this claim?

But amidst all these imaginative extrapolations, innate abilities and applications of acquired skills, two examples of the hidden qualities of contemporary oral storytelling can be identified from evidence collected for this chapter. The first is how such grassroots, community-based movements seldom attract a high public profile, even though they are ubiquitous in society. The last chapter reveals how career storytellers tend to participate less in complex network interactions compared with many cultural vocations, professions and walks of life. And in this chapter we learn that about 60 per cent of audience members have no knowledge of any other storytelling events anywhere in the country. Taken together these findings suggest a diminished interconnectedness between the component parts of today's storytelling movement. The Preface to this study also identifies a second form of hiddenness: how participants in storytelling events are generally unaware of the social contribution they are making to the event, and by extension, the multiple roles that contemporary oral storytelling now plays in our wider society. Here is the most sublime example I have encountered of this second hidden quality of storytelling.

> A middle-aged Norwegian couple holidaying in Edinburgh chance on a poster for the Scottish Storytelling Festival, and attracted by its theme, Northlands & Sagalands, purchase tickets for several events. At the outset of my interview with them they insist they have never heard of storytelling, either as a performing art or for adding social value in society, neither in Norway, nor anywhere else in the world. Yet during the interview they describe how they have always told stories as teachers, he to disabled children, she in state education, and how as weekend hobby farmers they regularly tell environmental and traditional Norwegian stories to disadvantaged children visiting from culture-poor communities. The following week she is to start a new job advising senior business managers on reducing stress in the workplace, a position she won by proposing what she thought was a wholly original idea: to meet these objectives by telling traditional stories. By chance the next festival workshop they attend is led by one of Norway's leading storytellers who opens to them a whole new world of storytelling opportunities in which they discover they are already acknowledged heroes.

As we shall see in subsequent chapters, the concept of co-creation by audience members is not unique to storytelling, but it would be hard to imagine another performing art in which audience members play such a prominent co-creating role.

Notes & References

1.   My thanks to Donald Smith, Director of the Scottish Storytelling Centre for access to this unpublished report based on 17,000 attenders.

2.   My thanks to Graham Langley of the Traditional Arts Team for access to this unpublished 2004-05 evaluation which was based on a sample of 436 respondents.

3.   *The Listening*, writer/director/producer: Michael Howes (Channel Four Television Company UK, 1991).

4.   John Davies, 'The Musical Mind', *New Scientist*, IPC Magazines UK, January 1991, pp. 38-41.

THREE

ORAL TRADITIONS IN A DIGITAL AGE

ℰ℧ℛ

I
n Chapter One our storytellers reveal they are engaged in a broad range of specialist genres. Chapter Two alludes to many specialist interests that attract members of the public to participate in storytelling events. For example, at one conference on Storytelling for Peace and Reconciliation the workshop leader asked the twenty eight delegates present, 'What personal interest does each of you have for attending this workshop?' My contemporaneous notes recorded twenty three widely varied answers.

This chapter does not attempt a comprehensive description of any, let alone all, the common genres of contemporary oral storytelling, nor does it obtrude on the territory of more narrowly focused studies by practitioners and academics, some dating from early in the last century. Rather it seeks to compare and contrast some of the working practices of eleven well-established storytelling genres; it explores the varied social zones where storytelling and storymaking interact with participants and co-creators; and it reflects on certain aspects of the efficacy and functions of storytelling and storymaking in our society. Research for this chapter has also been hampered by the confidential nature of many of these genres, so that direct observational and experiential evidence is completely missing from some of the examples described. Instead, evidence has been collected by multiple research methods that include: extended interviews with specialist practitioners, participant observation, reference to the literature where it exists, consulting third-party professionals where evidence is ambiguous or contradictory, and for two of these genres, I bring a certain personal expertise to the subject area under discussion.

My original intention, to draw up a comprehensive list of storytelling genres, proved utterly futile. No sooner did I think I was approaching this goal than the next storyteller I interviewed would recount how they tell leadership stories to Royal Marine Commando officers, or horticultural stories at garden centres, or trawlermen stories at supermarket fish counters, and on it went. My second approach focused only on the well-established, headline genres that are recognised as distinct by most storytellers. Of these, some are distinguishable by the specialist skills required to practice them; some require professional qualifications unconnected directly with storytelling; others again rely for their success on particular types of story told. Some aim to bring social change to individuals and communities by means of specialised storytelling practices, or particular forms of participation, and some it seems are only effective in certain social contexts. Yet, as ever, storytellers themselves express widely divergent views. Some hold that 'demarcation between types of storytelling, and therefore definitions of what storytelling is, has no place [in these discussions]'. Others outline clear demarcations and definitions of the storyteller's art. Others again describe precise roles and practices that distinguish their own specialisation from those of others. And one academic opined that 'Storytellers too often claim ownership to the *true* storytelling and make few concessions to other forms'.

'My favourite story was Lazy Jack. Do you want to know why I liked the story so much? Well, to tell the truth, I honestly think I'm a bit like him sometimes'[1]

This quote comes from a primary school pupil aged between seven and eleven. It illustrates how children of this age can be taught how to understand the central message of a story below the level of words and reflect it back on their own lives and behaviour. The value of storytelling in child development and education has been acknowledged, and has been the subject of a specialist literature, at least since Katherine Dunlap Cather's 1922 publication, *Education by Story-telling: Showing the Value of Storytelling as an Educational Tool for the Use of All Workers with Children*.[2] During the research period for this study, the teaching of storytelling core skills was embedded in the national curriculum for British primary schools and included

> [s]peaking clearly, fluently and confidently with appropriate intonation; choosing words with precision; listening to others' reactions; telling real and imagined stories; speaking to different people, taking part in group discussion and interaction; working in role; responding to performances; understanding fiction, poetry and drama; using their knowledge of sequence and story language; retelling of traditional folk and fairy stories from a range of cultures and composing their own texts; identifying how character and setting are created and how narrative struc-

ture and themes are developed in the broader context of English literature; learning how to listen and respond to stories; and finding out about the past from a range of sources, including stories, eye-witness accounts, pictures, artefacts, historic buildings and visits to museums, galleries and visitor attractions.

Those teacher-storytellers I have interviewed also report on 'the importance of teaching what a story is and why it matters' to people's lives, how 'storytelling can teach children social skills' and as an aid to 'playing with language'. There have also been many institutional developments in educational storytelling, amongst those brought to my attention during the research period include: A steady stream of research degrees awarded. An expanding literature on educational storytelling. Drama schools now offer storytelling workshops for school teachers. Experienced teacher-storytellers increasingly organize workshops for their less experienced colleagues. Most National Storytelling Week events (see Chapter Five) are currently staged by schools. The grant-aided Oxford Museum of Storytelling now tours storytelling events, exhibitions and teacher training workshops. The Scottish Storytelling Centre is now developing multimedia storytelling techniques for schools. And the Young Tongues Project (see Chapter Five) is now extending the reach of its campaign to promote a storytelling culture in schools.

Beyond the disciplines of storytelling in support of curriculum teaching practice, many storytellers report they are engaged by schools for more theatrical-style shows, or as part of history, arts, drama and after-school projects, or as part of recreational activities. From here, the application of educational storytelling becomes diffuse, merging with storytelling for community cohesion and identity, for religious and moral teaching, cultural and artistic understanding and as a form of theatre and performance. All these examples add weight to anecdotal evidence that suggests that up to 80 per cent of all storytelling in Britain and Ireland may now take place within the education system.

'Anyone who has a new idea and wants to change the world will do better by telling stories than by any amount of logical exhortation'[3]

This is a quotation from Stephen Denning, former World Bank executive, now a prolific writer on storytelling as a leadership skill and private consultant in knowledge management and organisational storytelling. These were the topics I discussed with a partner at a global management consultancy with over ninety offices in more than fifty countries worldwide. They describe themselves as 'consultant and facilitator, specialising in coaching senior executives to effect organisational change through storytelling'. Their formative experiences as a storyteller-consultant are markedly more disciplined, even methodical, compared with other storytellers I have interviewed and include an economics degree, rhetorical skills honed in university debating society, a graduate of two leading schools of coaching, employment in leadership and team-building capacities, an authority on communications and a student of Stephen Denning's storytelling workshops. Yet, some of their other formative experiences closely match those of storytellers in other genres: 'I care about the power of language and words and their effect. My [multinational] education illuminated the importance of oral culture. I love linguistics.'

A business of this size and prominence must take a pioneering approach to the services it offers to its clients if it is to survive in this highly competitive market and retain the loyalty of its government and corporate clients across five continents. For these reasons they employ a broad range of professional skills in the fields of communications, information, psychology and other social sciences. This leads to a deeper 'understanding of the psychological reasons why [organisational] change is needed, [how this] can be achieved through stories [and why] the power of the story is undeniable'. Research and development programmes to build on existing storytelling skills are also distinctive of this storytelling genre. They adopt 'an experimental method [of] trial and error; seeing what works; developing more deliberative techniques; defining [the client's] personal story [then applying this to] the business story'. Yet they also avoid an 'overly systematic' approach, so once the core skills have been acquired, they 'throw away the formalities for a natural performance [so as to] be fully present in the storytelling'. Their teaching methods also embrace practices that are 'chaotic' and 'entrepreneurial' (in the risk- and initiative-taking senses) and their practices aim at 'raising emotions', 'provoking action' and 'willing the audience to be part of the story beyond abstract thought and description'.

This interview was conducted in late 2008 as Britain was heading for the deepest and longest economic recession since World War Two. Yet this consultancy was already committing substantial resources to research and develop new forms of story and to 'tighten up storytelling skills' to support the leadership of public and commercial institutions 'in times of social and organisational turbulence'. This is the only example I have encountered of what might be called 'pre-emptive storytelling', to serve some future need in society rather than the redemptive, palliative or ameliorative needs more commonly found in other storytelling genres. When this interview began to suggest a rather doctrinal approach to the storyteller's art I mentioned that the words 'symbol', 'metaphor' and 'allegory' had not arisen in our discussion, nor do they appear in the index of two of Stephen Denning's best known works (although the word 'parable' does). My interviewee's rather crushing response did rather leave me wondering whether I was on to something here.

Beyond this rather hyper-rarefied specialisation, organisational storytelling is now widely practised in our society. About a third of the storytellers I have interviewed are engaged in some capacity with this genre, ranging from managerial advice to light relief for stressed-out middle-managers. There is now an extensive literature on the subject. The Society for Storytelling has a Special Interest Group dedicated to this genre. An internet search reveals companies offering hired-in storytellers and/or coaching as a function of management. And by way of post-script, this is the only storytelling genre I have encountered that attracts the overt disapproval of other storytellers (albeit an insignificant minority) on moral and/or ideological grounds. One respondent stated that, 'as a political left-winger I don't want to help large companies make more money than they already do'. And another, who approaches storytelling as a form of folklore, expresses the hope that commercial companies that offer coaching in organisational storytelling, and therefore 'know nothing about real storytelling' may not influence the future development of this art form.

'Reading the consultation as a story? I think Hippocrates[4] was doing much the same!'

This quotation was one of very few responses to a mini-e-poll conducted at one inner-city health centre to discover if general medical practice had embraced oral storytelling techniques. Several respondents were aware of what they called 'narrative-based medicine' and our family doctor (who had conducted the poll at my request) subsequently emailed a much-annotated, nine-page academic paper he had found in the practice photocopier, called 'A Narrative-based Approach to Primary Care Supervision'. One speaker at a storytelling conference I attended spoke in general terms about of the role of narratives in medical practice (as it happened, he did not; with some irony, he had lost his voice, his written answers to questions from delegates were read by the chair). But his latest book of personal stories from medicine's frontline was on sale downstairs. At this point, it had become clear this line of enquiry was leading nowhere, so was abandoned.

In contrast, a significant number of storytellers and storymakers I have interviewed apply the storyteller's art to therapeutic practices and most of these are professionally qualified social scientists, mainly in psychology, psychotherapy or dramatherapy (combines the techniques of drama and the goals of therapy). Their storytelling and storymaking practices are generally an adjunct to their professional practices, their teaching and/or primary research projects. Most describe their storymaking as a tool to bring about some 'transformative process' or 'healing change' in individuals and groups. The term 'therapeutic storymaking' (TSM) is often attributed to dramatherapist Dr Alida Gersie who has developed these techniques since the 1970s. Nowadays, the term 'storymaking' is widely used to describe any form of palliative or ameliorative storytelling that requires intensive activity and/or creative participation by participants. In the introduction to Gersie's *Reflections on Therapeutic Storytelling: The Use of Stories in Groups*, she says

> I work with stories because we not only make up and live our stories, we also need to tell them. [...] Two undisputed certainties remain. The first is that telling matters. The second is that not telling has many undesirable consequences for our health. [The work described in this book] builds on awareness gained in a range of fields – such as psychology (particularly developmental and social), philosophy (moral and educational), comparative mythology and folklore studies, group work and the arts therapies. [...] In the course of a TSM group a person's collaborative ability is evoked, nurtured and sustained by means of various activities and dynamics. [...] I shall explore how mutuality and reciprocity might be strengthened by means of structured response tasks. [...] Storymaking and storytelling are habits which people have used since time immemorial to vitalise both past and present, thereby to create trajectories into the future.[5]

This conjunction of storytelling and therapy now has wide professional applications. Research for this chapter has revealed storyteller-therapists engaged in hospital healthcare, care homes and hospices, family therapy, therapeutic counselling, psychiatric social work, dramatherapy and care of the dying and bereaved. Storyteller-therapists are now also engaged in advisory, managerial and consulting roles to develop mental health programmes in schools and other public institutions. In another extension of this genre, storyteller, consultant and speech and language therapist, Dr Nicola Grove is founding director of Open Story Tellers, the first professional company of storytellers for people with learning and communications difficulties. There is an expanding body of literature on this storytelling genre. A steady stream of postgraduate research degrees in this field of study is being awarded by British universities. Several professional conferences, including one jointly hosted by the Society for Storytelling and the British Association of Dramatherapists, have been held during the research period. And of the twelve participants at a one-day storytelling workshop I attended, three were BA or MA students of dramatherapy, one was a professional dramatherapist and one a professional mental healthcare worker.

As with some other storytelling genres, several of those I have interviewed have observed how many of their clients, mainly from disadvantaged communities and especially amongst the young, have no concept of narrative, no mental model for stories, so have grown up without recourse to this basic tool for life. In these cases the therapist has to teach the skills of what is sometimes called 'oral literacy' before therapeutic storytelling can bring any form of healing change. While these practitioners issue a warning that only those professionally qualified should attempt ameliorative treatment of mental health conditions, they do encourage storytelling as a palliative tool for personal distress or trauma. As one prominent storymaker and professional psychologist, hypnotist, therapeutic counsellor and psychiatric social worker put it, 'It's OK for the unqualified practitioner to share the therapeutic value of storytelling with their listeners, but only as an artist, not as healer or therapist.'

Still in the realm of the unqualified teller, the application of the storyteller's art to palliative care is broad and diffuse and now embraces any form of bounded community, care homes, charitable and community volunteering, religious ministry and the criminal justice system. As a form of entertainment there has been a steady growth of playback theatre (audience members tell personal stories that are then enacted by others as a form self-revelation). And a variation of this has even reached mainstream theatre where invited celebrities recount personal stories that are enacted by professional actors under the direction of a master of ceremonies. Nor should we overlook the phenomenon noted in Chapter One where a significant number of career storytellers have been able to overcome some physical, mental or social trauma in their lives and create new personal and professional identities through the self-therapeutic qualities of storytelling.

'How storytelling can save the planet'

The image of rural landscape is deeply embedded in oral storytelling. In the English language the word 'culture' has its roots in the cultivation of crops, hence 'agriculture'. Aetiological stories that attribute supernatural causes to geographical features are found in every culture. Teaching and morality tales frequently evoke images of landscape, as of course do many creation myths. Humankind's relationship with the natural environment inspires some of the most powerful metaphors, symbols and allegories in oral storytelling – presumably it has done since the first animist. Many of our best-loved folk tales are set in traditional rural communities and rural history is a rich source of traditional stories.

About a fifth of those I have interviewed tell stories to promote environmental awareness, ecology, conservation and a greater understanding of the landscape. Environmental and conservation organisations are regular employers of career storytellers. A group of environmental storytellers has formed Tales to Sustain to 'push the boundaries of where and how story is applied as a tool for positive, sustainable change'.[6] There is an established literature at this junction of storytelling and rural landscape. Amongst audience members I have interviewed some have discovered storytelling through their engagement with rural-based folklore and folk arts while others apply storytelling skills in their careers in rural conservation. And many storytellers are keen to explain how storytelling 'connects people with the ecology of the natural world which we can all associate with'.

This idea of storytelling as a conveyance for connecting people with the natural world is taken as a starting point to explore, contrast and compare some of the motivating stimuli for environmental storytelling with some of the motivating stimuli for real-world environmental initiatives. This latter phenomenon is a subject I am intimately familiar with because, by some freak misunderstanding between my decaying uncle and his deaf solicitor, the stewardship of an English Lake District landscape of internationally rare biodiversity and outstanding natural beauty was thrust upon me. The land was blighted by dereliction, legal dispute and financial loss and only the professional insights afforded as a former member of the Royal Institution of Chartered Surveyors and an absurdly optimistic sense of adventure persuaded me to accept this challenge. Seven years of life-affirming revelation and life-sapping drudgery found me honoured with a Sites of Special Scientific Interest Owners Award presented by Sir Martin Doughty,[7] Chairman of English Nature, amidst prolonged applause from conservation grandees at the 2003 Royal Show.

The heading of this section comes from the advance notice of a workshop for career storytellers on environmental storytelling that reads in full:

> [Name] offers insights into how storytelling can save the planet. What? You must be joking! Well, maybe it can play a part. Come and find out.

I was keen to attend this workshop because the leader was much respected amongst their peers, but also because, as an informed participant-observer, I was interested to discover whether the stories told did indeed connect me with the ecology of the natural world which I was so intimately familiar with. Obviously, this workshop offered no insights whatsoever into how storytelling can save the planet; however, I also searched in vain for personal connections with the ecology of the natural world. Many of the stories told here were about manmade features of the landscape not wild nature. Some were overtly polemical, judgemental and even hostile towards those who willingly accept a duty of care for the rural environment and its many stakeholders. And many seemed to be more about the storytellers' own personal landscape of mind than about any real natural landscape of shared experience and personal association. Incidentally, the supreme master of evoking a personal landscape of mind through a description of wild nature can be found throughout the work of the English Romantic poet, William Words-worth (1770-1850).

The facilitator at another environmental workshop I attended also seemed to be conscripting poor old Mother Nature in support of their personal landscape of mind; in this example, the doctrinal writ of their own professional training as 'a Jungian, psychodynamic counsellor, coach & eco-psychologist'. The form of this workshop required its participants to enact the story of The Prince in the Tower. I cannot claim to have followed the finer narrative detail here because, as an out-ward-facing window in the tower's walls, and unlike my inward-facing mirror-neighbours with whom I was holding hands, observation of this enactment behind me was restricted by a pain in my arthritic neck. But from what I could gather, we were all supposed to be marching in ritual lockstep with this facilita-tor's personal journey of reparation for some wrong or injury they had perpe-trated against the ecology of the natural world. Indeed, a later visit to their website confirmed how, 'as a child, my relationship with the Earth pulsed and flourished … and then I lost it. My life since has been a long journey home, unknowingly so until recent times. So I, too, have lived in the Princes Tower'. I cannot speak for other participants, but far from connecting me with the ecology of the natural world, this workshop left me with a pervasive sense of alienation, exclusion and collective guilt.

Meanwhile, this e-notice from the Society for Storytelling arrived in my in-box recently.

"Leave the great, dear tree unfallen so that birds may perch upon it."

Warning – A Lecture by [name of academic-storyteller].

At [address, www]. Booking recommended. [date, time]. [...] I will use these sto-ries from different cultures to clarify the ecological, social, and intrapsychic effects of a story-character's relationship with forewarnings. [...]

For the record, best practice nature conservation often requires the felling of healthy trees. For example, those that overshadow open water tend to suppress aquatic biodiversity in their shade. Also, fallen trees can be efficient recyclers of the molecular biochemistry of life – the elemental basis of all food webs – so sometimes fallen trees can be of greater benefit to birds than living trees can be for perching upon. For all I know, this lecture may have provided penetrating insights into the ecological, social and intrapsychic effects of a story-character's relationship with forewarnings. But I am suspicious its central thesis, even unheard, because its headline forewarning is itself a fallacious orthodoxy. Once again, our connecting pathway to the ecology of the natural world has been obstructed by the storyteller's personal landscape of mind.

No suggestion is intended here that polemics, doctrinal writ and fallacious orthodoxies are commonplace in environmental (or any other genre of) storytelling practice. I am only suggesting that personal landscapes of mind, as a driving motive for storytelling, can all too easily become counterproductive as a means of connecting people with the ecology of the natural world. Ideology, another form of personal landscape of mind, can also be a motivating stimulus in storytelling practice, as it can be in real-world environmental stewardship. My most formative years coincided with the 1960s protest movements, decades before the word 'environmental' gained its 'ism' suffix. I clearly recall pioneering conservationists pleading with an un-listening world to try and prevent this nascent movement from being driven by ideology, as were the peace and civil rights movements at the time. Fast forward to the early years of this century when many of Britain's laws and regulations for countryside governance were inspired by misguided political ideology and witness what became of the award-winning stewardship of my family's land.

Any first year student of Chartered Surveying could have told Sir Martin Doughty and his applauding grandees that environmental sustainability becomes fatally undermined unless mutually reinforced by both legal and economic sustainability. Sure enough, my family's land quickly became triply unsustainable. Worse, without some adroit managerial footwork, my award-winning stewardship would have become a crime punishable by heavy fines. When I returned my award to Sir Martin with a terse monograph on the follies of misguided political ideology, the high level enquiry he set up ended with one of his senior directors alleging that it was I who was 'trying to subvert the will of Parliament'. Under such explicit threats, the inevitable denouement of this story would lead to the sale of most of this family land into public ownership. At least this way the environmental, legal and economic costs of such political ideology would be shared amongst an unwitting public rather than borne alone by this award-winning environmentalist.

Some stories, like some real-world environmental initiatives, become so overlain by singular landscapes of mind, popular myth and utopian ideals, that the real cause and effect – the driving forces of a narrative – are completely lost from view in the telling. For example, no one has contributed more to the environmental sustainability of these Lake District landscapes than the children's author Beatrix Potter (1866-1943). However, it was not just the utopian ideals of popular myth that turned her name into a global brand, a Hollywood movie and a sourcebook for teaching English in Japanese schools. Her enduring legacy was also built on more solid foundations of pragmatism. Her research into biological symbiosis in lichens – environmental sustainability – was presented as a scientific paper to the Linnean Society of London in 1898 (actually it was presented by her uncle because women were not allowed to address the Society in person). It was the commercial sales of her anthropomorphic stories of Peter Rabbit and his friends – economic sustainability – that enabled her to purchase the land, farms and flocks of sheep that she later gifted to the National Trust. And it was the restrictive covenants (legal restrictions on land use) that her lawyer-husband imposed on landowners she had commercial dealings with – legal sustainability – that enshrined the preservation of these wildlife habitats in the laws of England. Here, fate seizes control of this story, because Beatrix Potter sold some land to my own Granny B in 1930 (the deed of sale lies on my desk as I write this) so all the land under my stewardship was protected under these restrictive covenants. But as the events described above attest, not even the laws of England were sufficient to protect this landscape from misguided political ideology.

Returning to a more life-affirming vision of landscape as inspiration for story-telling, some of the most visceral joys of managing this land followed from a policy of promoting it as a free educational, scientific and recreational resource under the currently fashionable title of 'a shared ownership of the countryside'. Farmers, visitors, scientists, students, bureaucrats, ecologists, all brought with them a powerful sense they were already primary stakeholders in this landscape. The stories they recounted were seldom born of polemics, doctrinal writ, fallacious orthodoxy, misguided ideology, utopian ideals or even popular myth (although I warmed to the one told about my redoubtable maiden aunt being a cross-dressing fighter pilot in World War Two). And all their stories connected them directly with the ecology of the natural world which we can all associate with, a real landscape of shared experience and personal association. I am grateful to them all for their vivid insights into this land that I, encumbered by officialdom and calloused by hard labour, would never otherwise have experienced. For example, Manchester University Department of Earth Sciences, were regular visitors here and were a rich source of personal stories about this land.

> And so it was that one day I came upon the gnomish figure of a geomathematician sitting cross-legged on a large boulder. 'For twenty years', he said, 'I have sat here alone for a whole day, imagining new mathematical ways of expressing the meanings of this landscape.' 'For instance?' I ask, as might an acolyte at the feet of his master. 'Alone' he repeats softly. So realising I am an intruder on his very private landscape of mind, and conscious that all science is to some extent metaphor, I leave him to speculate on the mathematical stories told by these old stones.

'This is the first time they have been listened to. They ask to be told stories, then they start to speak the unspeakable and say, "I am a person and I am not alone"'

Community storytelling as a distinct storytelling genre is one of the hardest to define, its outcomes so fugitive and its methods so subsumed in the fabric of everyday life. The quotation above comes from a storyteller who works with refugees and is well qualified to do so: widely travelled, of mixed ethnicity, speaks ten languages, a collector of folk songs, a musician and theatrical performer, a trained teacher, holder of a fine arts degree and suffers a permanent disability as a consequence of an act of mindless bigotry. As they outlined in interview, the particular distress of a refugee is their overwhelming sense of loss, of identity, status, belonging, homeland, community, language of communication, and their sense of geographical, cultural and social displacement. 'All life is a struggle'. Stories are the catalyst for healing, at first a shared greeting, a personal welcome, perhaps a familiar song, a game, some connection with their own culture, a personal story that might be told with as few as six words, a personal expression of self, a dialogue between cultures, the emergence of a cross-cultural community, and over time, the dawn of a new identity and of personal development.

Another inner-city, another disadvantaged community, an arts-based social project led by a church minister as part of his pastoral duties. He outlines how storymaking changes people's personal stories in order to change their real lives.

> It's about creating story-rich people, where their own stories are woven into the fabric of the community, gaining power and identity through the arts and creating a shared identity through storytelling. Then crime sinks. [...] The arrival of asylum-seekers is the best thing that's happened [here]. They're story-rich people, the adults are educated. Their children tell stories from their own cultures in school. The local kids are story-thin and demand stories from their own culture and their own parents. So storytelling becomes a shared cultural experience in this community.

In the early planning stages of this study, I asked Ruth Finnegan if I could assume that storytelling in communities performs the same role today as it always has done in the past. 'Yes and no', she replied. 'Yes, in so far as narratives have always helped us understand and make sense of our world. No, in so far as every storytelling event is unique, an act of personal expression by the storyteller, filtered through their own personality, while every audience member brings their own expectations and cultural baggage to the event.' Perhaps a more interesting question might have been: Would the aims and objectives of this study be better served by researching, contrasting and comparing the performance practices found in different types of community storytelling?

In this context, storyteller and Director of the Scottish Storytelling Centre, Donald Smith, has drawn my attention to how enduring storytelling traditions there are still more influential on storytelling practices than are the acquired practices of the individual storyteller, as described in Chapter Six. Meanwhile, community storyteller and folklorist, Simon Heywood, has drawn my attention to how an earlier draft of this chapter seriously underrepresents long-established storytelling traditions in minority communities throughout Britain and Ireland. Amongst these he includes travelling peoples, Roma, Jewish and immigrant communities from Africa, the Caribbean, South Asia and more recently, the Middle-East. In further discussions that followed, he revealed how the performance practices in these communities do differ in certain respects from what he called 'mainstream contemporary storytelling', and while these practices do 'appear to be undergoing change and contraction [they] are not dead yet'. Pressed further for examples of specific differences, he cited studies he has made of storytelling in Jewish communities.

> A working storyteller in the contemporary 'scene' will boast proudly of a repertoire of three or four hundred stories. Competent storytellers in a mature tradition, by contrast, will find little or nothing remarkable in a repertoire of several thousand tales, perhaps interwoven and organised into cycles and/or underpinned by various mental disciplines of cognition, expression and memory.

> Most [mainstream storytellers] encounter storytelling as young adults and begin public careers after a brief training, no training at all, or trained in something other than storytelling. By contrast, a traditional Jewish storyteller [might be] systematically trained as a storyteller by [their] grandmother from infancy; [might begin their] 'home schooling' at the age of about four and not tell stories in public until [they are] a young adult. Comparable early experiences are reported by Scottish travellers such as Sheila Stewart, who was mentored from childhood by several family members.

In discussing the physical performance of traditional community storytellers, Heywood pointed to the ritualised behaviour often associated with the formal, social and religious practices of these communities. Some folklorists and anthropologists define such ritualised behaviour as 'cultural performance', which this study discusses in some detail in Chapter Six. Meanwhile, he also made reference to the performance practices of audience members.

> Listeners in mature traditions have no particular *ex officio* reverence for the role of the storyteller; on the contrary, they tend to be seasoned, knowledgeable, intolerant and vocal critics. Storytelling is often interwoven seamlessly with everyday life,

and part of the storyteller's skill is the tact and discernment to know which story to tell when, where, how and to whom.

This is about as far as the available evidence on performance practices in traditional community will stretch. A re-examination of my notes from interviews and extended discussions with storytellers from traveller, Jewish and South Asian communities, and with several faith and religion storytellers, adds little of interest. The exception here is a passing reference to research in Scotland into an 'urban storytelling [genre] by the elderly – mainly men – with its black humour'. While openly acknowledging a strong London and south-east England evidential bias in this study – the very places where these community storytelling traditions are least likely to be found – we must just hope for more focused research on this subject before these traditions contract to the point of invisibility.

Three-quarters of those I have interviewed are engaged in community storytelling, most of whom affirm its primacy amongst other storytelling genres. Evidence for this study suggests it is prevalent in one form or another in almost every type of community where people gather together with others in common cause.

'Me as a sixteen or seventeen year old would have killed me sitting in this room now, given the views that I now have about the conflict and making peace with enemies'

This quotation comes from a leaflet published by the Glencree Centre for Peace & Reconciliation, a non-governmental organisation founded in 1974 as a response to violent conflict in Ireland. It is one of a number of such organisations that field counsellors and reconciliation practitioners to work for conflict resolution and peace-building within and between divided communities. Many counsellors use storytelling techniques as a practical and inspirational means to develop constructive relationships and mutual understanding. One such is Alistair Little, former member of a proscribed Protestant paramilitary group who served a twelve-year prison sentence for a sectarian murder committed as a teenager. His long and painful journey of renouncing violence came, as he says, 'at huge cost in terms of loneliness and isolation'. This has since led him into the world of conflict transformation and peace-building in Ireland, England, Kosovo, Bosnia, Serbia and South Africa, and he has shared a public platform with the Dalai Lama.

When I met him in 2008 I found it unsettling at first that we quite spontaneously started swapping humorous anecdotes about the darker days of the Irish troubles; he as a reformed paramilitary, I as an old soldier all too familiar with early efforts to establish constructive dialogue with, and between, paramilitary groups. Our robust exchange provoked strong memories of those days but also reminded me of the importance of humour in the peace-making and reconciliation process, even though such humour often takes the bleakest and most macabre forms. On one occasion a prominent figure in Northern Ireland – at best described as an apologist for his cause – played an elaborate practical joke on my military unit of such Machiavellian ingenuity (sadly, it cannot be recounted here) that we were left gasping in admiration.

The process by which humour can soften the hardest of hearts is analysed by anthropologist Mahadev L. Apte when he observes that humour 'is one of the most powerful tools available to humans in their communicative endeavors'.[8] Affirming that no single theory can explain the complex nature of humour he identifies three approaches to humour that can reveal valuable insights.

> Intellect-based theories [propose] that the human mind recognizes accidental or deliberately evoked incongruity, ambiguity, and/or oppositional dualism in external events and tries to resolve them by finding new relationships or by mediating among them.

> Emotion-based theories […] link humour to such preexisting feelings and emotions as hostility, aggression, disparagement, superiority, or malice toward others. These emotions then create a humorous state of mind when others suffer from various kinds of misfortunes [and] the mind compares one's [own] eminence with the follies and infirmities of others.

> Theories of cathartic release and relief [hold that] humor permits the release of pent-up energy or suppressed impulses, producing a mirthful state of mind. It is relief from the strain of excess energy or repressed impulses that leads to mirth.[9]

My on-going dialogue with Alistair Little led him to make a most generous offer: that I should recount a story he tells in his book, *Give a Boy a Gun*[10] as if it was my own personal story. This is a well-established method of teaching storytellers how to empathise with opinions and values that are not the storyteller's own. I warm to this story because it illustrates how fear and mistrust can coexist intimately with the mundanities of everyday life, and the degree of raw courage it takes to embrace reconciliation.

> I'd spent the day with Gerry. He's a Republican ex-bomber I'd met three years ago at Glencree. Since then we'd both been looking for a way forward without violence and revenge. Today, as we often do now, we'd been sharing our different stories with kids in a Republican school. The Peace Process may be underway, but I'm still not easy about driving in a Republican area of Belfast. Normally, I'd get a taxi home, but today I'd driven him to his flat so he could get his car and show me the way to a part of the City I knew. So now it's taken him ten minutes to get his car keys. I'm sitting in the middle of Andersonstown, a Republican stronghold.

It's dark, cold. Gable-ends depict Republican victories, slogans, heroes. People are looking at my car, whispering. It's my worst nightmare. Is it a set-up? Have I been recognised? I get on with Gerry; we've worked together but can I trust him? Sectarianism is still everywhere in the province and it doesn't take much to spark violence. A moment later he's in his car and I'm soon safe home. A week later we're story-sharing at a Protestant school. One kid asks if our friendship is really as easy as it seems. I say we've still got a long way to go. With our background it isn't easy and I tell the story of my long wait in Andersonstown. Gerry bursts out laughing. I say, 'What's so funny?' He says, 'I was scared too. I didn't want you to know which my flat was. It was my worst nightmare. Was I going to find myself at the wrong end of Loyalist gun when I next opened my front door? So I left the lights off. I was crawling about in the dark feeling for the car keys. It took me all of ten minutes to find them'.

Storytelling for peace and reconciliation is now well established in many areas of conflict and confrontation around the world and in many cases is sponsored by governments and international agencies as part of wider political initiatives. In less specialised forms, and requiring varying degrees of qualification and experience, this genre is now commonplace in our society.

'It's about using storytelling as part of the restorative justice system'

The speaker here is a former school drama teacher, storyteller, professional dramatherapist, and currently a Restorative Justice Coordinator for one of the countrywide, multi-agency Youth Offending Teams (YOTs). These agencies supervise young people under the direction of the criminal courts, set up community services and reparation plans and aim to prevent youth recidivism and custodial sentences. As they outlined in interview, restorative storytelling is an intensely co-creative process of emotional and behavioural healing, an enrichment process that blurs with many of the normal functions of society. It can help prevent a drift back into criminality and can ease youth offenders' re-integration into society. At the YOT I visited some of the story-sharing workshops are led by a uniformed police officer, which helps ease the relationship between youth offenders and these symbols of law enforcement. Prisons are another venue for story-sharing and here prisoners find opportunities to express their personal feelings in an atmosphere of greater conviviality, openness and tolerance. In a preventative role, restorative storytellers and dramatherapists work in schools, for social services and as counsellors for children with learning difficulties and behavioural problems.

'Storytelling promotes interfaith dialogue in society, creates an ethos and nourishes the soul'

This is the near-verbatim response of one storyteller to a question I asked them about the role of storytelling in faith and religion. As the web pages of the Faith and Religion Special Interest Group of the Society for Storytelling says, 'At the heart of every religion there are wonderful stories. There are also a great deal of stories with themes related to spirituality and spiritual growth that are not connected to a particular religion.' Storytellers I have interviewed report that faith stories are now told in community groups, at faith and interfaith meetings, book launches, libraries, private homes, conferences, on public stages, and storytellers of any faith, or none, now find themselves telling in places of worship of widely diverse religions. Storytelling is now commonly part of the pastoral care duties of religious leaders and often takes place in wholly secular contexts. The Church of Scotland is a partnership organisation to the Scottish Storytelling Centre. Bibliodrama (Bible stories enacted during religious worship) is a growing trend. And in response to the news that theological colleges now teach storytelling skills, one newspaper ran an article under the headline ATHEIST STORYTELLER TEACHES VICARS.

From a personal perspective, as an atheist of a scientific-rationalist tendency, I shall not be exploring further these multiple applications of faith storytelling. Instead this section raises the question, what happens when the personal beliefs, socio-cultural affiliations and value systems expressed in a story are irreconcilable with those of the listener of that story? 23 career storytellers were asked in interview about the assumptions they make about the private world of their audience members, and although this yielded no startling revelations, their responses suggest that few storytellers had ever addressed this question. Some insights, however, can be gleaned from one faith-based storytelling conference I attended.

Unsurprisingly, many of the stories told – even those of secular origin – were structured around some presupposed sin, followed by a quest for redemption by means of a prescribed course of conduct and/or belief. As one Dutch anthropologist I met there commented, 'I suppose the mother and father of all stories are set in the Garden of Eden.' Although the idea of eating from the tree of knowledge as an expression of original sin is alien to me, it was surprising how many other delegates freely discussed their discomfort when listening to such faith-based redemption stories. When late in the evening I was discovered by another delegate of my acquaintance deep-breathing cold night air outside the conference venue, they simply said, 'Oh, thank goodness for that, I thought it was just me.' I later recounted these events during interviews with two faith storytellers who had been at this conference. One responded: 'Ah, yes, thank you. I'd never thought about that.' The other, with studied concern for my apparent lack of enlightenment, recounted the story of Adam and Eve and ended it with the words, 'That's what we believe.'

Yet this kind of conceptual gulf that can so easily distance the storyteller from their listeners is not restricted to faith-based storytelling. One workshop I attended seemed to be based on a wholly speculative theory of narrative consciousness, and since many of the participants were themselves social scientists, it came as no surprise that the event turned palpably hostile. Nor did it surprise me that when I interviewed the conference organiser a few weeks later they reported that this workshop had been the subject of several formal complaints. This kind of unbridgeable divide between teller and listener was brought into focus recently by Emerson International School of Storytelling which held a week-long course called Dangerous Stories. The wording of its publicity is unambiguous.

> Of all human inventions, story is far and away the most dangerous. At the heart of every war, argument or dispute lurks a story. There are narratives of justification and blame, tales of persecution and revenge. [...] Stories have real power [...] they can stir passions that can lead to tragic consequences.

'Storytelling is a tool to give people a feel for Shakespeare and his world'

This quotation comes from a storyteller, actor, folk singer and freelance educational practitioner at the reconstructed Shakespeare's Globe Theatre on London's South Bank. It is a good example of how oral storytelling remains a living, breathing carrier of our own cultural heritage in today's digital age. From London's British Museum to the Mythstories Museum in the English West Midlands storytellers are now often featured in museum education programmes. Mounting evidence from academic research shows how 'museums are increasingly making use of professional actors, living history interpreters, performers and storytellers in their presentations [and how] stories, storytelling and narrative can provide a valuable tool for assisting learning about museum collections'.[11] And amongst a growing literature on the subject of storytelling for cultural heritage is Eric Maddern's *A Teacher's Guide to Storytelling at Historic Sites*.[12]

It would be hard to imagine a more evocative setting to hear the Anglo-Saxon myths than by firelight in a reconstructed iron-age roundhouse, and in the interval to sip mulled apple juice under a full moon with the call of a tawny owl in a nearby oak wood. Many of the storytellers I have met and interviewed tell stories to enhance some cultural or historical experience. A significant number of fellow workshop attenders and audience members I have interviewed were training to become Blue Badge tourist guides. Public libraries increasingly welcome storytelling as part of their education and life-long learning programmes.

> It's consistently the most successful event we've ever put on [...] audiences of 70-90 every month [...] all ages, sexes, minority groups. Nothing else has achieved that [...] it's given them a focus they didn't have. [...] It fits in with our programme so the library is seen more as a community venue. Other knock-on effects are not easy to quantify but [regular attenders do sometimes] become library members.[13]

Meanwhile, my south London borough council has introduced a whole new form of cultural learning through personal storytelling during Adult Learners Week. Abibat Olulode of Lambeth Libraries explains:

> The idea is that you can come into the library and meet and talk to someone you would never normally have any contact with. Instead of taking out a book, you can hire one of our volunteer 'human books' and hear what they have to say.[14]

Beyond the mainstream genre of oral storytelling in the service of cultural heritage, there are now companies of multimedia performers who offer guided tours, tell stories from history and perform historical re-enactments relevant to the cultural sites and visitor attractions that employ them.

'I admire their passion and energy'

The expectation of finding a concise definition of performance storytelling, that embraces all examples witnessed during research for this study, yet clearly distinguishes it from other storytelling genres, was very short-lived indeed. That said, there are some notable characteristics that provide us with clues. First, this is a term mainly used in Britain, whereas it tends to be called 'platform storytelling' in the USA and I have heard this latter term used in Ireland. As we found in the last chapter, performance storytelling often takes place in theatres and other public venues, at festivals or as site-specific events and mainly plays to paying audiences. Many such tellings are introduced by a master of ceremonies with the teller coming onstage to audience applause and the telling also drawn to a close in theatrical manner with applause and one or more curtain calls. The common exception here is Scotland, where even epic storytelling tends to follow the more informal practices of a community telling.

The precise relationship between performance storytelling and a theatrical performance is similarly difficult to define and I shall make no attempt to do so here. As we found in the last chapter, audience members often use theatrical terms to describe their experience of a storytelling, yet remain generally aware of how their experience differs from that of a theatrical performance. Stories are seldom told in character and are mostly told with the teller's naturally modulated voice. This genre is often associated with a more expressive style of telling, leading to a more immersive experience for audiences – yet exceptions abound. The storyteller's performance skills overlap with those of the actor only in part, mainly because few storytellers have learnt the skills of theatre stagecraft. And as we shall see in Chapter Six, some distinction between performance storytelling and other genres can be identified by observing the same storyteller at both an informal community-style telling and at a formal theatre telling in front of a paying audience.

About two thirds of those I have interviewed include performance storytelling amongst the genres they practice, though some who are best known for this genre report they enjoy more, or are more proficient in, other storytelling genres. So, in Chapter One we see how a storyteller who describes themselves as 'mainly a fireside teller' was booked the following week to tell to a conference audience of 2,500. Added to this, amongst all the storytelling events I have witnessed, I have been unable to make a clear distinction between the 'performance' and the 'community' storyteller. Nor can I find compelling evidence that different storytelling genres can be logically arranged along some sort of continuum with say 'fireside storytelling' at one end and 'performance storytelling' at the other. Once again the 'mosaic' metaphor seems more fitting here. That said, performance storytelling can refer to a very wide range of events, from a solo telling of almost any duration, to a tandem or multi-handed epic, with interval, with or without music and/or song, and/or dance, costumed or not, or a competitive story-slam or biggest liar contest and probably many other subgenres as yet unimagined. As we shall discover in Chapter Six, oral storytelling techniques are now embedded in all manner of stage performances and I can find no empirical distinction between the more elaborate forms of performance storytelling and theatrical performances which use original spoken narratives and call for highly reactive audience responses.

Reviewing all the evidence for this study it is possible however to identify two significant roles that distinguish performance storytelling from other genres. First, it has become the most prominent public face of storytelling in Britain and Ireland and the portal through which many people discover other storytelling genres. Second, the performance techniques developed by pioneering performance storytellers over the last few decades have become, and remain, a significant influence on the practices of storytellers in other genres.

'My favourite performances are those that are most daring, that blur the line between performance and self-revelation'[15]

There is one established storytelling genre that has not been included amongst those described above: personal storytelling, stories about the teller themselves, rather than traditional myths, legends, fables, folk and wonder tales. This genre has, of course, always existed in the telling of personal anecdotes and much story-telling in traditional communities also takes this form. From the literature and from several storyteller interviews I have learnt this genre is more popular in the USA than it is in Britain and Ireland. While most storytellers here tell traditional stories, one teller with a background in street theatre, expressed their deep regret that personal storytelling was spreading here from across the Atlantic. Yet already there are now informal local storytelling groups that focus their activities on personal storytelling. Many of the stories told at 'biggest liar' competitions I have attended are personal stories. And this genre can now be found as public performances at storytelling festivals.

This chapter also reveals elements of personal storytelling in the social zones of interaction between teller and participant in every genre reviewed above. The effectiveness of all these genres is dependent on an intensive engagement by participants in the co-creation process. As one community storyteller describes it above, storymaking 'changes people's personal stories in order to change their real lives'. Since changing one's personal story must surely involve a process of self-awareness, it suggests that all storytelling and storymaking contain elements of self-revelation. The quotation at the head of this section comes from an article by Tom Bland, Young Storyteller of the Year, MA student of storytelling as a healing therapy and driving force behind one-day conferences on this topic. He describes in very personal terms his journey of self-revelation as a student on the three-month course at Emerson International School of Storytelling. As a Waldorf Steiner school their website affirms how 'self-awareness is the foundation for making a difference in your personal life, your career and for the planet. [...] Transformational learning requires a deep and holistic engagement in the learning process as well as in the content of learning'.

To explore this theme further, an internet search using key words 'personal + development' reveals a number of organisations offering personal development courses, personal counselling, group-work and life coaching. The first such site I visited offered two consultant-coaches, both describing themselves as storytellers and one having trained at Emerson College. Following a different pathway again, several storytelling coaches and workshop leaders have confirmed my own impression that many of those attending workshops do so for reasons of personal development rather than career advancement or the acquisition of storytelling skills. It was also noted in Chapter One how the blurring of performance and self-revelation is evident amongst those storytellers who discover a new personal and professional identity through the self-therapeutic qualities of storytelling.

'Government wants quantitative results, so all research is bent to this'

In some of my interviews, where storytellers were also engaged in research projects, I raised the question of the efficacy and functions of storytelling in today's society. The quotation at the head of this section comes from one story-teller and social scientist currently seeking research funding, and seems to set the bar very high indeed, particularly as storytelling practices are mainly associated with the social sciences which are more likely to yield qualitative rather than quantitative research findings.

In educational storytelling, the earliest endorsement I can find for the efficacy of storytelling is Katherine Cather's 1922 *Education by storytelling* and referred to above. The most recent is Sir Jim Rose's 2009 report on the primary school curriculum for the Department for Education in England and Wales.[16] In organisational storytelling the partner I interviewed at the global management consultants came at the question of efficacy as an economist. If their clients are convinced that teaching storytelling to senior executives shows a good return on their investment then market forces alone demonstrate sufficient efficacy. They also pointed out the inherent methodological difficulties of assessing quantitative efficacy for their storytelling activities. This business measures its own financial success by the revenue earned under each of about 35 headline services they offer their clients. Although storytelling is a component of most of these services, it is not itself a headline service, and therefore its contribution to the company's revenues cannot be measured quantitatively. Incidentally, another storyteller I interviewed, who teaches storytelling to senior staff at two other global management consultants, noted that the issue of efficacy does not arise at all because it is manifestly self-evident.

Storytellers practicing in the public service – health, welfare, criminal justice and so on – report they often find three common impediments to demonstrating efficacy: a widespread misunderstanding of the difference between ameliorative as opposed to palliative care, the inherent methodological limitations available for demonstrating efficacy, and a widespread ignorance of the tools, processes and practices now available to the public-service-storyteller. So far as the public subsidy of festivals and other storytelling events is concerned, the Arts Councils in Britain and Ireland do issue tightly worded criteria by which they assess applications for grants. However, as I know to my own personal cost as a documentary filmmaker, these are subject to ever-changing whims of the relevant minister, current political priorities and the general state of the nation's economy. It may be no comfort to storytellers but all the issues discussed in this section on efficacy also apply to the documentary filmmaker, whether for broadcast television, business communications or the public service. The problem here is that the inherent strengths – and note, weaknesses – of the film medium, as with the storytelling medium, are not self-evident to an outsider, so decision-makers are often ill-qualified to judge the worth of a proposal or the track record of the filmmaker. For this reason the second task of the filmmaker (after exchange of contracts) is to begin the lengthy process of educating the client on the ways and means of the film medium itself. (Incidentally, making people feel better about the purchases they have just made is now standard practice in the world of sales and marketing.)

There seems to be a general consensus amongst storytellers and storymakers that their practices can be seen as a form of tool kit for bringing about some purposive outcome amongst their listener/co-creators. This closely mirrors the view taken by the psychologists of music in the documentary film I made and referred to in the last chapter: 'Music can be understood as some sort of coded instruction to get us doing something. We construct music in our minds, responding to it, using it for some purpose, however abstract.' As to the efficacy of these purposive outcomes, it can be seen from this comparative overview of storytelling and storymaking genres, that they are clearly wide-ranging in scope. As to the comparative efficacy of these purposive outcomes, that is a subject far beyond the scope of this present study.

Notes & References

1.   'Storytelling in Education', undated leaflet, Society for Storytelling UK, Education Sub-committee.

2.   Katherine Dunlap Cather, *Education by Story-telling: Showing the Value of Storytelling as an Educational Tool for the Use of All Workers with Children* (London UK: Harrap & Co, 1922).

3.   Stephen Denning, *The Leader's Guide to Storytelling* (San Francisco USA: Jossey-Bass, a Wiley Imprint, 2005), Introduction, p. xvi.

4.   Hippocrates: fifth century BCE Greek physician, known as the founder of medicine.

5.   Alida Gersie, *Reflections on Therapeutic Storytelling: The Use of Stories in Groups* (London UK: Jessica Kingsley, 1997), pp. 1-6.

6.   Charlene Collison, 'Tales to Sustain', *Storylines*, Society for Storytelling UK, Winter 2010, p. 7.

7.   Sir Martin Doughty obituary at www.guardian.co.uk/environment/2009/mar/09/sir-martin-doughty-obituary.

8.   Mahadev L. Apte, 'Humor', in *Folklore, Cultural Performances, and Popular Entertainments*, ed. Richard Bauman (New York USA: Oxford University Press, 1992), p. 67.

9.   'Humor', pp. 69-70.

10. Alistair Little, *Give a Boy a Gun* (London UK: Darton Longman and Todd, 2009).

11. Maureen James, 'What can investment in narrative contribute to museum education?' (unpublished master's thesis, Institute of Education, London UK, 2002), p. 20.

12. Eric Maddern, *A Teacher's Guide to Storytelling at Historic Sites* (London UK: English Heritage, 1992).

13. Unpublished extracts from interview notes for the Traditional Arts Team's Storytelling Café Evaluation Report, March 2006.

14. 'Borrow a person at the library', *Lambeth Life*, London Borough of Lambeth UK, May 2010, p. 12.

15. Tom Bland, 'Echo of "the now of storytelling"', *Storylines*, Society for Storytelling UK, Summer 2009, p. 8.

16. Visit www.education.gov.uk/publications/primary curriculum review.

FOUR

COMMUNITIES IN A LANDSCAPE

ℰℭ

his chapter follows multiple pathways that lead to the communities, groups, companies, organisations and representative bodies that give structural form to the storytelling movement today. It reviews their working practices, leaderships and interconnectedness, and reflects on the social roles they play in driving change, development and growth of oral storytelling. Evidence has been drawn from extended interviews with their leaderships, participant observation of their public activities, analysis of two of their evaluation reports and by monitoring their websites and e-newsletters throughout the four-year research period of this study. It is also hoped that this chapter may be read as a snapshot overview of the state-of-the-storytelling-nation today.

'We are a group of people who love to listen and to tell stories from around the world in a friendly club atmosphere'

This quotation comes from the website of one long-established local storytelling group. It lies at the heart of what the storytelling movement is all about and it goes some way to explain why this innate, human, social and cultural phenomenon is thriving in an age of digitised automata and mass culture theory. It is a group of people who gather together to share common social purpose. Telling and listening to stories is what gives individuals and communities their identity. Stories from around the world are, in a literal sense, the collective identity of humankind. And a friendly club atmosphere engenders a spirit of conviviality, openness, understanding and tolerance. Such groups are now scattered widely across Britain, Ireland and most of the developed world and they are torch-bearers of fundamental human values in doubting and uncertain times. Thirteen such groups have been studied in widely scattered regions of Britain.

A pathway can be found into the origins, history, practices and ethos of these local storytelling groups from their names alone, but to clarify a point made in the Preface, the term 'local storytelling group' or 'local group' is used throughout this study to describe these communities, whereas the most commonly used term is 'club', as in Eden Valley Storytelling Club and Tir Na Nog Storytelling Club. The craft skill of the storyteller is evoked by the word 'guild', as in Surrey Storytellers Guild. The word 'circle' in their title, as in Cardiff Storytelling Circle and Kings Heath Storytelling Circle, alludes to the ancient tradition of sitting in a circle with a master of ceremonies or host/ess who invites those present to tell their stories in turn – hence also the term 'story round'. Many groups link their identity to their geographical location as with The Borders (of Scotland) Bards, Mouth of the Mersey (river), Tales at the Watermill and Storytelling at Milgi's Yurt. Some hint at the social setting of their meetings, as do Storytelling at the Ostrich (pub) and Café Credo. Some names describe the performance style of their storytelling, hence Infectious Theatre, Stroud Story Cabaret, 40 Winks Bedtime Storynights and Life Stories Café.

Some groups incorporate in their names a veritable thesaurus of synonyms for the act of storytelling itself, for example: Yarnspinners, Fibs & Fables, Wordweavers, Meat of the Tongue, Spoken Word, Tale Tellers, Shaggy Dogs, Towncriers, Play it by Ear, Winged Word, Spinners, Word of Mouth, Blatherers, or its Scottish variation Bletherers. Like the Lunar Society pioneers of the English Enlightenment who met at full moon, some group names are calendar reminders of their monthly meetings, as are First Friday Fling and Second Tuesday Storytellers. Some career storytellers formed companies and the name stuck when they formed a local storytelling group, as in Greenwich Storytelling Company. Some groups incorporate the storytelling ritual of 'call' (from the storyteller) and 'response' (from the audience) in their names, hence 'Crick Crack', 'Guid Crack' and 'Bit Crack' according to regional variation. 'Ceilidh' is a common name for local groups especially in Scotland and Ireland and I hope I can spare readers the embarrassment this Englishman suffered when I first attended one, knowing neither how the word was pronounced nor what it meant. It is pronounced KAY-lee, with a silent D and just the hint of an aspiratory H at the end. It is a nineteenth century Gaelic word meaning 'visiting' and describes an informal social gathering for any combination of folk music, singing, storytelling and dancing. Some group names identify the nature of their own membership, as do Storytelling Dinner Ladies, Scandalmongers, African Story Group and Storytailors. And there are also group names that seem to conjure up worlds as fantastical as the stories they tell, as do Three Heads in a Well, Flying Donkeys Storycircle, Starkadder Spoken Word Society, Dreamfired Storynights and Spiders Web Storytellers.

All thirteen groups studied engage in multiple activities. Their regular events, which are variously called 'meetings', 'club nights', 'story nights', 'circles' or 'ceilidhs', are generally held monthly (one meets weekly), last about two hours and generally take one of two distinct forms. The first finds the teller(s) and their listeners facing each other. Here, the teller(s) may be group members or 'invited' or 'guest' tellers, may tell for the full two hours, generally with an interval, or may share the programme with one or more events that can include an open discussion with listeners. Part or all of the event may be taken up with opportunities for group members to tell their own stories, which can be variously called 'open evenings', 'open house', 'open mic/mike', 'floor spots', 'open telling' or 'stories from the floor'. These events can provide a platform for less experienced storytellers to gain confidence and for more experienced tellers to develop new stories in front of a sympathetic audience. Storytellers visiting from a nearby group will sometimes sign up a promising newcomer to tell at their own group. And as we have seen in Chapter One, there are even examples of reluctant storytellers launching successful careers at such events.

The second, less formal form, finds group members sitting in a circle or sit-where-you-can arrangement. Here the proceedings can be elaborated with warm-up activities that include storymaking games, skills-based exercises, technical discussions and friendly advice from others in the group. Alternatively, group members are equally welcome to just sit, listen and enjoy. One ceilidh I attended was a more boisterous affair, held above a pub, where tellers either took to the floor or remained seated for their story, song, joke, personal anecdote, reminiscence, or just challenged us with riddles. This event was greatly enhanced by being held at Halloween – the town was jumping, invaded by bellowing ghouls and sprites (or were they out-of-season Christmas tree fairies?). And one local group I have monitored has recently opened their monthly meetings to poets, writers, singers and musicians.

Some local groups stage rehearsed group tellings which are generally performed by between four and six tellers, the performance being either devised collectively or directed by a single lead storyteller. They often recount epic Greek, Arthurian, Hindu, Arabian or Nordic myths, may last two hours or more and may also involve musicians and occasionally dancers. Group storytelling events may also be themed: The Sea, Biggest Liar Competition, Comedy Night, Adult Stories (sometimes very and have recently included that perennial Welsh favourite The Princess with Two Cunts), Story Slams (competitive storytelling, audience votes the winner), Tribute Evenings to honour the memory of an iconic storyteller, and so on. Even the interval refreshments can be similarly themed as can the musical interludes. Exchange storytelling between nearby groups is also common.

There are only a few protocols governing the conduct of these meetings. Stories may generally be of any type and origin, must not exceed the allotted duration, should never, ever, be read from a written text or even notes, and as I discovered too late to avoid embarrassment, visiting anthropologists with notebook and pen are especially unwelcome. All these storytelling events are open to the public and those taking place in theatres and community or arts centres, where events are advertised, can attract public audiences of over a hundred.

Skills workshops are perennially popular, may be led by an experienced storyteller from within the group or by a hired-in specialist, and are held over a series of evenings, a single day or a weekend. Beginner's storytelling workshops are held most frequently, followed by voice coaching and movement (the physical performance) and occasionally workshops are held on subjects such as puppetry and mask. Some groups appoint a storyteller in residence, generally a promising newcomer, as one way of assisting their early careers. Storytelling on the move is also well represented by 'story walks' and I have been made aware of at least one local group that organises 'story bikes' (think bicycle rally follows narrative route with storytelling stops).

Beyond the near-ground of regular storytelling events, local groups are involved in many forms of outreach activity. They are called on to tell at community events at care homes, youth clubs, arts and cultural venues and other civic functions and these engagements can occasionally attract public funding. Experienced teacher-storytellers lead workshops for less experienced teachers in local schools and then mentor their on-going development. Local groups provide storytellers for special events such as Habitat Action Day, Refugee Week, local fairs, festivals and fetes, folk and literary festivals and sometimes for highly improbable events such as a pagan festival held in a Unitarian church (Yes, really, I was sorry to miss that one). Groups recommend storytellers for local conferences, university departments and tertiary education colleges, to write articles for journals, for interviews on local radio and as after dinner speakers. Or sometimes people just get in touch to organise storytelling at a private party or some other kind of local gig.

Any attempt to draw up a list of venues where local groups meet would prove futile. They range from hotels to private homes, arts centres to pubs, cinemas to student unions, British Legions to book shops, public libraries to cafés, cabarets to community centres, church halls to firesides. Some groups are regional hubs for the national Young Tongues scheme that promotes storytelling in schools and youth clubs and steers young people towards the national Young Storyteller of the Year competition (see Chapter Five). Some hold events as part of National Storytelling Week (see Chapter Five). One group studied has forged institutional links with arts organisations and the city authorities, and by this means, storytelling plays a significant role in the city's cultural life – their brochures are prominently displayed in the tourist office. Some groups, especially those that offer the only form of cultural activity in the neighbourhood, play an important role in community cohesion. And finally, some of today's regional, national and even international storytelling festivals have evolved from the activities of a single local storytelling group.

While this range of activities is representative of local groups throughout Britain and Ireland, no individual group aspires to more than a few of these activities and more than half the groups studied undertake no outreach activities beyond their regular meetings and perhaps the occasional training workshop. It is also unclear how many of these outreach activities are the result of initiatives taken by individuals, often associated with their day-jobs or personal interests, and how many by the collective leadership of the group as a whole. It is inevitable therefore that many of these activities are short-lived and depend on the continuing commitment of individual group members.

Chapter Two drew up a demographic profile of a typical storytelling audience and this can also be used as a rough and ready guide to the membership of local groups. Women are in the majority. The highest proportion is aged between their mid-thirties and mid-fifties, with proportions tailing off either side of these decades. Nearly half attend alone and diminishing proportions attend in larger groups. For about a third of attenders, this is their first experience of storytelling while a further third are storytelling veterans. About half have been attracted to local group events by word of mouth recommendation and a third by advance notices as regular attenders. Well over half has no knowledge of other storytelling events elsewhere. And a majority has interests and skills that inform their experience of storytelling events.

Most of the local storytelling groups studied for this chapter were founded by individuals or small groups of career storytellers with shared interests and passions. A few were inspired by early storytelling festivals or by storytelling in schools which have longer histories. Two groups studied are led by individuals without any form of organisational structure, the leadership reporting they spend about two days a month on organisation and administration. Most however are managed by between three and six core members, who volunteer their unpaid time as chair, treasurer and secretary, while other office-holders are appointed as required to manage special projects. Only one group studied (and one other brought to my attention) have office-holders that are not themselves storytellers. Most well-established groups can call on the managerial and administrative experience of teachers, public servants and professionals when negotiations with local authorities, arts organisations and funding bodies are called for. Most groups are incorporated as clubs with formal articles of association that afford them legal status. Most have bank accounts, most keep financial records and most leaderships report they would not attempt to attract public or commercial sponsorship without an established track record of these three administrative functions. Local group leaderships tend to meet between four and six times a year, with one of these being a formal annual general meeting. Only larger storytelling organisations with multiple functions, large cash flows and complex duties and liabilities are registered as charities.

Most groups are financed largely by door money (paid entry to storytelling events) or discretionary collections (more common at ceilidhs) and only one I have come across raises revenue by a combination of door money and a nominal annual membership fee. The leadership of the two groups managed by individuals report they sometimes subsidise their group's administrative costs from their personal financial resources. However, in both these examples, they state the extra storytelling commissions they receive as figureheads of their groups more than compensates for the minor financial deficits they suffer. Local groups sometimes raise revenue from outreach activities, training workshops, occasionally from arts funding bodies and commercial sponsorship, and occasionally for larger projects, from the Heritage Lottery Fund, local authorities and the Arts Council. I found amongst some groups a tendency to overlook the value of discounted costs, donations in kind and the goodwill value of volunteers who help with administrative duties. Local groups' costs are mainly the fees paid to guest storytellers, paid-for venues, refreshments and publicity. Most leaderships seem to be a bit vague about their contractual and other legal obligations, public liability insurance and the nature of intellectual property rights generally. No group studied undertakes regular evaluation of their activities except as required by funding bodies.

These leaderships also talked about the challenges and aspirations of their groups. One raised concerns that attendance of a high proportion of new members quickly dropped away, while another recently under new management, cautioned against building their membership too rapidly. Several reported that developing and/or redesigning their websites had repaid their efforts greatly with increased attendance. Two long-established groups lost their public funding during the research period, had returned to their original core activities and had not sought alternative financial support. Another, which had participated in a local folk festival in recent years, had withdrawn because they felt their contribution had been undervalued, but were then offended when the festival organisers hired high-profile storytellers from outside the region. Several spoke of how even low-key marketing and publicity had brought growing attendance. One group reported their commitments had outgrown their organisational capacity and were returning to a reduced range of core activities. Another aspired to start a Saturday morning storytelling club for kids as a way of raising the profile of storytelling amongst their parents, and by extension, in the neighbourhood generally. These challenges and aspirations are only a brief summary of the changes taking place in local groups and speak clearly of strong, proactive leaderships that are sensitive to the rapidly evolving world of storytelling today. All these trends are characteristic indicators of complex emergent systems, driven by hundreds of independent judgements and decisions, without any centralised, organising force. Like nature itself, it may seem chaotic from the inside, but as we shall see in the closing chapters of this study, complex emergent systems tend to evolve naturally into very beautiful and efficient things like rain forests and human minds.

Most local storytelling groups keep in touch with their regular attenders in person at group events and by email, and occasionally by post and telephone. Many groups have websites and several have spoken about the benefits of professional design quality. Some undertake sporadic marketing, leafleting and/or limited poster campaigns to promote larger events. Only the higher-profile groups manage to attract editorial coverage of their events in local journals, radio and listings magazines. Local group news is mainly disseminated by regular e-newsletters or via a tab on their website. Groups led by members of national bodies such as the Society for Storytelling can exchange news and information with other members and other local groups via SfS's Area (regional) Representatives.

Although many local groups have forged strong links with other local communities, organisations and public bodies, there is little evidence of networks of weak links developing, or of storytelling groups developing as powerful hubs in a wider communications network. Similarly, I am not aware of any of the groups studied engaging their own members and attenders as potential weak links to other local communities, organisations and public bodies. This is not a call to action, but is mentioned here only to highlight opportunities that exist for local area networking.

Storytelling without boundaries

Beyond these local storytelling groups there are an unknown number of communities, groups, organisations and public bodies that host storytelling for the public as an adjunct to their main purpose or function. Bookshops, cafés, pubs, social clubs, schools, churches, museums, libraries, visitor attractions, arts organisations, businesses, health centres, universities and government bodies now host storytelling in some form other. Meanwhile, rumours spread from resolutely arty backstreets of our cities about 'guerrilla storytelling' groups (don't ask, I have no idea).

Some informal groups form themselves into companies of performing artists to offer entertainment and learning to public audiences. One such is The Company of Players and Tellers that engage storytellers, visual artists, musicians, dancers and other performing artists for performances in schools and other public venues. At a recent exhibition in Birmingham to mark the bicentenary of pioneering engineer and manufacturer Mathew Boulton, I was greeted by a member of an acting company in late eighteenth century costume who told stories to visitors about Boulton's life and times. When I asked him whether he thought of himself as a storyteller, he replied, 'Well, I suppose I am, but I'd never really thought of it that way.' Reference is made in the last chapter to Open Story Tellers, a company with a mission 'to enrich the lives of people with learning and communication difficulties, and those who live and work with them, through the use of narrative and story; building relationships, sharing experiences, developing a sense of identity and helping people find their place in society'.[1] The Crick Crack Club, founded in 1987, describes itself as 'the UK's premier performance storytelling promoter and programmer – working with artists whose unique talents and incurable taste for narrative leads them to unleash the rich metaphorical content of international fairy tales, epics and myths on the imagination of contemporary audiences'.[2] The Story Museum 'exists to celebrate children's stories and to share 1001 enjoyable ways for young people to learn through stories as they grow. We take story performances, exhibitions, activities and ideas to schools and communities'.[3]

A broad range of cultural organisations and institutions, although not dedicated exclusively to storytelling, nonetheless feature storytelling in their programme of events. The Centre for Reconciliation and Peace in the City of London is led by a director with four staff and hosts inter-faith and peace and reconciliation projects, seminars and conferences, some involving storytelling.[4] At the Mythstories Museum of Myth and Fable in the English West Midlands, visitors can experience an exhibition, take part in hands-on activities, refer to the country's largest archive of stories and storytelling, and hear a story from a resident storyteller.[5] The Institute for Cultural Research, founded in 1965 by the late Idries Shah, an early pioneer of the storytelling revival, continues to hold lectures, seminars and conferences on storytelling.[6]

Kingston University, London, has recently opened the Institute for the Spoken Word, 'the first of its kind in the UK [that] aims to be an international centre of excellence for oracy – the study of oral skills as the foundation for literacy, comprehension, and advanced reasoning'.[7] The George Ewart Evans Centre for Storytelling at the University of Glamorgan, Wales 'is dedicated to promoting, teaching, developing and researching storytelling in all its forms'.[8] Emerson International School of Storytelling, 'founded in 1994, is the longest running centre of its kind, where the craft of the storyteller is practiced and honoured [...]. For 16 years we have taught people from 17 countries around the world and most courses have a truly international flavour'.[9] London's Central School of Speech and Drama now offers courses on storytelling for teachers.[10] The University of Derby now embeds a storytelling module in its BA courses in Creative Writing.[11] And Newbattle Abbey College, Scotland's only residential adult education college, is amongst a rising number of adult education colleges that offer accredited courses on storytelling.[12]

These are only some of the groups, companies, organisations, cultural institutions, educational establishments and public bodies that have been brought to the attention of this study during the research period. Any career storyteller could add greatly to this list. Many have done so. It must be assumed that such storytelling initiatives are now nurturing the art of oral storytelling in all parts of Britain and Ireland.

Oversight and coordination

Beyond this world of stand-alone companies and organisations there are others that coordinate and oversee storytelling at a regional, national and international level. Five of these have been sampled for study. The leaderships of two have been interviewed; the remainder studied by other means; storytelling events under the auspices of all five have been attended; and here their working practices and roles are described.

The Traditional Arts Team (TAT) was developed from a Birmingham folk club in the late 1990s by Graham Langley, and with a small support team, it now promotes and programmes a broad range of folk-related dance, music, song and storytelling events throughout the English Midlands and it also publishes a regional listings magazine, Folk Monthly. During the research period the storytelling component of TAT's programming has comprised between four and six Storytelling Cafés that meet monthly, several other regular storytelling groups, and regular training programmes held in Birmingham over five Monday evenings. Each of the Storytelling Cafés stage evenings of storytelling, meet monthly in a variety of venues and hold training workshops for all levels of storytelling competence. True to their name the Storytelling Cafés place great emphasis on creating a sociable, relaxed and welcoming atmosphere. Further storytelling initiatives by TAT include the Young Storyteller of the Year competition, staged in Birmingham annually in March, and the Young Tongues programme that develops 15-25 year-olds as confident public speakers through the medium of traditional storytelling (see Chapter Five).

A comparison of TAT's core functions at the start of the four year research period with that at the end reveals substantive changes over this time. Overall, their monthly calendar of events reveals a significant expansion in the number of events staged, but also accompanied by losses in other areas. The Young Storyteller of the Year has become a truly national event and local storytelling groups beyond this region are now joining the Young Tongues programme to develop storytelling in schools and youth groups. Meanwhile the well-established National Storytelling Tours that toured British and overseas storytellers around more than twenty local groups throughout England has become a victim of cuts in subsidy. Individual Storytelling Cafés have come and gone, their venues changed and new forms of local storytelling groups have been founded.

It would be wrong to leave the impression that TAT plays an over-dominant role in storytelling in the English Midlands when independent groups abound in the region and one of the country's larger annual festivals of storytelling is also held here. However, what makes TAT distinctive for an organisation with so few (mainly part-time) staff, is the critical mass of folk-related initiatives and programmes it has been able to sustain. The density of complex network interconnections maintained by TAT can be seen to have raised the public profile of storytelling in the region to a level that is not found elsewhere in England. Graham Langley's personal commitment to maintaining contacts with the Federation for European Storytelling (FEST) has also given the region an international identity. This combination of factors may account for why TAT continues to attract levels of public subsidy that are not generally available to single function groups or to individual storytelling events.

The Society for Storytelling (SfS), a membership organisation founded in 1993, is the largest representative body for storytelling in England and Wales. Membership is open to anyone with an interest in storytelling, and although most live in England and Wales, SfS also attracts members from other parts of Britain and Ireland, the European Union and as far away as Japan and the USA. At the time of writing SfS is led by an unpaid board of directors comprising chair, secretary, treasurer and three other directors. Other board members are responsible for the oversight of the website, Area (regional) Representatives, business and marketing, the Annual Gathering (of members), Special Interest Groups (SIGs), sponsorship, the quarterly magazine *Storylines*, publications and liaison with the Federation for European Storytelling (FEST). Funding comes from annual membership fees, the National Lottery, Arts Council England and occasionally from other sources for one-off projects.

Six Special Interest Groups (SIGs), each with its own organiser, promotes storytelling in business, health and therapy, faith and religion, education, libraries, and museums and heritage. National Storytelling Week, held annually in February since 2001, now promotes over a thousand storytelling events reaching some 17,000 people at a broad range of community venues nationwide (see Chapter Five). An Annual Gathering, held over a spring weekend, combines conference, AGM, storytelling performances, keynote speeches, workshops, debates, folk concerts, and for those with energy to spare, a Saturday night of dancing and regional merrymaking. SfS's publishing activities embrace Papyrus (peer reviewed academic papers), Oracle (texts of lectures and talks) and Artisan (practical guides).

A paid-for directory of storytellers is accessible through the website, it carries no recommendations or endorsements, but listing is conditional on minimum standards of accreditation. Area (regional) Representatives support a dialogue between SfS, individual members, and by extension, local storytelling groups. Its commercial operations include an on-line shop offering publications, stories on CD and fact sheets. The website contains pages to access details of membership, regional events, local storytelling groups, National Storytelling Week, the Annual Gathering, news, a directory of storytellers, on-line discussion forums, publications and useful website links. Yet SfS is a near-virtual organisation. It is managed by a board of directors scattered across the English regions, employs no fulltime staff, has no hierarchical structures, many of its core functions are delegated to individual members and has only recently acquired a permanent base. Nor has SfS been immune from the kind of institutional changes that are common amongst such organisations. The research period for this study has seen a complete replacement of the board of directors and a significant shift of focus in many of its core functions. These include developments in its representative functions, an on-line directory of storytellers, social networking capabilities, publications and a new business plan that foregrounds the need to raise a wider public awareness of storytelling. Taking a broader view still, it can be seen that SfS functions successfully as a powerful hub in a complex communications network from which it gains much of its authority and strength.

Storytellers of Ireland draws its membership from all over Ireland and its leadership is by unpaid committee members currently including Chair, Secretary, Treasurer, Child Protection Officer (there is currently no statutory vetting of people working with the young and vulnerable in the Republic of Ireland) and five other members. The website contains an on-line directory of storytellers which carries no recommendations or endorsements and there is currently no system for the accreditation of storytellers listed there. An on-line newsletter is available to members via the website, as are transcripts of recent speeches and lectures, and an events diary covering all of Ireland and Irish community centres elsewhere. The leadership maintains close links with other storytelling and arts organisations, academic institutions nationally and internationally, and acts as a representative body for storytelling throughout Ireland.

The Forum for Storytelling in Wales (FSW)[13] was founded in 2008 to 'promote and support storytelling and storytellers in Wales in all its forms, from the traditional bearers and professional storytellers working in the community through to creating new storytellers everywhere. It aims to be a resource for all those interested in storytelling to find out more and help stimulate interest and support in this enriching and diverse art form'.

The Scottish Storytelling Centre[14] is led by its Director, Donald Smith, supported by eight full-time staff and additional unpaid volunteers as required. It is housed in purpose-built premises in the centre of Edinburgh's literary and cultural quarter and its facilities include administrative offices, a ninety nine seat theatre, library, conference suite, exhibition space, shop, and a public café with direct access from the street. It operates under a charitable trust, and in addition to its own revenue-raising activities, currently receives funding from Scottish Arts Council, City of Edinburgh, Scottish Enterprise and the National Lottery. Through its partner organisations, the Scottish Storytelling Forum and the Scottish Storytelling Network, the Centre manages a membership organisation that promotes and facilitates the development of storytelling in Scotland and beyond. It supports a network of storytellers involved in outreach projects to bring storytelling to community organisations. And it develops relationships with people who wish to stage storytelling events at a local level called 'front-liners'. The Centre's core policies are directed towards engaging with all age groups and diverse cultures, providing opportunities for the socially and educationally excluded, sharing community-based cultural experiences, and reinforcing Scotland's contribution to the worldwide storytelling movement.

A directory of Scottish storytellers who have passed the requisite selection and accreditation process is maintained to assist those wishing to hire a storyteller for their own events. The Centre organises year-round public storytelling and theatre events, literature, craft and multi-media exhibitions, and stages the ten-day annual Scottish International Storytelling Festival (see Chapter Five). It also provides resources to develop and organise widely varied storytelling projects, festivals and community events. In-house and outreach training workshops and development programmes for career and aspirational storytellers are central to its remit. A three-week showcase for young storytellers, ending with national Tell-A-Story Day, is staged annually. A partnership with Newbattle Abbey College has recently been formed to create accredited courses in Contemporary Storytelling and an extension of this initiative into more specialised forms of training is currently planned. External communication is by quarterly newsletter, proactive relationships with press and other local media, and collaborative links with a broad range of cultural institutions and public bodies in Scotland and worldwide.

But a quick march through the organisational structures supporting Scottish storytelling does not reveal its most interesting qualities. Unlike other representative bodies, it has not evolved through piecemeal development to meet the immediate needs of its current stakeholders but through a strategic plan developed in the early 1990s. Its aims have been to put storytelling at the heart of every Scottish community, to represent and speak for storytelling at a policy-making level and to bring influence to bear at the highest levels of government in Scotland. There are historical, political and demographic reasons that favour this organisational model, and while the Centre expects to be judged on its ability to add social value to communities throughout Scotland, it is to serve these specific objectives that these structures have been developed. At the core of this strategy lies a highly developed network of relationships and complex network interconnections with cultural organisations and public bodies. It is by these means that the Centre can speak authoritatively at a strategic level for all storytelling in Scotland. And it should be noted that such organisational structures and network interconnections do not and cannot arise spontaneously by emergent processes, but require a very rare combination of leadership competences.

The recently formed Federation for European Storytelling (FEST) 'is an international collaboration between associations and projects devoted to the perpetuation and advancement of live oral storytelling. Membership is open to any national or regional storytelling association, or to other organisations which unite storytelling groups in a collaborative framework and subscribe to the aims and purposes of FEST'.[15] More detailed descriptions of both FEST and World Storytelling Day are beyond the scope of this present study.

Reflections

A review of these communities, groups, companies, organisations and representative bodies reveals just how multifaceted the oral storytelling movement has become. No two local storytelling groups studied for this chapter are administered or organised in the same way and this reflects the many types of change that are now sweeping through the storytelling movement. The same can be said of the companies of players, the specialist storytelling organisations, the venues that host storytelling, the university departments that research oral storytelling and the dedicated schools that teach storytelling skills. And even the membership and representative bodies for storytelling in Britain, Ireland and Europe are constituted to meet the particular needs, wishes and aspirations of their members and other stakeholders.

Our Chapter One interviews reveal divergent views on the nature of the storyteller's core skills and the multiple social roles they play in society. Chapter Three reveals multifaceted applications of the storyteller's art. And it follows that the perception of oral storytelling from the point of view of individual participant-co-creators is similarly multifaceted. For an audience member storytelling is mainly entertainment; for a school pupil it is a developmental skill; for the refugee it is an escape from cultural isolation; for the client in therapy it offers a personal vision of themselves without mental illness; and so on. It is for all these reasons that the communities, groups, companies, organisations and representative bodies described above are all structured, led and managed in different ways. And along with these kinds of diversity come doctrinal differences, contrary beliefs, factional disputes and the sense of personal exclusion that some storytellers describe. I do not share their deep regrets for these divergent views because they are a necessary part of the rough and tumble of any emergent social and cultural movement. In one respect though, the storyteller quoted in the Preface was quite right: any wide-ranging study of storytelling 'would be like a study of, say, singing, it's a whole world of human experience. It can't all be encapsulated'.

There is a healthy sense amongst many storytellers that their individual liberty and freedom of expression is in danger of being inhibited, intellectualised and even sanitised by bureaucracies and centralising organisational structures. Not one I have met has given a passing glance to additional oversight, coordination, supervision or management of the storytelling movement. Yet, this chapter has described a bewildering assortment of organisational structures, each in their own way, successfully driving change, development and growth in oral storytelling. In some storytelling genres these structures are sustained by other meta-structures, which in turn are beholden to other towering hierarchies of meta-structures. For example educational storytellers work within the organisational structures of best teaching practice, pastoral care of minors, school administration and management, the diktats of the curriculum, at least one government ministry and ultimately our parliamentary democracy. Therapeutic storytellers will be familiar with similar hierarchies of organisational structure. Even for performance storytellers there is no escape from some involvement with organisational, administrative, managerial and legal structures.

But during all my encounters with storytellers – committed guardians of individual liberty and freedom of expression that they are – I have had to keep reminding myself that status hierarchies and organisational structures are not, by and large, the invention of overbearing bureaucracies in post-industrial states. They are more commonly the invention of pre-industrial, traditional societies that are rigidly hierarchical, zealously illiberal, intolerant of dissent, ritually hidebound and dogmatic in their beliefs. (Mesopotamian city states were already overburdened by bureaucracy in the second millennium BCE.) In this respect I have never quite understood the fondness of today's storytellers for wonder tales, myths, legends and folk stories whose origins lie in such social hellholes, rather than in today's enlightened and liberal democracies, which by definition, we can more easily associate with. Chapter Nine returns to this structure/anti-structure theme.

A chapter entitled Communities in a Landscape begs the question whether the wider fellowship of individuals, groups, organisations and representative bodies can be considered a community at all. One prominent storyteller from the early days of the revival became truculent when I used the term 'the storytelling community'. Yet all the evidence gathered for this study points towards a remarkable sense of community amongst practitioners and participants. It seems self-evident that all storytelling is a community event. Local storytelling groups are quintessential communities. Storytelling reinforces the social and cultural identities of communities and societies. The social role of the storyteller in communities and society is more or less universal across all cultures. The sum total of world stories is the collective identity of the wider human community. And in today's wired world all storytellers and their participants are bound together by complex networks of interconnection.

In *The Storytellers' Journey: An American Revival*, storyteller, folklorist and musician, Joseph Sobol observes how, 'The storytelling world grew, as many such worlds do, through relationships and an intensity of interactive commitment that turns a job, a pastime, an idea, or a technique into what was once commonly called a "school" but now is more often dubbed a "movement".'[16] But how do such movements grow from simple relationships to a nationwide movement? Evidence for this study really has very little to say in answer. The Preface contains a sketchy outline of how complex network interconnections can bring about change, development and growth, in particular through weak-link connections. Each chapter describes varied multimodal means of communication, and for the storytelling movement as a whole, it is likely that the widest possible spectrum of communications media will bring the greatest benefits. It is a near certainty that complex network interconnections will evolve by emergent processes and will remain in a constant state of flux. In today's cyber world there are now plenty of virtual organisations that thrive almost without organisational structures, but none that I can think of that thrives without intensive, interactive relationships between all its stakeholders. I did however conduct a small-scale experiment by following the internet links displayed on a number of websites of high profile storytelling organisations. It was rare to find more than three generations of internet link that remained relevant to the subject of storytelling. Others will know better than I whether this level of internet connectedness is more or less than normal for such cultural, grassroots movements like oral storytelling.

It may be that network interaction is already optimal in the world of storytelling, given the multifaceted nature of this movement. If so, what remains of the common perception of storytelling as a worldwide community? Well, without stretching a metaphor too far beyond credibility, it might be possible to consider the storytelling movement as a form of social, cultural and creative ecology, rather like the hierarchy of self-organising complexity found in living ecosystems. Storytellers work as individuals or as one of a population of storytellers with more or less shared aptitudes and aspirations. Populations of storytellers work within communities of storytelling groups and other organisations as a form of cultural ecosystem that resembles the highly diversified mosaic of species found in a natural ecosystem. Such widely varied and interconnected cultural ecosystems co-exist and share many of the characteristics of natural climatic zones or biomes. There is an ill-defined sense amongst storytellers that an individual storyteller can be linked by infinitely complex processes and self-organising networks with some sort of worldwide cultural biosphere. As our natural earthly biosphere is bound together mainly by carbon-based biochemistry, so the cultural biochemistry of multicultural worldwide storytelling may only be observable at a molecular scale.

Notes & References

1. Visit www.openstorytellers.org.

2. Visit www.crickcrackclub.com.

3. Visit www.storymuseum.org.

4. Visit www.stethelburgas.org.

5. Visit www.mythstories.com.

6. Visit www.i-c-r.org.

7. Visit www.fass.kingston.ac.

8. Visit www.storytelling.research.glam.ac/GeorgeEwartEvans.

9. Visit www.schoolof storytelling.com.

10. Visit www.cssd.ac.

11. Visit www.derby.ac.uk/humanities/creativewriting.

12. Visit www.newbattleabbeycollege.ac.

13. Visit www.storytellingwales.org.

14. Visit www.scottishstorytellingcentre.co.

15. Visit.www.storytelling.eu.

16. Joseph Daniel Sobol, *The Storytellers' Journey: An American Revival*, (Urbana USA: University of Illinois Press, 1999), p. 88.

FIVE

CELEBRATING NARRATIVE

ॐ

S torytelling festivals, conferences and competitions form much of the public image of contemporary oral storytelling and are amongst the most popular events in the storytelling calendar. Four very varied festivals, ten conferences and two forms of storytelling contest have been sampled for study, their organisational structures and distinctive features are analysed and the social roles they play in a broader cultural context are reviewed here.

Small beginnings

Hampstead Garden Suburb in northwest London, conceived and built as a social experiment in urban planning, celebrated its centenary year in 2007. To contribute to the festivities, a junior school teacher, Jane Pendry, had the idea of staging a schools storytelling festival and I am grateful to her for details of the festival's evolution and for access to its records. Other members of the planning committee included the business development director at another local school and one parent helper. Monthly meetings, also attended by representatives from participating schools, were held over a five month period, each committee member spending about 4-5 hours per month on planning. The minutes of these meetings recorded the committee's most pressing concerns.

> There was a danger of 'over-administering' the event. Once the first few schools had committed themselves to participation, others joined more readily. Early decisions were made on the festival's theme, type of stories told, size of teller groups, programme of events, rehearsal times and a time limit for each telling. Staging and

housekeeping arrangements involved stage set, lighting, sound system, capacity of both stage and auditorium, seating, refreshments, toilet and changing facilities, marshalling, VIP guests and logistics. Legal matters concerned insurance, health and safety and press and photography approvals. Publicity for the festival was mainly by word of mouth at participating schools, plus a small poster campaign that 'stretched the resources of the committee'. An early decision not to attempt fundraising was justified when ticket sales to the festival covered all expenditure. Overhead costs were met from existing budgets of the hosting school and one other school. A small financial surplus was donated to a local charity.

The festival was held over an extended Sunday afternoon in November 2007. It brought together 700 children and adults from this culturally diverse community in a celebration of traditional storytelling. Ten schools and youth organisations and a local library took part. 150 children and adolescents aged five to eighteen and their attendant adults performed in 10 telling groups. The stories told had their origins in four continents and three diverse faiths. The performances involved classic storytelling techniques, choral speaking, drama, narration, repetition, song, music, movement, dance, mask, costume and props. The festival raised the profile of schools storytelling in this borough and within the wider storytelling community through an article published in *Storylines*, the quarterly magazine of the Society for Storytelling.[1] The planning committee's post-festival evaluation recommended it should be repeated and that it could be grown in scope to include storytelling workshops, events for adults and guest storytellers without significantly changing the management model.

No estimates can be made of how many such festivals are staged in Britain and Ireland today. Some are never repeated; others become annual events or change in style and scope. Since schools and youth storytelling is probably the dominant storytelling genre, it is likely that most such festivals are staged within educational and youth communities. Beyond such closed-community festivals, perhaps the most common forms are those staged by local storytelling groups in towns and cities where storytelling already enjoys a raised public profile.

City festivals

Cambridge Storytellers was founded in 1998, since when a small core of its most active members have successfully built a public profile for storytelling in this famous university city. Following the success of an inaugural festival in 2007, it was decided to hold The Second Cambridge Storytelling Festival in 2009. I am grateful to Marion Leeper, Chair of Cambridge Storytellers and her planning committee for their active support for this study and access to their records. An eight-member volunteer festival committee, one of whom has professional experience of arts marketing, committed 'significant investments of time and effort' over a seven month period. They were assisted during the festival weekend by 14 volunteer stewards from this local storytelling group. Marketing and promotion included print leaflets, word of mouth recommendation by local group members, free promotion by the County Council, e-notices to members of the Society for Storytelling and an article *Storylines*. The Festival was part-funded by the Arts Council, County Council and City Council, with further support coming from Cambridge University Press and one local business. The festival made a small financial surplus which will be used to develop the Young People's Project described below.

The core festival was held at St Andrews church in an attractive suburb of this city. Festival events were staged in the church building itself, its adjoining hall and ancillary rooms, which included on-site catering facilities. It took place between a Friday and Sunday evenings over a May weekend and was billed as 'a family weekend of story'. Ten stories were performed by established career storytellers, past winners of the Young Storyteller of the Year and by 'the best of local storytelling clubs'. The programme included two 'story walks' and, this being Cambridge, 'a story punt' on the River Cam. There were two 'open tellings' (anyone can volunteer a story), four 'story rounds' (seated in a circle, host/ess invites stories from participants) and 'an audience with ...' (known elsewhere as 'meet the storyteller'). Family events included making shadow puppets and a Punch and Judy show. And eight skills workshops were held on a wide range of storytelling topics.

Outreach programmes came in three distinct forms, all with the support of public funding. The New Directions Commissions enabled the festival committee to commission development of two new stories from career storytellers that were premiered at the festival. The first, a two-hour story from an experienced teller, will carry a credit for the commissioning body, The Cambridge Storytelling Festival, on all future promotional literature and for all future performances. The second, an hour-long story from a younger career teller, was commissioned by means of a nationally advertised competition and an audition held for shortlisted applicants. Development of the winning commission was mentored by a prominent performance storyteller and its premier at the festival attracted four immediate bookings for this storyteller from local storytelling groups nationwide.

The Young People's Project engaged experienced youth storytellers to mentor members of Cambridge Storytellers, who in turn led 12 storytelling workshops in local schools and youth clubs and a Young Voices Workshop was held during the festival itself. Several benefits followed from this initiative: the standard of youth storytelling in the region was raised; it provided opportunities for participating groups to perform in this public forum; several teenage storytellers went on to tell at the larger Festival at the Edge; and one group took group prize for under-eighteens at the following year's national Young Storyteller of the Year competition. The Traveller Project engaged a Scottish traveller who led two schools storytelling workshops, one family workshop and performed their own story during the festival.

About 350 people took part in the festival, not including outreach events. Most audience members were resident locally or in the wider Anglia region, some came from other parts of Britain, while one travelled from the Netherlands to attend. Five audience members were interviewed for this study and their responses more or less conformed to the profile of any public storytelling event as outlined in Chapter Two. A high proportion of the festival's own audience evaluation forms noted the friendly atmosphere of the festival, while the post-festival report noted how the close collaboration of the venue management had contributed greatly to the sense of celebration. Overall, the festival raised the profile of Cambridge Storytellers, significantly developed the art of storytelling locally, and the committee resolved to build on these successes to further develop storytelling in the Anglia region.

Several annual festivals using similar organisational models were held during the research period of this study. Bristol's storytelling festival is held in February to coincide with National Storytelling Week. The Ulster Storytelling Festival held at the Ulster Folk and Transport Museum in Belfast is another regular. The Farmleigh Festival of Story and Song is held at a large country house in Phoenix Park, Dublin, where a high proportion of attenders for the July 2009 festival reported they had been attracted by a report on local radio that morning. The rather larger Beyond the Border North, an international festival of performance storytelling was held in the city of Leeds from a Wednesday to a Saturday in April 2007. Here, performances took place in ancillary venues within the West Yorkshire Playhouse and outreach events were mounted at public libraries, a prison, a stately home, a museum of arms and armour and an industrial museum. Unusually for this type of festival, the Artistic Director, Assistant director and several production team members were from outside the region, although they were well supported by local volunteers.

Rural festivals

The Wales International Storytelling Festival, better known as Beyond the Border Wales, has been staged on the first weekend in July most years since 1993. It is held at the medieval castle of St Donats overlooking the south Wales coast which is also home to St Donats Arts Centre and Atlantic College. I am grateful to the festival's Artistic Director, David Ambrose, and the management and staff of St Donats Arts Centre for their support for this study and access to their records of the 2010 Festival. Further background details have come from contemporaneous notes of my own attendance in 2007. The festival shares many of the characteristics of a rural folk festival, with most attenders staying in tents, hired yurts or caravans in an adjoining field. The festival programme is wide-ranging and family-friendly to 'satisfy all-inclusive tastes'. Its cultural roots are expressed through Welsh language stories, poetry and song, and the promotional literature and festival programme are printed in both Welsh and English language versions. Some of the events are held within the castle buildings, some in marquees and several on open-air stages in the castle grounds.

Keynote tellers for the following year's festival are generally booked a year in advance. The first planning meeting is held six to eight months before the festival when a freelance production manager is appointed and work begins on site planning, licences, liaison with local authorities, marketing, print advertising, website updates and tickets are put on sale. In the months leading up to the festival, permanent staff members of St Donats Arts Centre are increasingly made available to the Festival's Artistic Director to assist with administrative planning. Further administrative, managerial, supervisory, production and technical personnel are recruited for the weeks leading up to and during the festival, and staffing is completed by recruiting forty unpaid volunteer stewards for the festival weekend itself.

The campaign to market the festival generally includes: a full-colour programme featuring sponsored advertising; cross-promotion at twenty-four cultural events in the region reaching some 1,800 people; the appointment of a marketing professional for the three-month lead-in period and a part-time press and marketing consultant for a final week's preparation.

Public funding, sponsorship and other support for the 2010 festival was provided by the Welsh Assembly (devolved government in Wales), Arts Council, County Council, Academi Cymraeg (Welsh literature promotion agency), National Museum, Atlantic College, St Donats Arts Centre, Canada Council for the Arts, two commercial sponsors, private trusts, festival friends and some in-kind services. Ticket sales make up the balance of the revenue and can be purchased on-line, by phone or post. Just under half the tickets sold were for the full weekend programme, just under half for day tickets and the balance for half-festival and single events. The capacity for the Festival is about 2,500 and in 2010 it attracted over 80 per cent of this number.

The programme for the 2010 Festival lists 56 individuals and groups of performing artists, either solo, tandem or multi-handed tellings, with or without musical accompaniment, MCs for open telling events, story walk tellers, poets, puppeteers, scholars (to give talks or lead discussions), musicians, singers, musical ensembles, a strolling entertainer, choir, Punch and Judy show, family of story-teller giants, community circus, face painters, yoga facilitators, and perhaps not quite qualifying as a performing artist, but certainly participating in an open debate, the Welsh Minister for Environment and Sustainability. The internation-alism of the Festival was underlined by artists, stories and music originating in five continents. The festival ran from 7.00 pm on Friday to 11.30 pm on Sunday. The shortest storytelling event lasted forty five minutes, the longest two hours forty five minutes. One tented venue was set aside on the Saturday for The Tales to Sustain Project (a group of environmental storytellers referred to in Chapter Three). On both Saturday and Sunday another tented venue was set aside for activity events for the under-fives and their parents and carers. In addition to the festival events, there was an in-house bar and café, eight careering outlets, a real ale tent and craft and gift stalls.

An extensive programme of community outreach events was staged during the previous twelve months, including 64 storytelling events at 30 local schools led by storytellers from Africa, Italy and Britain, a three-day Storytelling Summer School at St Donats, a summer school for blind and partially sighted children, and free monthly Sunday Lunch Hour Storytelling at the Wales Millennium Centre in Cardiff. And in the week before the festival, storytelling sessions in four primary schools were held throughout county.

Evaluation and feedback forms, completed by 10 per cent of attenders, invited their appraisal of the performances, performers, staff, venues, catering, access, value for money, management of the campsite, their personal experience of the festival and any other comments they wished to add. The most significant con-clusion of the 2010 post-festival report noted that it had not been possible to secure public funding till three months before the festival weekend and the con-sequential delays to the marketing campaign had caused a significant fall in attendance when compared with previous festivals.

Festival at the Edge, like many festivals, evolved from the activities of a local storytelling group and shares with Beyond the Border Wales many characteristics of a folk festival. Research for this study was conducted by interview with one fes-tival committee member, from published documents and contemporaneous notes from my own attendance in 2008. Festival at the Edge has been held annu-ally in rural Shropshire in the English West Midlands over a July weekend since 1992 and is billed as 'a family-friendly event'. An eleven-member volunteer festi-val committee meets monthly throughout the year at the nearby Mythstories Museum at Wem. Most festival events are held in large marquees or on an open-air stage. The programme offers story performances, story rounds, story walks, festival-commissioned storytelling, story bonfires till late, training workshops, concerts and other traditional music-making, dance performances, a dedicated children's festival, craft fair, catering, a real ale bar and most festival attenders stay on an adjoining campsite. Beyond the festival weekend itself Edge Extras is a series of winter storytelling workshops held at the Mythstories Museum.

The profile of the 15 attenders interviewed for this study more or less matches those of other storytelling festivals. However, since it was difficult to interview attenders inside the storytelling venues themselves, the interview sample showed a strong bias towards those attending mainly for the folk elements of the programme, rather than the storytelling elements. With this in mind, about half had heard of the festival by word of mouth, a third from prior experience of storytelling events and only a few knew of any other storytelling events elsewhere. Unsurprisingly, a third referred to this as 'a folk festival', or compared it favourably with 'other folk festivals', for its 'good feel', 'informal atmosphere', 'low cost' and for being 'safe for kids'. One had attended only for the real ale bar, one as a dedicated follower of the folk band and one nineteen-year-old had attended every year since she was two but had only occasionally attended a storytelling. The festival's own evaluation and feedback was by written questionnaire.

Several other annual folk-style storytelling festivals were held during the research period. The West Country Storytelling Festival held in August in South Devon is an annual event and its programme resembles both Beyond the Border Wales and Festival at the Edge. The Sting in the Tale – A Festival of Stories, also held in August, is unusual for being mounted by several local authorities and for its events being widely scattered across the south-coast county of Dorset. Storytelling is held in a wide variety of venues, including a reconstructed iron-age earth house, mediaeval castle, model town, open parkland as well as museums and libraries. The best known rural festival in Ireland is The Cape Clear International Storytelling Festival which is held on an island of the same name off the southwest coast (last ferry 6.00 pm) and attracts about 500 attenders. A further five rural storytelling festivals have been identified during the research period throughout Ireland and a further five throughout England and Wales. Some of these are occasional, some much changed in scope and some festival websites are now suspiciously obsolete.

The Scottish

The Scottish International Storytelling Festival, founded in 1990, is the largest in Britain and Ireland and is held over a ten-day period commencing on the last weekend in October. It comprises a Public Programme and two Outreach Programmes, is planned as a 'brand leader event' for The Scottish Storytelling Centre (see Chapter Four) and is integral to a long-term strategy to develop the art of traditional and contemporary storytelling in Scotland and beyond. I am grateful to Donald Smith, Director of the Centre in Edinburgh and his staff for their sustained support for this study, access to the festival records and the 2008 post-festival report. The festival is managed by its director, a working group from the Centre's full-time staff, the staff of other partner venues and, for the duration of the festival itself, unpaid volunteers from the community.

Great emphasis is placed on marketing, publicity and media relations. For the 2008 festival, promotion of the Tell-a-Story Day was by print flyers and a poster campaign, while for the Public Programme a twenty-page full-colour events guide was produced. During the month leading up to and during the festival itself, paid-for advertising was taken in Scotland's premier national publications, in one prominent listings magazine, and one classified advertisement was placed in a specialist periodical. The Centre's own website has seen a year-on-year rise in the numbers of those logging on to festival pages. An advance press campaign included the production of two videos leading up to the press launch held in the presence of the Scottish Minister for Culture. The festival itself attracted media coverage in regional print journals, listings and events guides, local radio and feature articles in regional editions of one on-line national newspaper and one Scottish Sunday.

The Festival's profile was also raised by building on existing relationships with the Centre's regular network of contacts, partner organisations across Scotland and, as an international festival, with the consular offices of the European Commission and other participating nations. In a background development, research by the City Council has established that Edinburgh is the world's third most famous festival brand name (after Rio de Janeiro and Glastonbury) and a policy has since been adopted to coordinate and brand Edinburgh worldwide as 'a city of festivals' under a coordinating body called Edinburgh Festivals. The Storytelling Centre's close collaboration with this representative body has brought significant benefits to the Storytelling Festival. Each year's festival also carries a strong international theme as part of the Storytelling Centre's strategy for raising the profile of Scottish storytelling as a network hub with global reach. To this end the 2008 festival was themed Northlands and Sagalands and other recent themes have been Out of Eden – Scotland & Africa, Eastern Routes: Authentic Voices and Island Odyssey: Scotland and Old Europe.

Public subsidy for the 2008 festival came from the Scottish Government's Edinburgh Festivals Expo Fund, Arts Council, City Council, European Commission and The Scottish Storytelling Centre's own venue subsidy. Revenue was also generated by box office takings for the Public, Partner and Workshop Programmes.

The 2008 Public Programme involved 44 Scottish storytellers and 15 guest tellers from Alaska, Finland, Denmark, Sweden, Iceland, Norway, France, Switzerland and Germany. Thirty three events were held at the Scottish Storytelling Centre and included ceilidh nights, meet the storyteller (stories and conversations with guest tellers), talks and discussions (panel events and presentations on storytelling-linked themes), training workshops and activity sessions for children and families. Twenty-two festival events were also held at partner venues in Edinburgh and across central Scotland.

Several festival events were held outside the Public Programme. Tell-a-Story Day is Scotland's national storytelling day and in 2008 attracted nearly 6,200 participants of all ages. It is promoted and supported by the Scottish Storytelling Centre which provides free publicity packs and on-line assistance to 75 participating groups across Scotland. The Festival Schools and Libraries Outreach Programme ran over nine days and involved 47 storytelling events and 5,500 children and young people at schools and libraries in the region. The Education In-Service Day attracted 60 local education authority, teaching and library staff from across Scotland to explore the theme of 'Scottish culture in the school's curriculum, using a storyline teaching approach'. And on the final day of the Festival, the Network Development Day brought together 25 Scottish and guest storytellers with diverse experience, to share ideas, approaches and stories, and to identify key subjects for the future development of the international storytelling network.

Altogether, nearly 17,000 people attended the 2008 festival, of which just under one third were for the Public Programme held at the Storytelling Centre and partner venues, and two thirds for community outreach events including, in near-equal proportion, the Tell-a-Story Day and the Schools and Libraries Programme. Feedback and evaluation of the Public Programme was by peer review, three external evaluators and an audience questionnaire that focused on attenders' personal perceptions of the festival. Participant feedback from Tell-a-Story Day, Schools and Libraries Outreach Programme and Training Workshops was by tailored feedback form. The post-festival report noted that the particular success of two partner events had been due to strong marketing, close collaboration between the venue management and the Storytelling Centre, and for one of these events had been due to additional funding made available for research and development.

My own interviews with 26 attenders at the Storytelling Centre revealed no significant variations from storytelling events elsewhere. However, worthy of note are: the high proportion of attenders from overseas; the high proportion who heard about the festival from publicity rather than by the more usual word of mouth recommendation; the significant numbers who came here for the Centre's convivial café rather than to attend storytelling events; and in common with London performance storytelling, a high proportion who have personal skills and interests that are relevant to storytelling.

These four organisational models for conventional storytelling festivals are not the only way to celebrate narrative. In London there are mini-festivals of performance storytelling, staged by the Crick Crack Club over successive evenings in studio theatres and other public spaces. And in at least one other English city a local storytelling group stages events in public theatres as part of regular arts festivals. And even as I write this paragraph today's national press reports that the Scottish Storytelling Centre is celebrating Burns Night (after the nineteenth century Scottish poet) with a midday 'ceilidh flash mob' in Parliament Square complete with a live band.

National Storytelling Week

National Storytelling Week (NSW) in England and Wales evolved out of National Storytelling Day and aims to 'promote an inclusive public awareness of the art, practice and value of oral storytelling in our society'. It has been held annually since 2000 over the first week of February to coincide with the Christian festival of Candlemas when blessings were traditionally made for that most precious of storyteller's organs, the throat. I am grateful to Del Reid and the Society for Storytelling for their assistance and for access to their records. The Society promotes and coordinates NSW, provides participating groups with a guide to managing events and advises them on organisation, promotion, media relations and funding. NSW has in the past received corporate funding and at the time of writing a small balance remains to match sponsorship raised by participating groups. The overhead and administrative cost of NSW is met from the Society's own Arts Council subsidy.

The promotion of NSW is by periodic issue of press releases to national and specialist journals from early in the previous summer. For the 2010 NSW these resulted in editorial copy in 5 national newspapers, 3 colour weekend supplements and 3 specialist magazines (including one in Japan). The Society's own members regularly write articles to promote NSW in the journals of professional bodies they are members of. A link on the Society's website promotes networking and the sharing of information and ideas between participating groups. Some local radio stations are supportive, providing airtime to local NSW events and even broadcast on-air storytelling. Groups wishing to participate can find details at www.sfs.org.uk and to qualify for support they are required to demonstrate they have identified a new audience for storytelling, hold the event at a venue not previously used for storytelling, plan to continue the event in future years and show how the objectives outlined in their application can be realistically met.

More than three quarters of applications are for events whose organisers are not members of the Society. Most successful applications are made by schools, although others regularly include museums, libraries, public archives, art galleries, visitor attractions, universities, theatres, prisons, retirement homes, childcare organisations, disability forums and clubs, social services charities, charity staff workshops, environmental organisations, zoos, aquariums, shopping centres, pubs, cafés, restaurants and bookshops. One recent NSW event was held in the window of an eighteenth shop in a darkened alleyway in London's West End and is reported to have attracted a crowd of no less than 50 people at any one time. Slightly less than a quarter of applications come from the Society's own members and have included the Young Storyteller of Wales Festival, Bristol Storytelling Festival and story-swap video links with schools as far away as West Africa and the Caribbean. Written evaluations are returned to the Society at the end of NSW and in 2010 revealed the youngest participant to be three years old and the oldest ninety three. The total numbers participating in NSW has grown steadily over the years and by 2011 had reached about 17,000.

All the celebrations of contemporary oral storytelling outlined above have storytelling as their core activity; however, there are other forms of festival that nonetheless feature storytelling as part of their programme of events. Literary festivals, including those held in both Cheltenham and Bath, have featured storytelling in recent years, as have large and well established folk festivals such as Sidmouth Folk Week, Whitby Folk Week and the smaller Tenterden Folk festival. Meanwhile, as we found in Chapter Four, local storytelling groups are often invited to tell at fairs, festivals and fetes. To put British and Irish storytelling festivals into a wider context still, the often quoted, but unverified figure of 45 storytelling festivals worldwide is now almost certainly an underestimate. A very superficial internet search reveals at least 21 in the USA and Canada; they are widespread in continental Europe; and recent revivals of oral storytelling in much of the developed world suggest that storytelling festivals are now commonplace worldwide. Nor should the growth of World Storytelling Day be overlooked. Founded in Sweden in the early 1990s, it celebrates live storytelling at the spring equinox in the northern hemisphere (autumn in the southern) and according to this movement's own website, has now become a global phenomenon.

Conferences

A further trend brought to my attention has been the emergence of academic conferences on the subject of oral storytelling. No systematic research has been conducted on this topic and no attempt has been made to enumerate or analyse them. However, details have been collected on several of those held during the research period and two have been attended as participant observer. Those described here may be taken merely as indicative of their scope and forms, the nature of their subject matter and their inferred prevalence throughout Britain and Ireland.

The Power of Stories, a weekend conference held in London over a March weekend in 2009, was organised by the Institute for Cultural Research. Founded in 1965 by the Sufi writer and thinker Idries Shah, the ICR is run by many of the people who were at the heart of the College of Storytellers in the 1980s and its aim is to stimulate study, debate, education and research into all aspects of human thought, behaviour and culture. This conference brought together leading writers and social anthropologists who sought to throw light on the question: Why do we tell stories? From brief interviews with fellow delegates here it seems there are few points of contact and few connecting links between academe and the world of practicing oral storytellers. Only one of the nine speakers was themselves a career storyteller, and although seven of the ten delegates I questioned had attended at least one oral storytelling event, only one knew of the full extent of oral storytelling practices and the roles they play in society today.

In 1993 the mediaeval church of Saint Ethelburga's in the City of London was destroyed in a terrorist attack and subsequently rebuilt as a centre for reconciliation and peace. It is dedicated to promoting an understanding of the relationship between faith and conflict. This centre mounted a three day conference in November 2008 called Narratives of Hope in collaboration with the Forgiveness Project and the Society for Storytelling. It was intended as a gathering for peace-workers, NGOs, interfaith groups, community development workers and educators, and it aimed to explore the many and varied ways that personal narrative and traditional storytelling can be used to build bridges and to make peace. The programme included storytelling, personal narratives, narratives of identity, story-sharing, video narratives, listening circles, talks, workshops, music, song and prayer. The conference was self-financing from ticket sales, although overhead costs were met from St Ethelburga's own public subsidy. At peak periods about 70 delegates were in attendance, close to capacity for the venue. Publicity was organised by St Ethelburga's through the Society for Storytelling's own websites and by e-notices to members of the Society. Delegate feedback forms invited comments on 'What was good about the conference?', 'What could have been better?', 'What was the most useful thing you are taking away with you?' and 'Any good ideas for follow up for the future?'

The Storytelling Ape, a three day conference in November 2007 was held at Cumberland Lodge, Windsor, in association with the London Centre for International Storytelling. It combined storytelling performances, talks, panel debates and discussions. The conference was aimed at academics, arts organisers, educators, students, researchers, sociologists, philosophers, writers, theatre directors, artists, actors and therapists. The programme addressed the topics of humankind's need for storytelling, why we tell stories, what happens to us when we listen to them and the cultural, political and social power stories can bring to our lives.

The Quest For Vision Conference, a one day conference and evening performance was held in London in September 2009. It brought together storytellers and psychotherapists to explore ideas of storytelling as a healing art and was conducted though talks, stories, poems and discussion.

Storytelling and Narrative in Healthcare, a one-day conference in September 2008, was mounted jointly by the University of Central Lancashire and the Northern Centre for Storytelling in the English Lake District where it was held. It attracted storytellers, healthcare professionals and academics for a day of workshops and discussion.

Celebrating Stories, organised by the British Association of Dramatherapists in association with the Society for Storytelling, was a one-day conference held in London in May 2010 to celebrate the art and craft of storytelling and the creation and dramatisation of stories.

The Annual Gathering for members of the Society for Storytelling regularly dedicates some of its weekend programme of events to debates, keynote speeches and panel discussions on the wider issues of storytelling in our society. As we have seen above the Scottish International Storytelling Festival also holds panel discussions and debates on wider issues.

Amongst those academic institutions closely associated with storytelling is the George Ewart Evans Centre for Storytelling, a department of the School of Creative & Cultural Industries at the University of Glamorgan. It was named after the socialist and oral history pioneer who lived nearby, and in addition to its role in teaching, research, publication and the wider support of storytelling initiatives, it holds regular conferences, seminars and symposiums.

Kingston University, London, founded the Institute for the Spoken Word during the research period for this study. The first of its kind in Britain, it aims to be an international centre of excellence for oracy – the study of oral skills as the foundation for literacy, comprehension and advanced reasoning. The Institute's inaugural one-day conference, the Spoken Word Conference, held in September 2009, explored themes as diverse as: classical texts as vehicles for developing communication skills; the current paucity of communication skills in business; language ideologies about, and attitudes towards, the spoken word; the effects of status, demographics and education on language in business; the rise of the spoken word in publishing; and cultural policy and the teaching of spoken word skills.

Competitions

The early inspiration for the Young Storyteller of the Year and the Young Tongues Projects was the traditional 'hiring fairs' that resulted from the 1351 Statute of Labourers which regulated the employment of agricultural workers in the aftermath of the Black Death and could still be found in rural England in the early twentieth century. (Mop fairs, as they were called, were for hiring housemaids.) In our more enlightened times I am grateful to Graham Langley of the Traditional Arts Team and Fiona Collins, coordinator of the Young Tongues Projects, for their support for this study and access to their records.

The Young Storyteller of the Year competition is held annually in Birmingham on a Saturday in March. It aims to provide a platform for launching storytelling careers, to inspire others to become involved in storytelling and to raise the profile of storytelling nationally. The Traditional Arts Team organises the event, it is hosted by two comperes, judged by three prominent storytellers and stewarded by nine volunteers. Support comes from Arts Council England, Birmingham City Council, West Midlands Folk Federation, Festival at the Edge and the Traditional Arts Foundation. Additional acknowledgements on the programme of events are afforded to several County and District Councils, local storytelling groups, storytelling and folk festivals, schools, museums, libraries, print periodicals and individuals who have donated prizes. Competitors are the winners of regional Young Tongues Projects, those promoted by local storytelling groups and those entered for the competition by colleges such as Emerson International School of Storytelling.

There are four competition categories: individuals, groups, those aged fifteen to seventeen and eighteen to twenty five. The performances are judged on the story, its staging, the performance and its artistic interpretation. The prizes are generally combinations of book tokens, Society for Storytelling membership, performance slots at Festival at the Edge and Whitby Folk Week, and the cost of professional liability insurance for one year. About 80 people attended the 2009 Young Storyteller of the Year and feedback evaluation cards were returned by about half of those attending. I have interviewed five competitors and four previous winners, all reporting the event had enriched their lives and/or their storytelling careers.

The Young Tongues Projects are a series of regional programmes involving between nine and twelve workshop sessions to help young people, particularly the disadvantaged, to become confident public speakers. Its aims are to teach the art of oral storytelling, provide opportunities for young people to perform in public, put them forward for participation in the Young Storyteller of the Year and to offer guidance during the run-up to and beyond the competition itself. Its wider aims are to develop a storytelling culture in schools and communities, and to support creative producers of storytelling events for young people. Eleven Young Tongues Projects were represented at the 2009 Young Storyteller of the Year, made up from schools and a theatre company in the English Midlands, schools and a youth club in East Anglia and participants from the Young Storyteller of Wales Festival.

In a very different example of competitive storytelling, storyteller Taffy Thomas recounts[2] how nineteenth century tourists to the English Lake District were captivated by tall stories told by one Auld Will Ritson, the landlord of the Wasdale Head Inn. To revive this tradition the borough council established The Biggest Liar in the World competition in the 1980s and it is still held on the third Thursday in November at the Bridge Inn, Santon Bridge. The rules are vague but, for obvious reasons, journalists, lawyers and politicians are excluded for having an unfair advantage. Competitors stand to tell their stories that must not exceed twelve minutes. Those who overrun are dismissed by the loud ringing of a bell by white-coated Bill the Bell-Man (a role he also plays at the gurning competition (grotesque face-pulling) at nearby Egremont Crab Fair). The stories are judged by the mayor and borough counsellors.

Biggest liar competitions are now popular at local storytelling groups and those regularly held in studio theatres and other public venues have included the recently staged 666th Grand Lying Contest. In a variant form of competitive storytelling London has recently hosted The World's First Ever International Story Slam when competing teams of slammers from Chicago's Windy City and the UK joined in combat at a book club in London's East End. Again the rules are sketchy but suggest: five minutes maximum, no restriction on topic or mode of communication, audience votes the winner.

Reflections

One recurrent theme of post-festival reports is the intensely time-consuming effort taken to stage such events, in particular for unpaid volunteer organisers who have to curtail their professional commitments to meet the pressing deadlines of festival organisation. It is for this very understandable reason that many storytellers report they do not become involved in festival management. Several have also reported that they do not organise even their own storytelling workshops because the fees they can charge attenders do not compensate them for their time, effort and the cost of planning such an event. An analysis of the organisational models of the festivals discussed above does however suggest ways of relieving some of the administrative burdens. Sharing responsibilities with, for example, partner organisations and/or the staff and management of event venues, has successfully brought administrative relief in some cases. Some organisers have recruited volunteer advisers with specialist expertise that is not available within the festival committee, for example, business or arts management or fund-raising. Co-producing an event by two or more organisations can bring multiple benefits, including the pooling of revenues and subsidies, organisational and promotional effort, and access to each other's lists of supporters and potential audience members.

Staging an event at a venue where all the logistics are available on site, say a university campus, may imperil the whole event budget and may bring an institutional atmosphere to the proceedings but will almost certainly save organisational effort. Venues, like folk-style festivals held on greenfield sites, may commend themselves by the friendly, sociable atmosphere they engender but require a large commitment to logistics. One such festival recently became catastrophically vulnerable to extreme weather. Good examples exist, both in storytelling and other arts, of festivals held at multiple venues, even spread over a large geographical area and staged on non-sequential days. It is difficult to draw conclusions about such an organisational model, but from the examples above, optimal decisions often seem to lie somewhere between attracting particular target audiences and retaining a sense of cohesive whole.

Although the financial details of festivals, conferences and competitions form no part of this present study, I did find some statistical correlation between the scale of public funding of the festivals studied and the proportion of their programmes taken up with outreach events in the community. I shared this observation during an interview with one regional representative of Arts Council England; however they affirmed this to be pure coincidence since 'grants are not dependent on outreach events'. They operate an 'open access' policy which permits grant awards for a wide range of artistic enterprises including such activities as 'research and development', while central to their judging criteria is 'artistic quality'. It goes without saying that other Arts Councils and other funding bodies may operate by different criteria. The analysis of audience interviews at those festivals studied, when compared with those at other types of storytelling event, reveals only insignificant variations in the responses given, and otherwise merely corroborates the general findings of this study, namely that the storytelling movement takes many forms and attracts those with many varied interests and motivations.

There is one quality that seems to be common to all storytelling festivals studied: their aspirations, organisation and sense of common social purpose are all deeply embedded in the places these festivals are held. It should come as no surprise, for example, that the one-day schools festival described above was a celebration of traditional storytelling in a culturally diverse community that was, in turn, celebrating the centenary of a London suburb built as a social experiment in urban planning. Everything about the Cambridge Storytelling Festival spoke of the enlightened traditions of this famous university City: its story walks and of course story punt, its emphasis on teaching through the Young People's Project, its sponsorship of new work through the New Directions Commissions, and the welcome it extended to other cultures through The Traveller Project. Beyond the Border Wales was as much a showcase of Welsh cultural identity as it was of storytelling in Wales. Its dual-language programme of events, its public funding mainly from Welsh cultural institutions, the involvement of the Welsh Minister for the Environment and the engagement of artists, music and stories from five continents, all draw the world's attention to the unique identity of Welsh storytelling traditions.

It would be hard to imagine a storytelling festival that is more imbued with the spirit of place than Festival at the Edge. This folk-style festival is held in open countryside at Wenlock Edge in the English West Midlands county of Shropshire, a bucolic landscape of rural beauty made famous worldwide through the lyrical poetry of A. E. Housman (1859-1936) and the song cycle *On Wenlock Edge* by that quintessential English composer and collector of folk music and song, Ralph Vaughan Williams (1872-1958). The Scottish Storytelling Festival quite consciously moulds itself on two separate public perceptions of its home city, Edinburgh. The first lies in its role as an iconic city of culture, laying claim to two UNESCO World Heritage Sites, the world's third most famous festival brand name and the clearest expression of Scotland's distinctive culture. (Those from Glasgow will disagree on this last point.) The second, as Scotland's ancient capital, Edinburgh has always maintained relations with the rest of the world independently from London. It is in this role that each year's festival carries a strong international theme which directly supports the Storytelling Centre's strategy to raise the profile of Scottish storytelling as a network hub with global reach.

Anyone who has ever been involved in organising a festival or conference with an international or even multicultural component will be aware of their adoptive role as a cultural diplomat. Hasty re-programming was forced on the organisers of one storytelling festival held during the research period when visas for a scheduled performing group were denied to them. As I write this paragraph, today's

93

newspapers carry an article about Asia's largest literary festival that has dropped one of its principal guest speakers from the programme after protests from local religious leaders. All storytelling for conflict resolution and peace-building is as much about political reconciliation as it is about social reconciliation. In Chapter Three we noted how the publicity for Emerson School of Storytelling's Dangerous Stories course warned us that, 'Of all human inventions, story is far and away the most dangerous. [Storytelling] can stir passions that can lead to tragic consequences.'

Yet, any form of cultural internationalism can equally well become an immensely powerful force for good in the world. The City of London Festival, held annually in this financial powerhouse of Britain's economy, is linked to the culture and economy of Britain's trading partners worldwide. It is no coincidence that major cultural institutions such as the British Museum hold blockbuster exhibitions that offer cultural rapprochement with the very regions or countries of the world where political rapprochement is proving most challenging. G. 'Buck' Buckland-Smith, referred to in the Preface as an early mentor of my own filmmaking and screenmedia consulting careers, built his reputation around such cultural diplomacy.

> In the immediate aftermath of World War Two the British occupying forces in a defeated Germany engaged Buckland-Smith and his colleagues to develop the media of film and radio as essential tools for nation-building, reconciliation and social reconstruction. One of their earliest projects was to stage an international film festival in Hamburg, an industrial city that had been systematically ruined by Allied bombing. Yet the enduring legacy of this initiative was to be far-reaching: it inspired a generation of young German filmmakers; it engaged a young media entrepreneur who would give his name, Axel Springer, to one of today's leading European multimedia corporations; and the film festival they founded is still held annually in this most cosmopolitan of cities.

In my personal experience the benefits of cultural diplomacy can be far-reaching. The 1981 and 1983 Mogadishu Pan-African Film Festival and Symposium, funded by the Arab League and UNESCO, succeeded in its cultural aims by attracting delegates from 40 countries and in its diplomatic aims as a vehicle for rapprochement with the neighbouring Republic of Kenya. Sometimes cultural diplomacy can be a harbinger of far-reaching political trends. So a commission for a feasibility study to educate China's estimated 150 million school-age children through the medium of film came just three years after the death of communist leader Mao Zedong and in the very early days of Chairman Deng Xiaoping's game-changing political initiative of 'opening up to the outside world'. Often it is difficult to detach cultural diplomacy from hidden political agendas, especially when popular culture in some counties is the exclusive preserve of the state. Sometimes, the core aims of cultural diplomacy have to be radically changed to remain credible and effective. So a British-funded initiative to put teaching films in Kenyan classrooms, where the medium would have proved ineffective, had to be redirected towards teacher training colleges, where the medium would have been a powerful teaching tool (although corruption eventually defeated the whole initiative). And readers can imagine the moral maze involved when conducting cultural diplomacy in the Middle East following al-Qaeda's attacks on New York in 2001. All cultural diplomacy is an emergent process and therefore leads to uncertain outcomes.

But on a more affirmative note, all the examples of storytelling festivals, conferences and contests reviewed above demonstrate how such celebrations can become a showcase and brand leader event for groups, organisations and representative bodies; can forge new identities and raise the public profile of communities and whole sectors of society; can provide forums for social and cultural understanding; can promote reconciliation, co-operation and social reconstruction; and become a powerful driving force for emergent socio-cultural phenomena like contemporary oral storytelling.

Notes & References

1. Jane Pendry, 'Many Cultures One Community', *Storylines*, Society for Storytelling UK, Spring 2008, p. 9.
2. Taffy Thomas, 'The World's Biggest Liar', *Storylines*, Society for Storytelling UK, Winter 2010, p. 4.

95

SIX

PRACTICE AND PERFORMANCE

ℰℛ

I
n Chapter One storytellers reveal widely varying and strongly held views on
the nature of their own core skills. Some hold these are 'innate human skills
[…] that rely on instinct, not an acquired technique'. Others state 'there is a
skills gap amongst storytellers; that relying on natural talent and instinct is not
good enough if storytelling is to survive in today's media-hungry world' and 'storytellers have to be as professional with their techniques as actors are with theirs'.
Chapter One also suggests these apparently irreconcilable positions may have less
to do with the core skills themselves and more to do with the lack of a shared language and a shared culture between the many genres of oral storytelling. This
chapter ranges widely across the landscapes of storytellers' core skills, human
communication, cultural performance and the techniques found in other of
today's performing arts. It seeks connecting pathways between these distinct
approaches to practice and performance and it attempts to reveal regions of
shared values and common interests.

Evidence for this chapter has been gathered from multiple sources. In the first
place from three academic publications: *Folklore, Cultural Performance and Popular Entertainments*[1] edited by Richard Bauman, an authority on folklore, linguistic anthropology and cultural performance (referred to here as *Folklore*); *Verbal
Art as Performance*[2] by Richard Bauman (referred to here as *Verbal Art*); and *Communicating: The Multiple Modes of Human Interconnection*[3] by Ruth Finnegan, an
authority on the anthropology of performance and human communication
(referred to here as *Communicating*). Evidence also comes from my own attendance as participant observer at nineteen varied skills workshops, of which thirteen
were for storytellers and included a two-day beginners' course led by performance

storyteller Ben Haggarty, and six with a duration of up to five days for practitioners in widely varied performing arts. Many observations and reflections on this original research also call on my personal experience as a filmmaker specialising in music, arts and humanities subjects, and my habitual attendance at over a hundred stage productions a year across widely varying performing arts.

In *Communicating* Finnegan provides us with a useful working definition of human communication.

> A dynamic interactive process made up of the organised, purposive, mutually-influential and mutually-recognisable actions and experiences that are created in a variety of modes by and between active participants as they interconnect with each other. [...] 'Communicating' is not one single once-and-for-all thing which you either have or don't have, but a bundle of features, themselves graduated rather than absolute. [And] humans use a *variety* of modes to connect with each other [that include] frowns or bows to sign languages and dance – but also the multifarious sum of human-made media.[4]

Nonverbal modes of expression and communication are now the subject of exhaustive research and come with their own terminology and system of classification. For example, 'proxemics (structuring and using space to communicate), haptics (using touch to communicate), chronemics (using time), kinesics (visual aspects of bodily movement), physical appearance (carrying messages to others), vocalics (vocal as opposed to verbal aspects of speech), artefacts (both as message vehicle and influencing other codes)'.[5]

In everyday human communication these distinct modes of expression come bundled as pre-formed packages of innate aptitudes. Yet mismatches between these individual modes of communication inevitably cause misunderstandings, or worse. For example, we are not calmed by soothing words if they are accompanied by a clenched fist and we tend to distrust anyone who cannot maintain eye-contact. Most multimodal forms of human communication are culturally learned and in our own culture have been systematically developed as organised, purposive art forms. There is no escaping it. Any successful applicant for an executive job will have learnt the behavioural techniques of a job interview. Successful teachers and coaches must have acquired both teaching and presentational skills. Most spokespersons for high profile organisations are now trained in media presentation skills. The priest must be a behavioural exemplar of their beliefs if they are to retain the confidence of their congregants. One drama school teacher of my acquaintance earns most of her income advising corporate employers on the body language of job applicants. We all prefer to be treated by a doctor with an empathetic demeanour and, it goes without saying, with clean fingernails. One government advisor recommends that teachers should be trained to control troublesome school pupils by adopting a more authoritative style of speaking and a more confident posture.[6] And there is also now an established literature on the subject of healthcare communication.

This detour into the wider territory of human communication is relevant to this chapter because storytelling and storymaking are organised, purposive art forms requiring not only innate skills of human communication but also the culturally-acquired core skills of the storyteller/maker and the culturally-acquired behavioural skills appropriate to the particular purpose of the storytelling/making. A psychiatric social worker story-swapping with a violent teenager requires both the acquired skills of the storyteller and the acquired professional skills of the psychiatric social worker. The chief executive of a global corporation inspiring organisational change with springboard stories requires both the acquired skills of the storyteller and the acquired leadership and behavioural skills of corporate life. The storymaker we met in Chapter Three who works with refugees is greatly advantaged by the multiple creative skills they have acquired and by their familiarity with many global cultures.

Both the acquired storyteller skills and acquired professional skills were clearly on display at one storytelling I witnessed for children aged between seven and ten years old. The storyteller's skills were manifest in the multimedia participation of the children which included pictorial illustration, costume and mask, role-play and making a magic rune. The professional skills of the storyteller, a specialist children's social worker, were manifest in appropriately adapted forms of vocal projection, body language and direct audience address (speaking directly and individually to listeners).

By contrast a mismatch of these distinct skills was painfully manifest at two storytelling events I witnessed when the same teller told similar stories a few days apart in very different social contexts. The first was at a ceilidh night in a crowded room over a noisy pub, beer glass in hand, their hilarious personal stories were a masterclass of anecdotal storytelling to a sympathetic audience in intimate surroundings. The second, in a formal theatre setting, alone on stage, under stage lights and telling to a paying audience on tiered theatre seating, was so adrift that the sense of collective embarrassment could be felt throughout the auditorium. The poor fellow had failed to acquire the culturally-learned skills of stagecraft needed to hold an audience in this formal theatre setting. I find myself persuaded by the anthropologists that there are no circumstances in which a storytelling can be detached from its purposive, actualised performance in the presence of a consenting and co-creating audience. Or as Shakespeare puts it rather more poetically, 'All the world's a stage, and all the men and women merely players' (see also Chapter Seven).

Cultural performance

Storytellers often state that 'actors do not make good storytellers'. Several spoke of 'letting the story tell itself', and as we find in Chapter One, there is a general if ill-defined sense amongst storytellers that 'performance and staging skills are no concern of the applied [non-performance/platform] storyteller'. Once again we look to the folklorists and anthropologists to find a pathway through the ideas and definitions alluded to here. In *Folklore*, Bauman brings us a definition of the word 'performance' in the context of formal ritualised social behaviour.

> A mode of communicative behaviour and a type of communicative event. [The word] performance usually suggests an aesthetically marked and heightened mode of communication, framed in a special way, and put on display for an audience. The analysis of performance – indeed, the very conduct of performance – highlights the social, cultural, and aesthetic dimensions of the communicative process.[7]

Surely there is nothing in this definition that the psychiatric social worker, the chief executive of a global corporation, the refugee storymaker, the children's storyteller, or even the stage-fright storyteller referred to above, would wish to disagree with.

In *Verbal Art* Bauman develops the theme of cultural performance and in particular the idea that any performance of the verbal arts, or spoken arts as they are also called, 'sets up, or represents, an interpretative frame [or context] within which the messages being communicated are to be understood, and that this frame contrasts with at least one other frame, the literal'.[8] The implication here is 'that in spoken communication no such thing as naked literalness may actually exist'.[9] He also explores the methods by which these performance frames are invoked by means of 'a range of explicit or implicit messages which carry instructions on how [a listener is] to interpret the other message(s) being communicated'.[10] In reference to such linguistic codes as 'Once upon a time ...' that all the verbal arts call on to evoke interpretative performance frames, he discusses how it is the formal patterns of these codes that 'elicit the participation of an audience through the arousal of [in Kenneth Burke's words] "an attitude of collaborative expectancy.... Once you grasp the trend of the form, it invites participation." This '[...] fixes the attention of the audience more strongly on the performer, binds the audience to the performer in a relationship of dependence that keeps them caught up in his display'.[11] The idea of an interpretative performance frame is also taken up by anthropologist Allessandro Duranti in an article in *Folklore* on the topic of oratory.

> For any orator the ability to communicate with an audience is not measured by linguistic skills alone. [These] must be accompanied by knowledge of [...] cultur-

ally and situationally appropriate nonlinguistic behaviors, such as body posture, gesture, eye gaze, and facial expression must accompany a speaker's verbal performance. The importance of such nonverbal expertise in a public speaker has long been recognised in the Western tradition of rhetoric, as documented by the special term, *actio*, given by the Romans to the nonlinguistic behavior that was supposed to accompany any public address.[12]

In a later chapter of *Verbal Art* Bauman discusses the emergent qualities of any performance, and by its very nature, the inherent potential for creating social structures as the performance proceeds.

> It offers to the participants a special enhancement of experience, bringing with it a heightened intensity of communicative interaction which binds the audience to the performer in a way that is specific to the performance as a mode of communication. Through his performance, the performer elicits the participative attention and energy of his audience, and to the extent that they value his performance, they will allow themselves to be caught up in it.[13]

Also relevant to a chapter on the practice and performance of oral storytelling is a point made by Bauman about the arts in general, but is equally relevant to the performing arts.

> Art is commonly conceived as an all-or-nothing phenomenon – something either is or is not art – but conceived as performance, in terms of an interpretative frame, verbal art may be culturally defined as varying in intensity as well as range. We are not speaking here of the relative quality of a performance – good performance vs. bad performance – but a degree of intensity with which the performance frame operates in a particular range of culturally defined ways of speaking.[14]

As a practitioner of the filmmaker's art I came to these ideas as something of a sceptic, but have since been persuaded by the folklorists' and anthropologists' definitions, descriptions and observations of 'cultural performance'. They seem to fit well with this study's primary research into the storytellers' and audience members' descriptions of the co-creation process of oral storytelling. They also seem to fit well with the many and varied genres of storytelling and storymaking, and the many and varied intensities of cultural performance found in the broader landscape of storytelling and storymaking. But research for this chapter has also revealed other storytelling and storymaking voices that are clamouring to be heard.

Shared performance cultures

As Chapter One reveals, there is a significant body of opinion amongst storytellers who say, 'we need a new theatrical form for our own narrative heritage'; 'we have to embrace the skills of others, invent a new artistry'; 'most storytellers have too limited a range of performance and staging techniques'; 'I'm aware of the benefits [to storytelling] of having a theatre background, but while theatre companies now engage storytellers, so storytelling ought to reciprocate'; 'storytelling [...] needs to be more open to outside influence and inspiration'; and 'storytelling is an adolescent art form and we should look at other art forms and learn from them'. Unexpectedly, several prominent storytellers, who would never consider formal coaching to improve their own performance skills, have urged me to take the broadest possible view of performance skills in this chapter, including a review of those found in other performing arts. So that is what this chapter now aims to do.

By broadening the scope of this study to embrace other performing arts, the first surprise comes from realising that Finnegan's definition of the purposive, multimodal nature of human communication can be read as forming the elemental building blocks of Bauman's interpretative performance frames in cultural performances. In turn, Bauman's observations can be read as forming the foundations of performance and staging techniques found in the performing arts. I have searched for some validation that directly links the intuitive aptitude we all have for human communication and the hard-learned techniques of the performing arts. The best I can find comes from Konstantin Stanislavski (1863-1938) who's system of actor training revolutionised theatre in the West and remains a strong influence on all theatre today.

> Acting is above all intuitive, because it is based on subconscious feelings, on an actor's instincts. That, of course, does not mean that an actor should be an ignoramus, that he has no need of knowledge. Quite the contrary, he needs it more than anyone, because it provides him with material with which to be creative. But there is a time and place for everything. Actors should educate themselves, build up a store of learning and real-life experiences, but onstage, while they are acting, they should forget what they have learned and be intuitive.[15]

The storyteller quoted above who said, 'while theatre companies now engage storytellers so storytelling ought to reciprocate', is obviously unaware that all the performing arts have already embraced the storyteller's core skills and regularly embed storytelling episodes in otherwise conventional productions. This is not merely the inclusion of storytelling techniques like direct audience address but the suspension of traditional performance and staging skills and the seamless adoption of the core skills of the oral storytelling medium. Recent examples I have witnessed include: A Royal National Theatre production of Christopher Marlowe's *Dido, Queen of Carthage*, during which Aeneas came out of character to tell a first-hand account of the sack of Troy. *Kafka's Monkey*, an adaptation by Colin Teevan for solo performer of Franz Kafka's short story *A Report to an Academy*, opens with the lines: 'Esteemed members of the Academy! You have done me the great honour of inviting me to give you an account of my former life as an ape.' *Eonnagata*, is a large-scale work of devised performance art, conceived and performed by leading performance artist Robert Lepage and acclaimed dancers Sylvie Guillem and Russell Maliphant. It opens with Guillem, dressed from head to foot in a sumptuous robe, recounting in heavily accented English the life-story of Charles de Beaumont, Chevalier d'Éon. And *In-i*, a two-hander devised and performed by Oscar-winning actress Juliette Binoche and acclaimed Kathak dancer/choreographer Akram Khan, in which the sometimes tumultuous action is interrupted to allow Khan to tell us a heartfelt personal story from his own youth.

Even the concept of co-creation by audiences is not exclusive to oral storytelling. As early as the 1950s Jerzy Grotowski (1933-1999), often referred to as father of contemporary experimental theatre and a pioneer of what became known as 'poor theatre', was describing how actors co-create theatre with their audiences and how theatre could not exist without the actor-spectator relationship of perceptual, direct and live communion. In a recent private conversation with Simon McBurney, pioneering director of Complicite, he spoke of theatre taking place in the heads of individual audience members. And the very words 'complicit' and 'complicity' are now widely used in the performing arts to refer to the emergent relationship of performer and audience member. (I look forward to reading a monograph on the comparative nature of co-creation in oral storytelling and other performing arts.)

Chapter Two reveals overwhelming support by audience members for active participation in public storytelling events, but this tradition has a much longer history. It was certainly well established in the mid-nineteenth century supper rooms (the forerunners of the English music halls and the origin of the expression 'singing for your supper') where luckless audience members might find themselves dragged on stage and put on trial for some heinous sexual crime. And come to think of it, bantering between stage and audience was well established in Elizabethan theatre. Recent examples I have witnessed include requests from the audience in a classical music concert; sing-alongs and dance-alongs; pre- and post-show discussions; open workshops; performance participation in art exhibitions; and I have paid the penalty for preferring front row seats and found myself on stage three times recently, the butt of very public jokes. In the very week this manuscript goes to the publishers I have just played xylophone with the London Symphony Orchestra – well, three of them – in an open workshop that explored the

103

structural motifs of Shostakovich's Leningrad Symphony (hence, it did not matter that I was playing all the wrong notes!). Just how far today's audiences are pre-
pared to go with their active participation was demonstrated in one recent show.

> Circus Klezmer is a riotous theatre-circus staged around a very slight story of an
> eastern European Jewish village wedding that goes horribly wrong. The only way
> to save the day is to enlist increasing numbers of the audience to play vital roles in
> the story – musicians, long-lost relatives, canopy bearers and even a substitute
> bride is hauled from the front stalls and put through an impromptu on-stage Jew-
> ish wedding. 'Am I really married?' she asks her on-stage companions amidst rap-
> turous applause.

This production, I suggest, attracted such wholehearted participation because
both audience and performance shared many cultural conventions – story, social
context, Western circus traditions and popular ethnic music. This meant we were
also familiar with the conventions of appropriate participation (although I should
mention that one young woman wearing a Muslim hijab did walk out as the on-
stage wedding ceremony began).

In contrast, a production of Japanese grand kabuki was brought to London
recently that demonstrates how shared cultures between stage and audience cannot be assumed in all circumstances. The performance and staging skills were
demonstrably of the highest order, but beyond that, we could identify little in the
way of a shared culture. We were therefore startled when our traditionally-dressed
Japanese neighbours suddenly shouted out or applauded their apparent appreciation when nothing whatsoever appeared to be happening on stage. In the interval they kindly explained this was a convention called 'kakegoe' that signalled
turning points in the narrative when lead performers adopt symbolic poses of
great cultural significance.

While it is widely acknowledged that there is no such thing as a universal theatre and absolute limits to shared performance cultures, the many intuitive media
of human communication can be seen as part of a shared culture when they are
mutually-influential and mutually-recognisable. Oratory, mime, clothing, song,
dance, music, humour, gesture and artefacts are all intuitive media of human
communication. They are also subjects of exhaustive study by folklorists and
anthropologists in the context of cultural performance (*Folklore* contains articles
on all these topics). The term 'performance tool' is also widely used in the performing arts, and amongst some storytellers, to describe the techniques that can
turn the intuitive media of human communication into the organised, purposive
performance of the orator, the cantor or the Shakespearean actor. It is to this
realm of performance tools that this study now turns.

Hearing voices

It hardly needs stating that the human voice is probably the most sublimely subtle auditory instrument for adding sense and sensibility to the spoken word. The acoustics of the vocal tract alone can inspire a national movement, lull a child to sleep or can set up a performance frame and determine how an audience listens to a storytelling. Anthropologists now study the sonic qualities of speech, quite separate from the literal meanings of the words spoken. Here is Finnegan in *Communicating* on some qualities of the human voice.

> It can produce infinite numbers of distinctive sound combinations differentiated by specific uses of (for example) teeth, lips, tongue, nose, and palate. It can differentiate along a spectrum of rhythm, pitch, tempo, timbre, tone quality, phrasing, melodic and other musical elements, pacing, volume, intensity, breathiness, roughness, low and high registers, vibrato or plain delivery, abrupt or sustained phrasing, silences … only some of its powers.[16]

Most storytellers modulate their speaking voices to add emphasis to their telling and some adapt their telling voices to represent different characters in the story. But in the wider world the performing arts there are literally thousands of modes of heightened vocal projection that lie somewhere between the our everyday conversational voices and the many forms of singing voice – everything from the more familiar sprechgesang (the German for spoken-song) to the husky modulations of the Korean Art of Pansori, described by storyteller Sef Townsend in a recent issue of *Storylines*.[17] In contemporary performing arts heightened speech can include the vocal mimicry of any human or animal sound, any human-made object and any sound from the natural world. In a recent National Theatre performance of Aristophanes' *The Birds* the metre of its rhyming couplets was occasionally sustained with human/bird calls to express an appreciation of, or an objection to, the lines just spoken. Yet few of the storytellers I have interviewed are aware that vocal delivery alone can hold or loose an audience's attention, or are aware of the causes and consequences of breathing problems, voice strain, laryngeal damage and psychological distress, or are even aware these conditions can be remedied in the care of a good voice coach.

To understand these issues better I signed up for a Voice and Text Summer School at London's Central School of Speech and Drama, five days of highly technical workshops that I approached with some degree of confidence as a filmmaker whose credits include the critically acclaimed *The Singing Voice*,[18] a technical analysis of the human voice as a musical instrument. First big mistake. Within the first hour I was lost, disorientated in a fog of humility. These highly intensive workshops were driven by individual and collaborative exercises, many in the form of games, which sought to develop the qualities of a student's own conversational voice so that it sounded natural in an expanded range of perform- ance contexts – from whispered confidences to a hectoring bellow. The teaching revealed how breathing techniques are the basis of all voice work and how every part of our anatomy, from the soles of our feet to the resonant cavities in our heads, is employed in every utterance we make. The exercises revealed deeply felt issues of how the colouring and intonation of our voices originate in our some- times subconscious minds. And one group exercise that left us all in tears revealed how our most heartfelt emotions can be connected with, and expressed through, our speaking voices. But my initial shock and my enduring impression of this summer school was not just a better understanding of vocal articulation, or the teaching of performance tools for public speakers, but of a life-enhancing experi- ence and the acquisition of life skills with practical applications in all human com- munication.

Body language

Amongst those career storytellers I have interviewed, few seem to be aware of their own bodies as powerful communicators of meaning and emotion. Even amongst those, like teachers and therapists, whose professional credibility depends on an appropriate body language, few seem aware that kinesics is a well understood symbolic language with its own grammar, syntax and meaning within a culture. Fewer still have undertaken any formal training in any of the common forms of physical performance. To put these common responses into a broader context, anthropologist Adam Kendon defines the word 'gesture' in these terms:

> Bodily action other than speech that is recognized as being done in order to express something. It is considered separate from emotional expression and sepa- rate from other bodily actions such as tics, mannerisms, and nervous move- ments.[19]

In the realm of body language as total performance, prominent choreographer, Wayne McGregor, whose pioneering work is much inspired by today's scientific thought, practice and method, writes 'My primary aspiration [is] the communi- cation of ideas through the medium of the body [...] to make sense of the world [...] through choreographed language and form.'[20] Somewhere between these two extremes, and in common with many storytellers, I rather thought the teaching of ritualised performance in traditional and folkloric contexts was a rather infor- mal, easy-going affair. Not so.

Trekking in remote Himalayan Bhutan, we climb through deciduous forest to an ancient, mountain-top dzong (those administrative and monastic fortresses that seemingly float between heaven and earth) where, on the worn paving of a balconied courtyard, an elderly dance master is drilling young monks in the highly ritualised movements of Tantric Buddhism. There is nothing informal or easy-going about it.

Most of us, I suppose, are strangers to our own physicality and have never reflected on the relationship between our innate body language and the formalised languages of physical performance. So to correct this oversight and to further the research for this chapter, I signed up for a broad range of performance workshops, kicked off my street shoes, left a lifetime of social inhibitions at the studio door and got up close and personal. These included: A two-day workshop with London-based Theatre de L'Ange Fou, an international school of corporeal mime based on the work of French master Etienne Decroux (1898-1991) and often referred to as the father of modern mime. A five-day Physical Theatre summer school at East 15 Acting School, based mainly on the techniques of Jerzy Grotowski (1933-1999), Rudolph Laban (1879-1958) and Jacques Lecoq (1921-1999). (Teacher's report: overall 'outstanding' but marked down on 'ensemble acting' and 'ability to accept criticism', both fair comment.) *The Art of Laughter*, a public, non-participatory masterclass by Jos Houben, writer, director, performer and teacher at Ecole Jacques Lecoq. (One of his favourite demonstrations: miming the taste of various cheeses by means of body language alone.) A week of half-day workshops with London-based Complicite, using movement, games and improvisation to devise ten-minute dramas from Anton Chekhov short stories about fishing. (Fondest memory: life as a river carp, infatuated with a frigid English governess.) And a season of two-hour, weekly evening classes on improvised contemporary dance led by London-based Independent Dance.

From a summary and analysis of my contemporaneous notes of all these workshops, certain recurrent themes stand out. Many performance tools are common to all these workshops. All are driven by highly structured exercises including children's games, improvisation, contests of quick-wittedness and close physical contact. Theory is not taught but emerges spontaneously through an individual's engagement with the exercises. Coaching standards are generally excellent and at two of these workshops inspirational. Performance tools are acquired first, only then comes 'a personal theatre of the body'. A primary performance tool is the power of intense observation and an analysis of human behaviour, life and everything. The term 'physical theatre' is not a distinct performing art but the language and grammar of all bodily expression. The 'bigging-up' of movement is not more expressive; smaller movements are generally stronger; moments of suspended motion are often strongest of all. Observers can often interpret the meaning of movements more effectively if their component parts are separated by momentary pauses. As to physical transformations, like frog to prince: do not signal, do it small, deftly, move on, never describe it. One overriding conclusion drawn from these workshops was how a natural body language in a performance context only exists amongst rare geniuses. For mere mortals like the rest of us, it requires discipline, rigorous training, regular practice, and often, as I experienced at the East 15 Summer School, blood on the studio floor (thankfully not mine).

As with vocal development, it came as a surprise that these performance tools are not merely the means to a personal theatre of the body, but life skills with practical applications in all human communication. For me, with no ambition to become a performer, the most important skills learnt were: the power of intense observation, a breathing technique for the whole body and a physical flexibility especially of the neck, spinal column and pelvis. If pressed to say how these workshops changed my life for ever I would add: a heightened awareness of my own physicality, insights into how others read and judge my body language, the shedding of many life-long social inhibitions, tics, mannerisms and nervous movements, and – this may sound a bit affected – a resolve to live my life more rhythmically.

Organised sound

Storytelling has always been accompanied by music and these traditions remain well represented amongst today's storytellers. Several of those interviewed however show a certain reticence or reserve when they accompany their story with song and one accounted for this observation in interview by saying they were 'not expert enough'. Isn't this rather paradoxical? Why judge their own expertise against today's professional singers when their singing would have seemed miraculous in the age of the story being told – in this example, the age of Arthurian legend? Isn't authenticity what storytellers seek? Anyone who has heard original recordings made by ethnomusicologists of traditional folksongs struggles to recognise the same song when it has been interpreted by Western, classically-trained composers. And aren't many of today's best-loved popular singers living examples of the triumph of self-confidence (and probably sex appeal) over musical expertise?

Beyond the realm of song and instrumental music the performing arts abound with examples of improvised soundscapes. Our voices are infinitely adaptable mimickers of human, animal and natural sounds. Any combination of blowing, scraping, plucking or striking bits of our own anatomy can evoke sonic associations and become an effective medium of human communication. Almost any object can be employed as a musical instrument, as did the French-American composer Edgard Varèse (1883-1965), the author of the term 'organised sound' and often referred to as 'the father of electronic music'. Some storytellers use everyday objects as percussion instruments, one I have witnessed played the spoons, and one recent theatre-circus production featured a whole one-person orchestra of kitchen utensils. A microphone can also be employed as an adaptable generator of soundscapes and musical accompaniments when blown into, struck or scraped against all manner of surfaces and textures. In one ingenious example of this, a dancer provided her own discordant accompaniment with a live microphone attached by its cable to one of her feet. And even the now-fashionable beatboxing (vocal percussion with closely-held microphone) has found a niche role in orchestral music.

One of the early lessons that filmmakers learn when commissioning an original musical score is to make sure there is a clear understanding with the composer about what precise grammatical role the music is to play in each scene. We have all seen films where the music seems to mix its metaphors, as it were, and for the same reason, a musical accompaniment to a storytelling can sometimes appear as little more than displacement activity. Nonetheless, whether a vocal solo, an atmospheric sound effect or a virtuoso instrumental accompaniment, storytelling audiences affirm that organised sound greatly heightens the immersive experience of a storytelling.

Artefact

Any study of folklore and anthropology reveals a rich source of stories embedded in artefacts of nearly every form. The word itself implies a process of making or modifying by human hands and signifies these objects are themselves interpretations, objectifications and materialisations of human experience. Artefacts are studied as signs, signals and signifiers of some quality of human existence and storytellers use them as vehicles and vestiges of human communication and interaction. As Finnegan says in *Communicating*, 'There seems no end to the manifold human-made objects and arts we use in visual communication. Textiles, carvings, pictures, dwellings, furniture, utensils, books, scripts, graphics, films, photographs',[21] all come imbued with their own social and cultural significance, quite apart from any functional significance they may carry. As the Museums and Heritage Special Interest Group pages of the Society for Storytelling website notes: 'Museums are places with objects, but the objects in themselves mean little, only by telling about them, interacting with them and assigning meanings to them (discursive interaction) can we understand their significance.'

Some storytellers use small artefacts that give specific meaning to their stories. One literally unpacks the artefacts of their stories from a suitcase. Educational and therapeutic storyteller/makers engage their listeners' participation by getting them to create some cultural artefact inspired by the story being told. One story-teller of the ancient Egyptian Isis myth, calling on a very different form of embod-ied artefact, quite literally fashions (or rather unfashions) a classical statue of the goddess from her own naked body.

The creation of artefacts in real time as part of a performance is found in many traditional cultures and in today's performing arts. In a spirited recent example the cast of the Cloud Gate Dance Theatre of Taiwan performed in socks and mit-tens that had been saturated in variously coloured paint, so leaving a wild trace of their choreography on the canvas surface of the stage. This was later cut up and sold as art works to the following night's patrons. Artefacts can also cross media boundaries. So a juggler who bounced six (I think) balls off the treads of a short flight of steps that had been tuned to sound musical notes was simultaneously cre-ating a visual artefact (circus act) and a sonic artefact (popular tune). In another recent dance performance a giant hand fan became, in turn, skirt, peacock's tail, headdress, lateen sail, not-so-modesty screen, fashion bag and more.

Puppetry, under its generic title of 'object manipulation', now takes centre stage in pioneering theatre productions. Some forms of puppetry, involving nothing more than advanced skills of observation and dexterity, can animate eve-ryday inanimate objects to startling effect.

> Once, auditioning puppeteers for a dramatised campaign film in a semi-basement
> kitchen, one puppeteer suddenly seized a floor mop, shook it in my face with a
> menacing cackle and instantly it became an old crone, and in the basement half-
> light, the kitchen became her broken-down hovel.

While folklorists and anthropologists agree that much of our social and cultural life can be expressed through artefacts, the interpretation and communication of their meaning can sometimes be ambiguous and/or misleading. Professor of Eng-lish, Barbara A. Babcock, discusses some of these issues in an article in *Folklore*.[22] First, artefacts can carry several meanings over a continuum between the wholly functional and the wholly symbolic and our interpretation of these meanings is heavily influenced by our personal and past experiences. Second, the meaning of an artefact can change according to the context it is observed in: as the subject of worship in a temple, as an ethnographic artefact in a museum and as a work of art when hung on a living room wall. Third, similar artefacts can be interpreted dif-ferently according to a range of observable variables; for example, the symbolic significance of a knife may vary according to its design or shape, materials of man-ufacture, size, method of its making, purpose of its use and its colour or structure.

Fourth, the significance of an artefact can be deliberately changed by recycling, assembling or juxtaposing objects for purposes unintended by the original maker; so coins that lose their monetary value as they cross an international frontier may gain aesthetic value as jewellery or add status to the wearer in hierarchical societies. And fifth, artefacts can lose all their meaning or significance through redundancy, ephemerality, and/or consumption; for example, an icon of a forgotten religion, a firework display or a ritual meal.

Costume and adornment

This and earlier chapters have shown how most storytellers have only patchy knowledge and experience of the tools and practices of the performing arts, but when questioned about costume and adornment as a mode of human communication, they mostly express clear and considered views. Most wear their everyday clothes as a reflection of their own personalities, and since most storytelling takes place within a vocational context, they dress appropriately for the social role they are playing at the time – teacher, health professional, business manager, church minister, and so on. Some performance storytellers wear everyday clothes but with subtle changes to capture the mood of their stories; for example, one sometimes wears a conventional day dress that is printed, not with flowers, but human skulls. Some emulate a common genre of stand-up comedy by wearing suit and tie. Those telling historical stories, especially at visitor attractions, more frequently dress in full historical costume. Some who tell in character – from history, fiction or their imagination – dress as their adopted persona. Some reflect their ethnic origins in their costume; some dress as they think their audience will be dressed; several wear distinctive hats; and one that tells stories from Arthurian England dresses 'neutrally' but is careful not to project a 'hippy' image.

Another sometimes tells in a National Lottery-sponsored 'tale coat' – more a work of art and conversation piece than garment – which has now become the inspiration for a musical composition. Chapter Three recounts how a serving police officer leads storytelling sessions at a Youth Offending Team wearing full uniform to ease the relationship between these symbols of law enforcement and those under the supervision of the criminal courts. Although none of those I have interviewed uses mask in their telling it has been reported that at least one storyteller does. This is a much studied subject in both the performing arts and in anthropology but does not necessarily involve full theatrical mask. Almost any object with mimetic association – hat, spectacles, scarf, hand gesture, make-up, facial adornment, hair – when covering even parts of the face can carry strong meanings within the context of a story.

Multiple senses

Educational and therapeutic storytellers underline the value of multimedia involvement of participants – seeing, vocalising, writing, making, painting, props, costume, mask, performing – which turns a storytelling experience into a storymaking experience. Several storytellers use the sense of smell and taste by serving food and drink to provide an associative social context for their telling. I have only heard tell of using the sense of touch, haptics, in the context of children's games which call for physical contact between participants, but other examples may exist. Proxemics, the structuring and use of space to communicate is addressed in Chapter Seven – All the World's a Stage.

Telling technology

The perennial debate held at the interface of storytelling and technology is simply stated. On the one hand instinct tells us that any attenuation or weakening of raw human expression by technology breaks the social bond of spoken dialogue and diminishes the power of oral storytelling in its elemental form. On the other hand, from the back row of a large storytelling, or in a challenging acoustic, most storytellers without recourse to sound technology and/or a trained voice have a problem of audibility. This is not just an issue for those of us with job-related hearing loss but is commonplace in our society from the age of thirty five, prevalent amongst the over-fifties, and yet I still meet young and able-eared audience members who cannot hear the finer nuances of a storytelling.

I hold in particular contempt those who try and introduce ideology into this discussion. In four years of research I have not met one single storyteller or audience member who is averse to technology. Nor have I found one shred of evidence that the social value of storytelling is somehow diminished by technology; or that the function of storytelling should somehow act a bulwark against the sinister intents of those controlling the world's technology; or indeed that the globalisation of technology is somehow blighting community solidarity, indigenous culture and social diversity. Just ask those Middle Eastern rebels who are now overthrowing despots and ushering in a new dawn of democracy with the help of mobile phone cameras, social networking internet sites and the world's television networks – all of which are controlled by global corporations. And incidentally, one of the best productions I have ever seen of *The Caucasian Chalk Circle* by Bertold Brecht (1898-1956, German playwright and winner of the 1954 International Stalin Peace Prize) had a stage set consisting entirely of technology. Technology is just another type of performance tool, its power lies exclusively in the hands of the end-user and there is nothing inherently sinister about its use in storytelling or indeed in society as a whole.

Although sound technology is widely used to great effect in storytelling, there is only a sketchy understanding amongst storytellers of the three distinct competences required for its full beneficial use: a mastery of the technology itself, in particular its inherent limitations of sound fidelity; the placing of speakers in relation to the audience and the telling space (see also Chapter Seven); and microphone technique that calls for a specialised form of voice modulation to prevent sound distortion. (Incidentally, stretching the neck towards a stand microphone can compress the larynx and lead to a husky voice and muscle strain in the vocal tract.)

Vision technology (on-stage video, film and stills projection) is now so ubiquitous in the performing arts that it is surely only a matter of time before we witness a tandem storytelling with a storyteller's own electronic image – if indeed it has not already happened. As an old fashioned film/video-maker I remain sceptical about its use in live performance because the psychology of human perception determines that we experience different media in different ways; the inherent strengths of one medium tend to reveal inherent weaknesses in others. That said, I have witnessed several effective uses of vision technology recently. First was where the technology was validated by the story being told; for example, English National Opera's modern-dress production of Handel's opera Agrippina where the title role was played as a manipulative, media-savvy spin doctor. Second was where the medium itself was a significant part of the message; for example, in one of French director Philippe Decouflé's recent productions the vision technology was integral to the performance choreography. Third was where still or moving images were front/back-projected as part of a stage set. And fourth was where video images stood in for objects that, for practical reasons, could not be brought on stage; for example, Complicite's *The Elephant Vanishes*.

Working technology embedded and playing an active role in a performance is also now ubiquitous. One of the most imaginative applications of this trend was an open-air dance show called *Transports Exceptionnels*, which took the form of a pas de deux for dancer and mechanical digger, with music from Camille Saint-Saëns and credits for choreographer, dancer, and of course, the digger driver.

Research and development

Chapter One notes how very few storytellers have any kind of forethought of how they, or storytelling generally, might develop in the future and much of this study has looked at storytelling phenomena at singular points in time or within narrowly defined research periods. It is perhaps timely therefore to try and gain some sense of progress in the practice and performance of storytelling, for which I can offer no direct, but only anecdotal evidence.

There is a steady stream of publications being brought to market on all aspects of storytelling. Global management consultants are committing large budgets to research and develop organisational storytelling. The Scottish Storytelling Centre has developed a formal system of R&D for their co-ordinated community story-telling projects and has recently formed a partnership with Newbattle Abbey College. There has been recent government support to promote storytelling in schools. The Crick Crack Club now stages what they call 'experimental storytell-ing' at London's Soho Theatre and at other venues in and beyond London. Many universities and other tertiary education colleges now teach oral storytelling in some form. Universities are awarding a steady stream of storytelling-related research degrees. At least one BA degree course in creative writing now includes a storytelling module. Academic conferences are held regularly to debate storytell-ing topics. And Kingston University has recently opened an Institute for the Spoken Word.

The Centre for Performance Research in Wales makes reference on its website to the study of storytelling skills from around the world. London's Central School of Speech and Drama now offers stand-alone workshops for teachers and story-telling components in their Drama, Applied Theatre and Education BA courses. The recently established Storytelling Observatory plans to study the impulses to, and processes of, oral storytelling. Substantive improvements have recently been made to the Society for Storytelling's administration, website, on-line discussion forum, area (regional) representatives, peer-reviewed publications and Special Interest Groups. Cybermouth is a membership internet discussion group. Neu-rolingistic programming is now applied in some quarters to the teaching and practice of storytelling. There is an active and international exchange in workshop leadership and performance storytelling at international festivals. And the Feder-ation for European Storytelling (FEST) is actively engaged in international col-laboration.

If, and it is a very big if, this anecdotal evidence is representative of all story-telling in Britain and Ireland, then it suggests there is indeed much active research and development by individuals, small groups of practitioners and storytelling organisations. There is however little evidence of this R&D being shared and coordinated between the diverse genres of storytelling, or their representative organisations, or between different regions of Britain and Ireland, or the scattered centres of learning, or shared with other performing arts. And there is little evi-dence of any form of coordinated network interaction between storytelling hubs or even an agenda for sharing the product of this R&D with a wider public. These observations are worth underscoring because a comparative study in Chapter

Eight reveals a very different picture within and between other performing arts and in the physical and social sciences.

Accreditation

Chapter Four outlines various systems of accreditation for those storytellers wishing to have their names included in the directories of membership and representative organisations, but the wider issue of accreditation is a perennial debate which I have no wish to join. However, there are other more informal systems currently in use which attract little attention. Those storytellers qualified as teachers, dramatherapists, psychotherapists, professional counsellors and mediators, health-care professionals, performance-arts therapists and probably others, bring with them professional qualifications and some years of practice and/or presentational skills in these specialist fields. Training and qualification in religious leadership calls for a certain level of competence in a broad range of narrative-based communication, mediation and counselling skills. Many of the consultants who coach senior management in organisational storytelling have studied with established experts in the field and many senior executives are trained in media presentation skills.

Accreditation for storytellers engaged by the Traditional Arts Team (see Chapter Four) is personal to its leadership as it is to the leadership of the Crick Crack Club for its productions. Similarly, most guest tellers at local storytelling groups are selected informally by the individual or collective leadership. Members of some local groups who wish to be hired out for public events must achieve a minimum level of accreditation, for example, two completed bookings, two future commitments, a valid indemnity insurance policy and a current Criminal Record Bureau check if telling to vulnerable people.

Beyond the world of storytelling, two other models for accreditation might be worth noting here. Apples & Snakes is the leading representative body for performance poetry in England and Wales, it has an administrative presence in most English regions and its work is coordinated by a full-time director and a small London-based staff. Inclusion on an approved list of performance poets is by invitation; those aspiring to qualify must demonstrate a proven track record; an informal selection process is overseen by Apples and Snakes' director; and qualification is endorsed by peer recommendation and paper-based audience surveys.

A different model for accreditation is adopted by the National Association of Decorative & Fine Arts Societies (NADFAS) which has a London office with full-time staff and over 340 local societies in the UK and further afield. It holds monthly lectures and study days, and organizes visits and study tours for its members. Those wishing to become paid lecturers must demonstrate specialist knowledge of their chosen subjects and an ability to illustrate their lectures. They must bring extensive experience of delivering one-hour lectures to audiences of more than a hundred. They are required to supply references from satisfied clients and obtain the formal approval of at least one NADFAS-appointed observer. And they must deliver a twenty-minute lecture to the satisfaction of a panel of NADFAS representatives.

Interviews for this chapter have been conducted with representatives of five cultural organizations that commission storytelling events, ranging in size from a large national institution, though mid-sized visitor attractions that hire storytellers, to small local centers that host storytelling events. Some sort of rough and ready consensus emerges from these interviews on the subject of accreditation: most only hire the same tried and tested storyteller(s); few actively seek new talent as part of their remit; those wishing to widen their choice of storytellers generally rely on word of mouth recommendation; and most would probably use an efficient one-stop shop with a reliable accreditation system if such existed. From the experienced storyteller's point of view there is little call for raising the standards of accreditation so long as they are getting plenty of bookings. From the inexperienced storyteller's point of view, accreditation works two ways: it is another barrier to cross before their name appears in an approved directory of storytellers, but once included, it becomes easier to promote their services. In the final analysis any accreditation system has its limitations – too restrictive and masterly mavericks may be precluded, too open and standards cannot be relied on by clients.

Reflections

Three other topics have been repeatedly written into and then discarded from this chapter, but after nearly a year of dithering, here they are, for better or for worse.

The first asks: Are there any performance tools that cannot be taught? Obviously we all have different capacities for learning (those of us in our seventh decade do not need reminding!). But from personal experience of the workshops described above I would judge that all such techniques can be taught to a certain degree; after all, there are now even workshops for such abstract skills as 'stage presence'. As for the skill of improvisation, I am less certain, but would suggest the foundation tools can be learnt. I cite here the example of one improvisation workshop for late renaissance musicianship which I attended as a non-participating observer but with some experience as an instrumental player. It was clear that only those with a complete mastery of both their instrument and the musical idioms of the period made much progress.

The second, of particular relevance to storytellers, asks: Can performance tools be learnt alone? I have discussed the issue with several performing arts coaches and stage directors and they are clear in their view that stagecraft can only be learnt in a formal workshop setting, within the collegiate atmosphere of a bounded community, taught by an inspirational coach, supported by empathetic yet critical peer reviewers and inspired by the incremental power of collective creativity. I find myself persuaded by this view and that only great geniuses like Konstantin Stanislavski, whom we met earlier in this chapter, can be wholly effective autodidacts. Orlando Figes, in his cultural history of Russia, *Natasha's Dance*, describes Stanislavski's working practices.

> He trained himself as an actor by standing for hours before a mirror every day and developing his gestures over several years to make them appear more natural. His famous 'method' (from which 'method acting' was to come) boiled down to a sort of naturalism. It was acting without 'acting' – which fitted in so well with the modern dialogue (where the pauses are as important as the words).[23]

The third asks: Is this chapter still sounding too prescriptive? Is it suggesting particular ways that storytellers' practices and performance skills might evolve? This is not my intention. I am merely following the lead of those storytellers who say, 'We need a new theatrical form for our own narrative heritage'. 'We have to embrace the skills of others, invent a new artistry'. 'Most storytellers have too limited a range of performance and staging techniques'. 'Storytelling [...] needs to be more open to outside influence and inspiration'. 'Storytellers have to be as professional with their techniques as actors are with theirs'. And 'Storytelling is an adolescent art form and we should look at other art forms and learn from them'. Taking them at their word, this chapter has followed the many divergent pathways that lead through this speculative landscape.

Notes & References

1. *Folklore, Cultural Performances, and Popular Entertainments*, ed. Richard Bauman (New York USA: Oxford University Press, 1992).

2. Richard Bauman, *Verbal Art as Performance* (Long Grove USA: Waveland Press, 1984).

3. Ruth Finnegan, *Communicating: The Multiple Modes of Human Interconnection* (London UK, Routledge, 2002).

4. *Communicating*, pp. 28-31.

5. *Communicating*, pp. 36-39.

6. Jack Grimston, 'Deepen your voice, Miss Squeaky, to tame that class', *The Sunday Times*, 22 April 2012, p. 4.

7. Richard Bauman, 'Performance', in *Folklore*, p. 41.

8.   Richard Bauman, *Verbal Art*, p. 9.

9.   *Verbal Art*, p. 10.

10. *Verbal Art*, p. 15.

11. *Verbal Art*, p. 16.

12. Allessandro Duranti, 'Oratory', in *Folklore*, p. 156.

13. *Verbal Art*, p. 43.

14. *Verbal Art*, p. 24.

15. Konstantin Stanislavski, *An Actor's Work: A Student's Diary*, trans. and ed. Jean Benedetti, (Abingdon UK: Routledge, 2008), p. xxiv.

16. *Communicating*, p. 67.

17. Sef Townsend, 'The Art of Pansori', *Storylines*, Society for Storytelling UK, Summer 2008, p. 4.

18. *The Singing Voice*, writer/director/producer: Michael Howes, (Channel Four Television Company UK, 1991).

19. Adam Kendon, 'Gesture', in *Folklore*, p. 179.

20. Wayne McGregor, programme notes for *Entity*, Sadler's Wells Theatre, London UK, 2008.

21. *Communicating*, p. 137.

22. Barbara A. Babcock, 'Artifact', in *Folklore*, pp. 206-210.

23. Orlando Figes, *Natasha's Dance* (London UK: Penguin Books, 2002), p. 205.

SEVEN

ALL THE WORLD'S A STAGE

෨෦ඥ

T he last chapter follows in the footsteps of anthropologists and folklorists who propose that in the verbal arts there can be no such thing as 'naked literalness', only an individual listener's interpretation of those words in a broader frame, or context, defined by the speaker's performance skills – their vocal technique, body language, musical expression and their use of costume, adornment, artefacts and so on. This chapter aims to conduct a kind of thought experiment to explore whether the concept of a performance frame can be broadened to embrace the places and spaces where storytelling events are held. It also speculates on whether the physical environment of a storytelling event can promote an audience's participation in an attitude of collaborative expectancy as part of the shared culture of teller and listener. The path this chapter treads is ill-defined and garners evidence from multiple sources: interview evidence from the performing artists we shall meet in the next chapter; experiential evidence from my own film productions and screen media consulting; by reference to the literature on performance disciplines, architecture and the built environment; attendance as participant observer at many storytelling events; and habitual attendance at over a hundred live stage performances a year.

The 134 audience interviews conducted for Chapter Two make it clear their experience of a storytelling is significantly determined by their physical surroundings. The 48 extended storyteller interviews conducted for Chapter One did not specifically address how the physical environment impacts on their audiences' experience; however, under a general question about their awareness of staging techniques in other performing arts, they expressed some awareness of the communicative potential of the telling environment. Some described how they incorporate the physical features or ambient sound of the telling places and spaces in their stories; or rearrange the furniture as props or stage set; or change the layout of the audience seating; or tell their stories from different parts of the performing space; or tell as a story walk or promenade performance (audience follows the performance through one or more spaces). Storyteller-dramatherapists report they use the performance space as part of their therapeutic practice. Some therapeutic storytellers have drawn my attention to techniques in neurolinguistic programming (NLP) involving what they call 'clean space'. Alida Gersie's booklet *Storytelling, Stories and Place*,[1] addresses the subject of the listener's place-related competencies. And the organisers of the Young Storyteller of the Year have recently introduced 'use of stage space' as a judging criterion.

Beyond this, however, storytellers seem to have only a patchy understanding of the communicative power of the physical environment and their use of it to enhance their audiences' immersive experience. In contrast, the psychology of the built environment is now a mainstream social science and even architectural schools teach this topic as part of their undergraduate curriculum. As we shall discover in the next chapter, the performing arts have been transformed in recent decades by a greater understanding of the communicative qualities of physical movement within a performance space. And London's Hayward Gallery recently put on an exhibition of sculptures and installations called Move: Choreographing You, 'that directly affect the movements of exhibition-goers, turning spectators into active participants – perhaps even dancers'.[2]

Place stages

There is a broad agreement amongst social scientists that physical environments impact on our behaviour and carry meanings for individuals, communities and cultures. These meanings can be triggered by personal association, perhaps a childhood home; or by the cultural role a building plays in society, perhaps a criminal court; or by reputation, perhaps a brothel; or because these places carry inherent symbolic, metaphoric or allegoric meanings for us or our culture. Any student of the history of architecture and the built environment is aware of particular architectural designs and styles that evoke certain feelings of, say, authority, conviviality, veneration, domesticity, opulence, dominance, durability/fragility, nostalgia/modernism, and of course agoraphobia/claustrophobia. Even natural environments can carry strong meanings and associations, for example, trees in different seasons, environmental damage, April showers, migrating birds, managed regeneration, full moon, harvesting. The relevance to the storyteller of these painfully self-evident observations is the astonishing diversity of places where oral storytelling is now staged. It is one of the defining characteristics of this art form. As we have seen in preceding chapters, from abode and anchorage to ziggurat and zoo, there will be found a storyteller and their attentive listeners.

Take for example a cursory survey of storytelling venues within one kilometre of my own house in London's South Bank cultural quarter. Storytellers are employed in the physiotherapy department of our local hospital. Three local educational establishments stage storytelling: a university college, an adult educational college where courses for the disabled are tutored by a blind storyteller, and a primary school which happens to have played an historic role in the emergence of educational storytelling in England three decades ago. Storytelling also takes place at three of the seven theatre venues in this immediate neighbourhood: at the multi-venue Southbank Centre (incidentally, the venue for Britain's first-ever storytelling festival), at one of the two studio theatres under a Victorian era railway viaduct, and at the recently reconstructed Shakespeare's Globe theatre. Storytelling at the headquarter offices of a global corporation is conducted in a modernist working environment. A mini-festival of performance storytelling was recently held in a disused warehouse ('Wrap up warm and come on in …'). Those visiting the evocatively named Imperial War Museum can hear a programme of storytelling called Once Upon a Wartime – Classic War Stories for Children. Storytelling at Britain's premier modern art gallery takes place in a converted power station. The elegant early nineteenth century church at the end of my street is another regular venue for storytelling, as is a modernist local neighbourhood centre. Storytelling takes place occasionally at a nearby public library, bookshop and café, and several story walks criss-cross the neighbourhood. Perhaps I should add that 17 very varied storytelling venues within such a small geographical area must be a very rare occurrence indeed.

The idea I am working towards here is that the physical surroundings of each of these venues is uniquely different, each acts as a unique performance frame and each visitor to these venues brings with them unique expectations and associations. It is for these reasons that I am proposing here that all storytelling venues have the potential to promote an attitude of collaborative expectancy in the minds of an audience. The physiotherapy patient's collaborative expectancy will differ from that of the school pupil's educational expectancy. At the reconstructed Shakespeare's Globe theatre the design of the building itself is now used as a laboratory to study the cultural norms of Elizabethan stagecraft and audience behaviours. At the museum of war, the exhibits themselves unavoidably become powerful performance frames that promote a distinct attitude of collaborative expectancy in the listener. The very fabric of the nearby church is an enduring symbol of Christian faith, purpose-built as it were, to promote an affirmation of religious belief. If this approach to the role of storytelling venues is anywhere near correct then it suggests that William Shakespeare got there four-hundred years ago when he said 'All the world's a stage, | And all the men and women merely players'.[3]

Some physical environments are themselves the inspiration and source for traditional stories, as are aetiological stories about the fanciful origins of natural features in a landscape, or the places where historical events occurred. On the other hand storytelling venues can also introduce conflicting meanings in a story, or even disrupt the narrative of the story itself.

> One such storytelling took place under crystal chandeliers in the ballroom of a very grand early nineteenth century house built by one of Ireland's wealthiest families. We sat on reproduction gilt chairs of the same period and our young woman storyteller's dress and accessories would not have caused embarrassment at a ball held here any time in the last half a century. My sense of visceral displacement arose because we were being told a harrowing changeling story (child secretly substituted by supernatural beings for its parents' real child) set amongst the abject poverty and social deprivation of nineteenth century rural Ireland…

Some places can evoke strong meanings and associations although they only exist in our imagination, say Shangri-La, or in literature, say the Zanadu of Samuel Taylor Coleridge's 1797 poem *Kubla Khan*, or places we only know by reputation, say Mecca or Beijing's Forbidden City. Sometimes the evocation of place in a performance context can be the most powerful communicating feature of the whole performance.

> A recent performance of Small Metal Objects[4] offered a piece of devised, site-specific theatre staged in the modernist Stratford railway station at the height of London's commuter rush hour. The audience sat on tiered seating overlooking the station concourse, thereby becoming passive actors in a play observed by commuter travellers, who in turn, were unwitting actors in a play being staged in their midst. There was virtually no storyline: a drug deal never quite happens. There was no character development: we could hear their minimalist dialogue through our headphones but it was only when the commuter crowds began to disperse that we could identify the actors. Yet this was a thrilling piece of visceral theatre, conjured up by an unwitting public, the movements of commuter trains and the epic engineering of the stage set. And then, by coincidence of almost miraculous serendipity, the evening I attended was 5 November, firework night, and as the plot reached its denouement, the darkness outside the vast glass wall of the station building exploded into an apocalyptic vision of a drug addict's mind. Physical performance frame induces cognitive overload.

Storytellers report they seldom have a choice of venue for their tellings and often the available alternatives offer no overriding benefits. A school classroom at least offers the benefits of a formal controlling environment and a structured design. For the psychiatric social worker story-swapping with a violent teenager there may be no better venue than the bus stop shelter, which at very least offers shelter from the rain. The convivial atmosphere of a pub may indeed be the optimal environment for the biggest liar competition. Yet, at least for the chief executive, they can hopefully pull rank and organise a more powerfully metaphoric or symbolic venue for their storytelling – perhaps the clinical white of their own factory's paint shop. The refugee centre storyteller might find a less institutional environment. And the story walk teller might find a more symbolic, metaphoric or allegorical route that promotes their listeners' participation. In the film medium, as with storytelling, the communicative power of the locations where a film is shot needs no explanation. As any producer of television commercials (sales films) will affirm, the meanings and messages embedded in the film's location are carried directly, often subliminally, into the viewer's mind.

Space stages

The researchers of an evaluation report commissioned by the Traditional Arts Foundation were in no doubt about the benefits of well-selected and well-prepared storytelling spaces.

> The Storytelling Café format is eminently versatile [with venues that] can include village and school halls, libraries, galleries and indeed cafés [where most spaces] can be adapted for the café or coffee house style of Storytelling Café events – complete with multi-coloured table cloths, candles and food. The atmosphere is relaxed, welcoming and sociable, creating an ambiance that reinforces the intimacy of audience-performer relationship characteristic of good live storytelling.[5]

Another evaluation report on the Storytelling Café's programme of events addressed the subject of how the ambiance of the telling space could be improved to make audience members' experience more enjoyable. Respondents suggested a very wide range of changes.

> Venue layout, signposting, seating plan, less heating, more heating, better lit stage, softer lighting, a better room, more comfy chairs, lovely cushions, don't even think about a larger space – intimacy is essential, a raised platform – help people at the back, can't always hear at the back, and so on.[6]

It goes without saying, that while these findings are important to the particular aspirations of the Storytelling Café, other promoters will seek to create widely varying environments to meet the needs of their own audiences. But the benefits of

123

a well-planned performing space and some awareness of proxemics (communication by structuring and use of space) can also be found in the animal realm. The male bowerbird creates an elaborate stage from twigs and an array of collected and arranged objects which appears to a potential mate to enlarge his size and exaggerate his mating rituals by means of an optical illusion known to humans as 'forced perspective'.

The lesson we can all learn from the art of 'poor theatre' is that telling spaces can gain communicative power without the need of elaborate sets and props. Some of these techniques invite physical interaction from both performer and audience member. For example, a recent London Mime Festival show, called La Porta, was inspired entirely by our innate physical relationship with doors. Another involved audience members pulling on ropes that caused unexpected reactions, which in turn drove the narrative forward in weird ways. Common in the performing arts is the introduction of some totemic manifestation whose presence adds a silent commentary on the story being told. More generally the last twenty years has seen the development of a whole new order of choreographed movement that owes more to the symbolic use of space than it does to traditional acting. And no storyteller needs to be reminded that a story told while standing on a table is not the same story if told while squatting beneath it, or while carrying it on their head. In many such examples these techniques can act subliminally on the listener, adding an additional layer of meaning to the story.

Soundscapes

At one gathering of storytellers I attended, the host opened the proceedings with a medley of welcoming anecdotes and was followed by several others who told brief, well-delivered stories. But it was only when musicians took to the floor that one of them asked for the doors to the adjoining kitchen to be closed to reduce the noise from an extractor fan. This transformed the acoustic space, the tellers became audible at the back of the room and audience detachment turned to attentive concentration. None of the storytellers I spoke to later had been aware of how the qualities of the acoustic space had compromised the telling and listening experience. This micro-vignette of storytelling life suggests three distinct processes going on in the auditory experience of a storytelling, quite apart from the teller's vocal qualities discussed in the last chapter.

The first concerns the natural acoustic of a telling space, a highly specialised scientific discipline beyond the scope of this study (and of my understanding). In the more formal performing arts, staged in theatres, concert halls and opera houses, a sympathetic acoustic will probably have been built into the fabric of the venue. This is not generally the case with storytelling where there is seldom any choice of venue and seldom an opportunity to improve its acoustic qualities. For this reason, perhaps a very crude film-maker's method of assessing acoustic qualities may be some help here. Use a hand clap in different parts of the telling space to estimate the duration of the venue's echo (reverberation time). If more than a second, get help from a friend to select by trial and error the least reverberant location for teller and audience. If possible, hang soft fabric in front of hard surfaces and otherwise expect the presence of the audience to reduce reverberation time by at least a quarter. If less than a second, which includes most outdoor venues, arrange the audience as close to teller as possible. Incidentally, the kitchen fan venue mentioned above had near-zero reverberation time, while the higher pitch of the fan's rattle overwhelmed the lower pitch of the storytellers' voices.[7]

The second process that frequently compromises the auditory experience of a storytelling is the disruption of sonic intrusion by uncontrollable external sound: flapping tents, rain on roof, road works, animal or human noises off, aircraft, and so on. Some quick-witted storytellers improvise reactions to intrusive sounds, sometimes even incorporating them into their stories, but often there is no alternative to bigging-up the physical performance and adding power and resonance to their voices. A better choice of venue and/or the structuring of the telling space can sometimes help; a point overlooked by the organisers of one storytelling festival I attended, where anyone wishing to visit the public toilets had to pass between the teller and their audience. Inevitably much of the story was lost to the urgent cries of desperate children echoing round the stone walls of this courtyard venue. Otherwise I can offer no succour to storytellers in such situations, except the sympathy of a filmmaker whose teeth have been ground to stumps with the frustration of location filming disrupted by sonic intrusion.

The third process involves the way the human mind processes the medley of sounds that form our local sonic world and the way we instinctively weave them into cohesive sound-pictures, or soundscapes, to navigate our way through our daily lives. Many storytellers use sound technology to great effect during their performances, to build atmosphere, enhance musical performance, create illusions of place or space, focus their audiences' visual attention, as sonic metaphor, and so on. However the misuse of amplification sometimes leads to a mismatch between what audiences see and what they hear – a phenomenon known to filmmakers as 'sound perspective'. This is most commonly found when, for example, the teller's physical performance signifies heightened emotion but their voice remains expressionless so as not to distort the amplified sound. (Check out microphone technique here.) Auditory mismatches also occur between two or more sound sources and can lead to audiences becoming confused by, or disengaged from, a storytelling. Storytellers also report that amplification is often set up for musicians without thought for the teller's voice, which can create a mismatch in the sound quality.

Light and colour stages

Some storytellers put stage lighting to good effect when telling in a theatre venue, while a few local groups I have visited enhance the telling space, and therefore the storytelling experience, with special lighting. One storyteller described how they like to 'create a magical space with candles', however most storytellers I have interviewed show little awareness of the potential of enhanced lighting effects. In the film medium lighting is not only a generator of atmosphere and mood but can also be a metaphoric and/or symbolic driver of the narrative itself. One of my favourite lighting directors, who also taught at the National Film & Television School, used to make the point to his students that without lighting technology there can be no filmmaking. But the technology required to make movie magic may be something as simple as a sheet of white reflective poly board, some coloured gel over a light bulb, car headlights, or daylight reflected off a half-open door. In the live performing arts 'poor theatre' has once again shown us the way to conjure startling effects from objects that are readily to hand.

But the real source of effective lighting lies not in the improvisation of technology but in the total mastery of the lighting director's art. Every storyteller is instinctively aware of the magic of a story told by firelight, but in many situations slight adjustments to the existing lighting in a room can transform its atmosphere. Daylight in a classroom can be turned to eerie moonlight with blue/green gel over a window. Some lights can be switched off, or on, or moved. Since we tend to trust people more if we can see their eyes the psychiatric social worker story-swapping with a violent teenager may ensure their eyes are not in shadow. Similarly, the biggest liar competitor may wish to tell from a well-lit part of the room, rather than a dark corner which can appear defensive. The chief executive can appear less threatening if they avoid speaking in silhouette with their back to the light. (In 44 of my 48 storyteller interviews I was able to arrange the dominant light-source on my face, not my back.) The refugee centre storyteller might be able to organise less institutional lighting, or better still, natural daylight. Ghoul and ghost-walk storytellers often illuminate their stories with Victorian cartoon body snatcher-type lanterns but the daylight story walk teller may be able to reverse the direction of their route so that sunlight illuminates the sites they visit rather than shining in the eyes of their listeners. The filmmaker knows this use of readily-available lighting sources as 'practicals'.[8]

A few storytellers talked about the use of colour to complement or enhance their storytelling, citing their choice of costume, set and/or lighting as a medium of expression. Most of us assume that our responses to colour are a matter of intelligent observation and intuition. So it came as something of a surprise, while visiting a recent exhibition of work by the late nineteenth century Dutch artist, Vincent van Gogh, to learn that he was not the madman of legend gone wild with an unorthodox colour sense, but a diligent student of colour theory (as many of his pioneering contemporaries were) who looked for inspiration to the 1839 discoveries of French physicist Michel-Eugène Chevreul.[9]

Stages of the mind

If, as this chapter proposes, there can be no such thing as naked literalness of the physical environment, but only a personal interpretation within the social and cultural frame of the audience's own experience, it suggests that much of our perception of the physical environment is also a product of the mind. In the early 1990s BBC Television invited me to develop *Cities of the Mind*, a series of four half-hour programmes that explored the psychology of the built environment. Although the project crashed out late in the commissioning process, the surviving research documents and outline scripts reveal themes directly relevant to this chapter. In the first instance the opening voice-over commentary reveals just how misleading our common sense observations and intuitions really are.

> Everyone knows that high-rise housing causes antisocial behaviour. Introverts need more privacy than extroverts. Green is a more calming colour than red. Disasters in enclosed spaces tend to render people helpless. Social planning schemes cause psychosis or new-town blues. Urban overcrowding causes stress. And all these psychological phenomena are the result of building design and urban planning. Except that none of these statements is true.

Under the supervision of psychologists of the built environment, well attested experiments would have been recreated in front of our cameras to reveal a broad range of psychological phenomena. Programme One explored how architecture and building design interact with our emotions, even allowing us to create emotional maps of a building or neighbourhood. Programme Two revealed how we create mental maps of our surroundings, use them as an aid to navigation and even allow us to anticipate what lies beyond our personal knowledge and experience. Programme Three put to the test just how beauty can indeed lie in the eye of the beholder, even how fictitious reputations can change our perception of architectural merit. And Programme Four demonstrated how building design can change our body language and our behaviour, and how so-called sick building syndrome really has very little to do with the building design itself. Many of these observations are understood in the performing arts: how we tend to read a stage from left to right; how a performer's movements can direct our attention to aspects of the stage design; and how the child within us has no trouble imagining a line of chairs as the interior of a bus, or an upturned table as a shipwrecked mariner's raft. Some of the very best storytellers can conjure up vivid images of places and spaces in the mind of the listener by their words and voice alone, and of course the supreme master of word-pictures is William Shakespeare.

> Piece out our imperfections with your thoughts:
> Into a thousand parts divide one man,
> And make imaginary puissance;
> Think when we talk of horses that you see them
> Printing their proud hoofs I' the receiving earth;
> For 'tis your thoughts that now must deck our kings,
> Carry them here and there, jumping o'er times,
> Turning the accomplishments of many years
> Into an hour-glass:[10]

Social and cultural stages

Friends often ask me: What actually happens at a storytelling? Of course they know perfectly well what a story is and what the word 'telling' means, but their question is really about the social roles that teller and listener play, and about the ritual and cultural norms of a storytelling event. Nearly five years into this study and I still stumble over a concise reply because the social and cultural variables amongst all the storytellers, audiences, local groups, organisations, genres, festivals, conferences and competitions I have studied are bewilderingly varied. There are certain slight regional variations too. When I mentioned to a prominent London-based storyteller that I was continuing my research in Scotland, they responded, 'Oh, Scotland, they do things differently up there.' And so they do. Storytelling in these storm-tossed islands of ours is richer for it.

Another phenomenon well known to social scientists is that social and cultural norms can vary more between similar types of communities, even within a single community, than between different types of community. As we found in Chapter Four, one storytelling group I studied split into two during the research period; one part adopting the distinct social and cultural norms of a performance storytelling group, the other decamping across town to adopt the distinct social and cultural norms of a ceilidh group. Meanwhile some storytelling festivals adopt the social and cultural norms more associated with literary festivals, while others adopt the social and cultural norms more associated with folk festivals. And some performance storytelling events more closely resemble theatrical events than they do community storytelling events.

These distinctions matter because, as Chapter One proposes, storytelling is a social art, listeners are social co-creators, and I am proposing here that the story-telling phenomenon works best when teller and listener share the norms of a social and cultural stage. So the educational storyteller and the school pupil make storytelling magic when they share the social and cultural norms of a classroom; similarly, when the psychotherapist storyteller and their client share a stage that promotes healing; and when the chief executive storyteller and their management team share a stage defined by good corporate governance; and when the priest and their congregation share a stage of religious belief and modes of worship; and when the storytelling police officer and the youth offender share an institutional stage set up under the criminal justice system; and when the biggest liar compet-itor and their sceptical listeners share a social and cultural stage defined by the rules of the competition; and when the performance storyteller and their paying audience conform to the social and cultural norms associated with theatre-going, rather than with a community storytelling. Contrast these shared stages with that of the refugee centre, where storyteller and refugees may share very few social and cultural norms and often not much in the way of a shared language.

Nor is it surprising, as Chapter Three discusses, that some storytellers speak from religious, ideological or political stages. In the foreword to Michael Wilson's *Storytelling and Theatre*, Jack Zipes states: 'There are many different ways to clas-sify storytellers today: traditional storytellers, teachers and librarians, performers, and amateur enthusiasts. Of course, almost all of them must contend with the fact that storytelling is becoming more and more institutionalized and commodi-fied.'[11] 'Of course'? 'Almost all'? 'Must contend'? 'Fact'? 'Commodified'? Really? He continues: 'The second function [of storytelling] is to question, change, and overthrow the dominant value system – to transform what has been preserved so that the values, norms and customs enable a group of people not only to survive but to improve their lives and make the distribution of power and wealth more just.'[12] 'Second'? 'Overthrow the dominant value system'?

Personally, I cannot see this kind of politico-ideological manifesto sparking a firestorm of youth revolutions across continents as it might have done half a cen-tury ago. So in case I had misunderstood Zipes's meaning I have just looked up my notes of Professor Wilson's lecture for first year BA drama students at the Uni-versity of Glamorgan on 12 January 2009. At one point he claimed that some of the characteristics of today's storytelling emerged from what he called 'the 1968 youth-led revolutions'. No, just no. I was there, a twenty-one year old student in

London. 1968 was the year when the world's youth was supposed to link politico-ideological arms with militant trades unions, overthrow the dominant value systems of the world's most liberal democracies and lead the proletariat into a golden age of utopian socialism. Even some college and university lecturers would pepper their teaching with Marxist theory. Two of my housemates were ringleaders of a protest and lengthy occupation of London's Hornsey College of Art, supported by sympathetic staff, which inspired a major television documentary film broadcast the following year. But by late summer this movement had morphed into a generalised protest movement against anything and everything. By autumn it was all over. Even the popular press agreed.

> The October "revolution" in London yesterday failed to live up to its name. [...] An estimated 6,000 marchers broke away from the main demonstration against the war in Vietnam to go to Grosvenor Square after a carefully planned tactical diversion by four Maoists with loudspeakers. With them went about 300 anarchists, who were mainly responsible for such violence as ensued, all of which was masterfully handled by 1,000 police under Commander John Lawlor. [...] Eyewitnesses and television coverage alike made it clear that police had not only carried out their duty to protect life and property but had also won a resounding moral victory. An accolade they will appreciate more than most came from Mr Tony Smythe, general secretary of the National Council for Civil Liberties, who said: "In general the police handling of the demonstrators has been exemplary."[13]

To this veteran of 1968 it just seems quaint that such revolutionary fervour should still smoulder in the green valleys of south Wales. I can find no evidence that today's storytelling owes anything to the so-called 1968 youth-led revolutions. And nothing I could read of the notes being written by my youthful companions during Professor Wilson's lecture would suggest there was any form of shared social and cultural stage in this lecture hall.

Written word stages

Many storytellers seem to have an ambiguous relationship with the written word. On the one hand, by common custom, all written-word documents are precluded from storytelling events. One storyteller expressed their regret that 'all our traditional stories are told through the prism of outdated, scholarly, Victorian, Christian culture'. And of all the storytellers I have interviewed only one develops their stories by recourse to the written word (perhaps not unconnected with their first degree in English Literature). On the other hand most tellers of traditional myths, folk and wonder tales use published sources as the prime inspiration for their verbal art, and research for this study has yielded much evidence that storytelling, along with most other verbal and even sung arts, is performed on a stage built from written-word documents.

Glossing over for a moment the forty-year debate between scholars who give greater priority to the entextualised words as opposed to the actualised performance of storytelling and other verbal arts, today's storytellers navigate their way through a forest of written-word documents. Of those storytellers I have interviewed about a quarter are published authors of magazine articles, monographs, fiction, treatises, histories, children's stories, story collections and scholarly monographs. Some storyteller's skills can be learnt from published guides and handbooks. Much professional expertise that teachers, therapists and other professionals rely on for their storytelling is learnt from standard textbooks during their professional training. The published literature on storytelling subjects is now enormous. Almost all complex network interaction that drives the day-to-day administration, coordination and organisation of storytelling is conducted by electronic written mail. And many administrative documents such as employment contracts, insurance policies and legal checks for those working with children and vulnerable people are paper-based documents.

The public face of many storytellers, local groups, organisations, representative bodies, festivals, conferences and competitions is made manifest in their websites which mostly comprise written-word documents. Much promotion and publicity for storytelling events is supported by printed documents and sometimes poster campaigns. All applications for grants and funding subsidies, festival evaluations and advance notices of storytelling events are generated as written-word documents. Storytelling academe is awash with academic publications, papers, booklets and research dissertations. The websites of the four representative bodies covering Britain and Ireland comprise written-word information, databases and discussion forums. The Society for Storytelling publishes a quarterly journal *Storylines* and peer-reviewed monographs, lecture texts and practical guides under their three imprints – all written-word documents. So are entrance tickets for storytelling events, festivals and conferences (even if some are worn as wrist bands). This relationship between oral storytelling and the written word is clearly one of mutual dependency and it is of little surprise that performance theorists conclude that nearly every aspect of nearly all the performing arts is rooted, one way or another, in written-word documents.

Wherever there is a written-word document, there is also a designer who has made conscious choices about headings and font styles, print colours, page design, illustrations and graphics. These are presentational qualities and I am proposing here they are also forms of visual stage that, like performance frames, can arouse an audience member's expectations and provide a broader context within

131

which they judge the qualities of the performance itself. To apply these ideas to the world of storytelling I have held an extended discussion with a marketing guru and called on experience of my own (seldom happy) dealings with advertising, public relations, marketing and communications companies. From this experiential evidence some questions arise for any storyteller who creates electronic or print documents for public distribution: Is the visual design itself an effective invitation to read the text? Do the design and the text enhance or detract from each other? Who is it written for? And for what purpose? Is a storyteller's telling style reflected in their writing style? Print journalism is all about compelling stories, so do press releases for storytelling events themselves tell a compelling story? And if a potential client visits a storyteller's website do they really want to read about the general merits of storytelling, or only about the merits of this particular storyteller? Chapter Eight returns to the parallel worlds of the written and the verbal arts.

Broader stages

Several people have asked me whether links can be made between the recent growth of oral storytelling and the recent growth of courses on creative writing that are now being offered by British universities and tertiary education colleges. From all the research for this study, only one rather attenuated link has emerged: a recent winner of the Young Storyteller of the Year had been encouraged to take up storytelling as a career by their university lecturer who was also a prominent performance storyteller. I have also interviewed a group of ten undergraduates on a BA creative writing course which includes a storytelling module but, unsurprisingly, only six months into their first year, it revealed little awareness of, and only muted interest in, the wider world of oral storytelling. So, nothing much of interest here and this question must await more focused research.

Another form of stage that plays a valuable supporting role in oral storytelling today is the economic stage. This is the market place where storytelling services are bought and sold; paying audiences exchange money for an entrance ticket; storyteller-therapists, guest tellers in schools and management consultants are hired for a fee; festival organisers can apply for public funding grants; and teacher-storytellers and academics can study, research and teach this art form with the comforting reassurance they are earning a regular salary.

There are also myriad organisational stages, real or virtual, where the leadership of local groups, festivals and conferences, schools administrators, librarians and museum curators, theatre managers and all the organisers of storytelling events actually make these events happen. They employ tried and tested organisational methods developed over decades and some of these organisational stages can literally boast a cast of thousands. Organisational stages can also be immensely powerful hubs of network interactivity. Real physical hubs, like local storytelling groups and festivals, attract large numbers of people who meet a wider circle of acquaintances, which spontaneously generate complex network interactions, and in turn, form the foundations of emergent properties and behaviours. In virtual communications hubs the capacity for exchanging information between individuals and other hubs is almost unlimited – effectively a stage that speaks with a million voices.

What has taken me by surprise while teasing out and analysing the evidence for this chapter is the degree to which many forms of storytelling stage can profoundly influence our behaviour as well as the unexpected outcomes of that behaviour. Rudolph Laban, whom we met in the last chapter, has profoundly influenced the development of dance, movement and the use of performance stages since early in the twentieth century. One of his own formative experiences might be taken as a lesson to us all.

> When the pioneering stage director, Joan Littlewood, asked Laban what had attracted him to a career in dance, he replied, 'I saw this man polishing a ballroom floor with two dusters tied to his feet.' Imagine this humble servant of a decaying Hapsburg Empire, totally alone, amidst crystal chandeliers, gilded stucco and mirrored walls, gliding elegantly around the floor, his mind a swirl of silk ball gowns and plumed officers. 'What a lovely job', Laban thought, 'that is the way I shall go.'[14]

Notes & References

1. Alida Gersie, *Storytelling, Stories and Place* (Society for Storytelling UK: Oracle Series No.10, 2010).

2. *Exhibition Guide* (London UK: Southbank Centre, 2010), p. 34.

3. William Shakespeare, *As You Like It*, Act 2, Scene 7.

4. *Small Metal Objects*, produced by Back to Back Theatre, Australia, in association with Theatre Royal Stratford East, part of the Barbican International Theatre Festival (BITE) London UK, 2007.

5. Unpublished Evaluation Report, for the Traditional Arts Foundation on their Storytelling Cafés, May 2005, p. 5.

6. Unpublished Evaluation Report, for the Traditional Arts Foundation on their Storytelling Cafés, March 2006, p. 6.

7. Reverberation time: this former Chartered Surveyor noted that the near-zero reverberation time of this venue was caused by a very crowded room, ceiling-to-floor curtains and a low ceiling made of sound-absorbing acoustic tiles much favoured by institutional architects in the 1970s.

8.   Practicals: much of the lighting designer's craft can be learnt from books on lighting for stills photography and practiced with any digital stills camera.

9.   Roelie Zwikker, 'Colour and Japonisme', the exhibition catalogue for *The Real Van Gogh: The Artist and His Letters* (London UK: The Royal Academy of Arts, 2010), p. 94.

10. William Shakespeare, *The Life of King Henry the Fifth*, Chorus.

11. Michael Wilson, *Storytelling and Theatre: Contemporary Storytellers and their Art* (Basingstoke UK: Palgrave Macmillan, 2006), Foreword p. xv.

12. *Storytelling and Theatre*, Foreword pp. xv-xvi.

13. 'On this day', *The Times*, 27 October 2012, p.119.

14. Adapted from a story told in Jean Newlove & John Dalby, *Laban for All* (London, UK: Nick Hern Books, 2003), with kind permission of the publisher.

EIGHT
BEYOND STORYTELLING

৪০৫৪

T here is a pervasive body of opinion amongst storytellers that storytelling stands, and in the opinion of some, should stand apart from other performing arts and creative enterprises. This chapter aims to put this view to the test by taking several lengthy detours on our journey and by looking beyond the world of storytelling at other forms of creative enterprise as a form of rough and ready control group. It compares and contrasts their working practices with those described in previous chapters and it aims to reveal extra dimensions and perspectives on the condition of contemporary oral storytelling today. Evidence for this chapter, as with other chapters, has required casting the research net very wide indeed and the methodology employed is outlined in each section below.

Performance poetry

One emergent creative movement closely associated with oral storytelling is performance poetry. Several storytellers I have met are also accredited performance poets. Both art forms require compositional skills, are primarily verbal arts, are realised as actualised performances and are generally staged alone. The leading representative organisation for performance poetry in England and Wales is Apples & Snakes (established in the Adams Arms pub – it took me a moment) and was founded in 1982. As its director told me in interview, 'artists are at the heart of the organisation' and a driving force behind these initiatives is a policy of inspiring, commissioning and producing new work, working with emerging artists, developing performance poetry as a professional art form, and breaking down barriers between artistic disciplines by sharing skills and methods. Research programmes, promotion and marketing and a formal accreditation process for emerging talent (outlined in Chapter Six) lie behind Apples & Snakes' core functions: to promote and produce poetry performances and cross-arts projects, manage artist development workshops and to stage national and international tours.

Apples & Snakes also manages an extensive social outreach programme in schools, arts centres, museums, libraries, teacher training centres, young offender institutions, prisons and city learning centres, and develops relationships between artists and grassroots, city-centre communities. Performances take place in a wide range of venues, from poetry cafés, book shops and arts centres to large public venues. The performance poetry I attended at the 2008 Imagine Childrens Literature Festival at London's Southbank Centre played to a capacity family audience of three hundred and sixty and also included storytelling, song, puppetry, movement, costume, magic, sound and vision technology, stage lighting and audience participation. At the 2004 Poetry International, also at London's Southbank Centre, Messa di Voce[1] staged what the programme described as 'audiovisual fireworks and sound performance' which involved two 'sound poets' who performed a medley of abstract speech, song and other vocalisations, which a computer translated into wildly coloured visuals on a large upstage screen to explore 'the poetic implications of making the human voice visible'.

Even the benefits of participation in performance poetry share much in common with storytelling. Ten year-old Yazdan Isfahani, winner of the 2009 Off By Heart poetry reciting competition, who spoke no English when his family came to Britain from Iran as asylum seekers, said in interview with The Times: 'It's so much fun, I've learnt to be more sociable [...] and it has helped me loads, especially with remembering things and keeping them stored in my head. I'm also a lot more confident.'[2]

Yet discrepancies do emerge between storytelling and performance poetry when considering the public perception of these two art forms. The term 'performance poetry' hardly needs any form of explanation whereas storytellers often struggle to explain the term 'oral storytelling'. As Chapter One reveals, one storyteller explained how 'the role of storytelling as a term hasn't displayed itself well, [its definition] has become diffuse. [The public knows] what the role of a doctor is, but not a storyteller'. And as one board member of the Society for Storytelling said recently, 'Being an oral medium, it has always been a challenge for all of us to explain to friends just what exactly storytelling is.'[3] To this dispassionate outsider, performance poetry projects a very youthful, dynamic image – something that may have its origins in the contemporary language of spoken poetry – and this image is also reflected in the contemporary style of graphics and typography of Apples & Snakes' website and promotional publications.

Comedy

During my interviews with career storytellers a significant number referred to stand-up comedy as an influence on their performance practices. Most readers will probably be more familiar with this performing art than I am, but to focus more closely on the shared culture of these two disciplines, I attended an evening of comedy in central London with a prominent actor-storyteller and our subsequent discussion seems to corroborate widely-held views on the comparative qualities of these two art forms. Both are mainly intimate forms of theatre; generally more spontaneous and responsive than other performing arts; share many of the qualities of the performer/audience relationship; rely for their popularity on audience participation; seem to place reliance on the performer's personality and stage persona; engage similar performance and staging techniques; and often embrace other performing arts like music, song, mime and illusionism. Both comedy and the more performance-type storytelling also follow what is called a 'headline' or 'showcase' format where a host/ess or master of ceremonies makes announcements and introduces the 'featured acts'.

The main dissimilarities lie in the youth of stand-up comedy's audiences and the harder-edged nature of its performances. These often involve a more aggressive delivery, riskier storylines, an underlying cynicism and much youthful anger. Its impact is often enhanced by a discordant use of sound, and in marked contrast to most storytelling events, comedy can thrive on a rather threatening atmosphere. This approach invites a more anarchic, provocative form of audience participation, which in the most experienced of hands can lead to public humiliation of audience members, and in less experienced hands, to the comedian's own public humiliation.

This more demonstrative, high-impact performance style highlights another difference between these two performing arts. The best comedians can command and hold a live audience of thousands, including those paying top-price tickets that are always the most demanding of audience members. In contrast, I interviewed a senior manager at a multistage theatre venue where storytelling takes place on one of the small studio stages, and while discussing the relative impact of mainstream theatre and storytelling, they commented, 'I would love to put storytellers on our main stage [capacity 1,500] but none could attract large enough audiences.'

Two other clear distinctions might be made between storytelling and stand-up comedy. First, the practices and performance of comedy seem to reside exclusively within the realm of entertainment and are not generally applied as a core function in education, management, healthcare, the criminal justice system and cultural understanding as discussed in Chapter Three. Second, although comedy as a form of paying entertainment can trace its origins to the nineteenth century music halls and later to pub, social club and a wide variety of non-entertainment venues, its recent emergence in Britain as a popular mainstream art form owes much to the Edinburgh Festival Fringe and to the mass medium of broadcast television. Arts journalist Richard Morrison has called this 'the rise of the comedy mafia, [those] chillingly ambitious stand-up comics [who] employ retinues of pushy publicists to beat off the opposition and treat the festival merely as a stepping-stone to TV fame'.[4] Add to this the driving force of commercialisation and broadcast television, which have turned comedy into a mass media phenomenon, and stand-up comedy could stand as an icon for everything that most storytellers would not wish storytelling to become.

Calligraphy and the lettering arts

Calligraphy and the lettering arts have always been at the back of my mind as a comparative art form for this chapter, but it was only when I looked out the rather yellowing files of an Arts Council commission to develop a one-hour documentary on the subject in 1992, that I realised just how fitting it might be. What attracted public funding to this proposal was that it was essentially ethnography, but treated in the televisual medium as much as a performing art as it is a visual art. The applications of this art form in society are probably as wide as in storytelling. A walk down any high street in the land reveals literally hundreds of examples of lettering that have originated under human hand – everything from the price of cucumbers on a market stall to the futuristic letter-style of a cinema poster. In the realm of high art, *The Saint John's Bible*, commissioned by the Benedictine Monastery of St John's, Minnesota USA, with a budget of over two million pounds, was hand-written and illuminated in Donald Jackson's Welsh scriptorium and was the subject of a special exhibition at London's Victoria and Albert Museum of decorative arts. My contemporaneous notes of research interviews with prominent calligraphers and lettering artists bring strong echoes of the storyteller interviews for this study.

> Handmade lettering is intimately tied up with the identity of the person who makes it. While cautioning against the claims of the graphologists, writing is nonetheless a very personal mark left to the world, and indeed for most people it is the only creative mark they leave behind when they depart this world.

Much of the creative force of calligraphy comes from emotional instincts, not from intellectual analysis. [Its scale] is one that we can associate with: words to read, textures to stroke, spaces to share, energy to feel. Its use of words gives it a directness that instantly appeals – from heart to mark without the intervention of any art garbage. But calligraphy is also about fear – there's no going back, no over-painting, no erasing of your mistakes in calligraphy. This sense of danger plays with your emotional vulnerability; it attacks the senses; it makes you live on a sensual edge. And it is this that calligraphers try and pass on to the viewer.

Preparatory rituals and ceremonies are essential for assembling the emotional tools before ever a single mark is made.

The written word is often an instrument of manipulation, for better or worse, but seldom is it neural in its intention. It is a powerful force in our lives and lettering artists see their role as revalidating the written word in a humanising tradition.

In an echo of Richard Bauman's performance frames, described in Chapter Six, calligraphers are also aware of the broader context of the lettering they make.

The sequence of events that links the spiritual, emotional, intellectual, physical and visual processes […] is central to calligraphy because the lettering style contains its own meaning, quite apart from the meaning of the words it spells. [It is] a product of the whole body, not just the hands and arms. The words are a product of both expressive gestures and motionless concentration with even the calligrapher's pauses visible on the paper.

Other calligraphers also spoke on the same theme: 'All the tensions and relaxations of feeling are visible even without knowing what the letters say. But then a reading of the words transforms the work from abstract to representational art.' 'Most of the meanings of the document can be read even with the legibility of the words compromised to the point of abstraction.' 'The choice of materials, colours and textures used predispose [the observer] towards certain responses to the finished work.' 'Even the construction of the finished work proclaims its function and imposes on the reader a certain mode of behaviour.'

The processes of co-creation and the role of community identity in storytelling also seem to have parallels in the lettering arts.

Calligraphy is a reflection of the community that made it: documents and letterforms flow from agreed conventions – what anthropologists call a 'community practice' – and these agreements are revealing of how people perceive themselves, the world around them, their consciousness, identity, their collective memory and their mode of relating to each other.

While Chapter Seven considers the role of the physical environment in an oral storytelling event, lettering artists also seem to take a similar approach when they say their art matters in our lives 'because it is part of some environment that demands from us some response'.

> The best documents, quite apart from the words they contain, should be con-
> structed as environments around the activities of human beings, with places to
> meet, make decisions, love, laugh, fight, relax, pause, [...] share in a street life, or
> be private, or temporarily subvert the main objective, take short-cuts, enjoy
> chance meetings, offer windows and doors to tempt your vision, open spaces for
> reflection. These are compelling qualities for reinvigorating documents if they are
> to help us make decisions, not on the basis of information, but on the basis of
> experience.

In parallel to the roles that storytelling plays in our society, calligraphy and the lettering arts have 'liberated the written word where it increasingly performs [...] divergent functions in our society'. Amongst calligraphers I interviewed were those who work in the education system to develop improved ways to teach writing skills. And there are good reasons why calligraphy evening classes at the high-security Manchester prison were always oversubscribed.

> Writing special letters, poems and greetings beautifully, even passionately, is one
> of the few ways that inmates can express their attachment to those they are sepa-
> rated from. It is a form of feel-good therapy and it gives them some minimal con-
> trol over their own destiny, some momentary sense of order in an uncontrollable
> environment.

Ultimately, like the often quoted remark, 'everyone is a storyteller', the rising popularity of calligraphy in our society can be attributed, in part, to the fact that anyone with a pen, a piece of paper and a kitchen table can do it, and get a great pleasure from it.

In the wider world of public image-making our initial impression of almost any type of organisation, even nation states, is often gained through the printed or electronic documents it publishes or displays. In a more intellectually challenging application of the lettering artist's art, one calligrapher I interviewed was currently engaged by a global corporation, as part of a multidisciplinary team of image-makers, thinkers and social scientists, to research and redefine the very nature of documents, in the widest possible definition of the term. This involved not only the design of the words they contain, but also the power of the physical qualities of documents themselves as a medium of communication. This could be anything from the surface texture of a sheet of paper to the symbolic shapes of complete buildings that can be read as a form of document by a passer-by.

Leading practitioners in both oral storytelling and the lettering arts are acutely aware of their historical precursors and both art forms have experienced revivals or renaissances in recent history. While the revival of interest in the lettering arts in Britain can be traced to the Arts and Crafts movement in the second half of the nineteenth century, today's practitioners affirm their art has now been 'consciously developed as a radical artistic medium for its own sake'. The oral storytelling revival/renaissance followed late in the twentieth century and, as we found in Chapter Six, it is perhaps for this reason that some leading practitioners can say 'storytelling is an adolescent art form and we should look at other art forms and learn from them'.

My research notes on the lettering arts also reveal two encounters that reflect on the professional teaching of this art form. The first was to witness a masterclass, part of the Advanced Training Scheme for prospective fellows of The Society of Scribes and Illuminators, where career calligraphers must present their own work in progress to their peers. Participants must account for their personal motivations, the stylistic content of their work and respond to comment and criticism. There was a pervasive atmosphere here of soul-searching, self-doubt, loss of face and resignation that projects will have to be started again. Snatches of dialogue speak of an acuteness of observation and rigorous self-discipline.

> What are the frames for and how do they relate to the document itself? ... What influenced this work? ... The effort of trying to read the words is part of the art, whereas total legibility does not command attention. ... It was the beer that freed me of my critical homunculus and liberated the style. ... What are the arched letters trying to do? ... Some letters are still too hesitant. ... By reducing the end-of-line spaces you can increase the illusion of spaces between the letters. ... You're too controlled, trying to make things happen, when you should be relishing the accidents. ... So why shouldn't each page of a book have different shapes and sizes? ... Can you see the change of weights across the page when I add these little black blobs? ... How will the viewer and the calligrapher see this differently?

The second was a visit to the studio of leading lettering artist David Kindersley (1915-95) which underlined the importance of formal workshop apprenticeships and the collegiate atmosphere of a bounded community as powerful drivers of this art form.

> I am talking to a young Canadian apprentice as he hand-polishes a piece of slate. He recounts how he had been forced to sell all his possessions to pay his passage to England in the faint hope of becoming apprenticed to David Kindersley. But to anyone familiar with the story of the revival of the calligraphic arts there is a poignant backstory lurking here that reflects on the importance of continuity in the teaching craft skills. David Kindersley was one of the last surviving apprentices

at the workshop of Eric Gill (1882-1940), a dominant figure in the British craft movement between the two World Wars, who in turn had been an outstanding apprentice to Edward Johnson (1872-1944), who in turn had almost single-handedly rediscovered the historical techniques of this ancient craft at the turn of the twentieth century and is hailed today as 'the father of modern calligraphy'.

Everything about this workshop carried echoes of the craft guilds and their workshop traditions from late medieval Europe before the age of the printing press: the experience of community learning; the power of collective creativity; the master's patient guidance of the apprentice; the arrivals and departures of journeymen/women from all over the world; incessant discussions around the communal lunch table; their client's aspirations guiding everything they do; and the sparsely decorated upstairs accommodation – apparently no radio, television or consumer gadgets. And in the grander sweep of history it should be noted how such continuities can be broken, in the example of the European lettering arts, by a period of five hundred years following the invention of the moveable type printing press. There are also other more recent quirks in the history of calligraphy. Several calligraphers recounted how cultures like those of the Middle East and East Asia, whose calligraphic traditions have endured without a break to the present day, often look to Britain's lettering artists for inspiration in developing their own contemporary forms of this art.

These insights into the historical precursors of the lettering arts also highlight another significant dissimilarity with contemporary oral storytelling in the way these two art forms are studied. Scholars of the former have ready access to a large body of direct evidence in the form of surviving documents from every age, as well as historical records of the period to aid interpretation and analysis. I recall one calligrapher describing his doctoral thesis as a comparative analysis between two copies of the same illuminated manuscript made in the late middle ages but in different monastic scriptoria. The calligraphic style of the first reflected, precisely, the Christian doctrines set out in the original document. The calligraphic style of the second revealed unmistakable dissenting, even heretical views! In contrast, scholars of oral storytelling have little direct evidence from before the age of personal recollection.

Dances with Ink, as this project was provisionally titled, never did raise sufficient support from television broadcasters to allow production to go ahead. It is seldom possible to discover the reasons why, but from comments and asides of television executives I was dealing with, it is likely they judged it to be too 'nostalgist' an approach to a contemporary art form and therefore had no valid application in an age of populist media and mass society theory.

Performing arts

Chapter Six explores many of the performance cultures that storytelling shares with the performing arts. This detour on our journey explores some of the practices that have driven change, development and growth in the wider world of performing arts over the last three decades. To this end extended interviews have been held with six prominent figures from the world of the performing arts, all of whom have worked at the forefront of developments in their own disciplines for at least a quarter of a century. The six were identified as having very varied skills and experience and in most cases were approached through personal introductions or by their association with organisations I am acquainted with. Actor Scott Handy is a veteran of the Royal Shakespeare Company, has been directed by some of the foremost figures of stage and film and is a Visiting Director at Central School of Speech and Drama and the London Academy of Music and Dramatic Art. Rosemary Brandt, originally a classical ballet dancer and teacher, later discovered the much broader 'vocabulary and repertoire' of Laban dance and movement techniques, which she now teaches as a senior staff member at London's Laban Conservatoire. Annabel Arden co-founded Complicite (originally Theatre de Complicité) in 1983, which has since become a syllabus subject in the Drama and Theatre Studies A Level curriculum. Her performance and directing credits include theatre, radio drama and opera, and she teaches widely at performance and arts organisations. Amanda Maxwell joined the Royal Ballet School aged ten, has been a company member with The Royal Ballet's Ballet For All, London Festival Ballet and a principal dancer with Northern Ballet. She now teaches character dance at the Royal Ballet School. Siobhan Davies, for many years a leading contemporary dancer and choreographer, founded Siobhan Davies Dance Company in 1988. She currently holds academic appointments at four universities and in 2002 was appointed Commander of the British Empire (CBE). German-Swiss-born Lilo Baur is a theatre, film and television actor, contemporary dancer, co-founder of Cabaret Chanson, international stage director and workshop leader, and is winner of the Dora Canadian Award and Manchester Evening News Award for Best Actress. All six were asked the same open question: From your personal and professional experience what has driven developments in the performing arts over the last thirty years?

The driving force most frequently mentioned in these interviews referred to a purposive 'pursuit of experimentation, […] starting again from a blank slate'; a 'relearning of everything'; 'a continuous cycle of experiment and reinvention'; a 'lifelong quest for originality' and a 'process of reinvention'. When I mentioned these responses to one prominent storyteller during interview they expressed the view that the performance and staging skills of 'the storytelling community were not good enough to rip up the existing rule book'.

143

In Chapters One and Six reference is made to how 'many storytellers have a natural resistance to the influence of other performing arts'. This is in notable contrast to our six performing artists who refer to 'long-term trends that have helped make theatre what it is today [which include] looking to other, non-theatrical disciplines and media for inspiration, technique and method'. One talks about 'the ever-widening search for inspiration in other art forms'. A second states how the 'most important [of my] driving motivations is the experience of working in very varied cultural environments and diverse theatrical traditions'. A third explains how 'there are always direct contributions to a work from other disciplines, both sound and visual.' A fourth refers to how 'further elements [of every new work] are sought from mainly outside the realm of dance [and] from a broad range of other artistic disciplines'. Several point out how 'Many of the performing techniques of stand-up comedy have been absorbed into mainstream theatre to capitalise on the rapid emergence of this performing art'; and how 'the language and structure of a performance has also been profoundly influenced by the cinematic language, particularly the grammatical forms that the film medium uses to manipulate time in the minds of an audience'. (One storyteller did recount how the film medium influences their performance skills.) And Brandt's adaptive teaching method 'seeks inspiration from people and events beyond the disciplines of dance and performance. [...] What makes recent developments in Laban so important is the dialogue that it has established between a broad range of creative disciplines.'

Following on from the discussion in Chapter Six about the use of technology in oral storytelling, our performing arts interviewees unanimously affirm that science and technology are powerful drivers of change, development and growth in all these performing arts. In the words of my respondents:

> Science and technology are the friends of the performer, not the enemies. Science is an intimate companion to art, their mutual exclusiveness no longer being a tenable view to hold. [The study of science and its methodology] adds greatly to my layers of knowledge and creativity. Advances in technology have also transformed theatre. [Both on and off stage, these] are all are driven by audiences who demand an ever more immersive theatrical experience. Even the design of theatres [is now] responsive to scientific advances in acoustics and the psychology of the performing space. Science and technology have also transformed the staging of classical ballet [...] so that today's choreographers can realise their wildest creative imagination in a performance [and thereby bring] a heightened emotional impact to today's audiences. More recent [theatre] productions have tended towards an increasing use of on-stage technology and an awareness of contemporary scientific method to drive the narrative forward. The application of technology to all aspects of performance and staging technique has opened up creative opportunities unimaginable before their development and their widespread availability.

Recent developments in the performing arts have also been driven by 'a more complicit relationship between stage and audience [...] as the public becomes more creatively informed'. While we have observed in previous chapters how the storyteller/listener relationship has evolved over recent decades, Handy describes a parallel process in contemporary theatre.

> The symbiotic relationship of stage and audience has driven recent developments too. Society has become more emotionally intelligent. Recent developments continue to break down the traditional transmitter/receiver relationship between cast and audience, and direct audience address – where actors come out of character and speak personally to the audience – is now commonplace. Audiences' understanding and insights into theatrical techniques have also progressed greatly, and many of these developments have called for a wholesale abandonment of traditional notions of what theatre is.

Arden also describes this phenomenon in similar terms.

> The founding ethos of Theatre de Complicité [embraced] a powerful will to create a more complicit, direct, immediate form of human communication by theatrical means, [...] a new theatre of popular storytelling that appeals across languages, cultures and continents. [...] A sense of complicity imbues every aspect of [our] productions: between performers, with their audiences, on stage and off, in question and answer sessions, and in the theatre bar before or after the show.

Other comments on the same topic include: 'Creatively informed audiences demand technically informed performances' and 'experimenting with unusual performance spaces [...] enables an audience to experience the piece primitively or as plain movement – the choreographic equivalent of making poems with complex forms but simple words'. When I asked Davies what assumptions she makes about her audiences' interpretative abilities, she spoke of 'the imperative of giving them clear indications of how the language of movement works; how this language should never be elitist or inaccessible. [It] should reveal the nature of [my] input as choreographer, and how these shifting assumptions should be the source of much of the excitement the audience feels.'

Again, in parallel with oral storytelling, all the performing arts have reached out into the wider community, into the worlds of education, healthcare, public service, business and the criminal justice system. Outreach programmes are now supported by BA degree courses in such subjects as Drama, Applied Theatre and Education. Most performing arts companies I am familiar with now run educational and/or community outreach projects as part of their commitment to sponsors and funding agencies and as a condition of their charitable status. And, as

Baur said, the 'teaching of drama and theatre skills in schools has made an outstanding contribution to the development of contemporary theatre'.

New teaching practices are also a significant factor driving developments in the performing arts. 'Formal teaching methods have now been developed for subjects as diverse as dramatherapy, theatre directing, improvisation and participatory theatre, when formerly these skills were believed to be innate in some individuals and un-teachable in the rest of the population.' My own experience of performance workshops described in Chapter Six corroborates statements made during these interviews that intense observation of innate human behaviour, life, the universe and everything is now central to the learning process in the performing arts. It was also noticeable from these performance workshops that significant numbers of students were seeking to learn the personal skills of everyday life or to apply lessons learnt to careers unconnected with the performing arts. As Brandt said of her Laban classes, 'Students are of all ages, from all walks of life. They come for both personal and career development and include architects who need a vision of human movement in space to design beautiful buildings.' And of teaching practices in classical ballet, Maxwell commented, 'Other recent drivers of improved technique include more exacting qualifications for teachers and more precise criteria for the objective judging of creative competences.'

These interviews also reveal a wholesale reinvention and relearning of production methods over the last thirty years. 'One of the greatest advances has been an explosive growth in new forms [genres] of theatrical production', a point reinforced here by Handy:

> Stardom and hierarchical structures have largely given way to a more collaborative, consensual, ensemble-based approach to production. The creative inspiration of both subject matter and its realisation on stage has become ever more divergent and now includes such improbable concepts as metaphysics, stranger aspects of human life, scientific practices and even theoretical mathematics.

Devised theatre (every aspect of production is developed in rehearsal) as opposed to a traditional text-based theatre has become commonplace. Conventional narrative forms in theatre have given way to innovative, even abstract structures more commonly found in dance. 'Theatre has become more spontaneous, reactive, immediate, improvisatory, happening in the here and now.' Amongst the development of many new performance tools has been a 'trend towards abandoning traditional styles of acting in character, and instead, adopting a style of the performer's real self, but in the manner of an objective, third-person storyteller'. Progress has also been made in 'understanding the human body as a communicative presence, a performer's self-awareness in space, their spatial relationships with other performers and how these relationships are interpreted by an audience'. All

146

these respondents discussed how 'the design of performance tools' is driving the performing arts. As Maxwell added, 'It is technique that makes audiences gasp, cry and laugh, and makes classical ballet more popular today than it has ever been.'

Two of these interviews reflect on a perennial debate amongst storytellers: Is the recent emergence of contemporary oral storytelling in Britain and Ireland a revival, a renaissance, an awakening, or as one storyteller affirms, a reinvention? If comparisons can be established between two very different performing arts (I don't have an informed view here) then Maxwell's interview may reflect on this subject.

> The world of classical ballet does not refer to the revival of character dance in the 1950s but to its reinvention. Early exponents did not uproot folk or court dances from Central and Eastern Europe and attempt to replant them in Western classical ballet companies. They studied folk traditions in their surviving state, analysed their component movements and rhythms and invented wholly original dance techniques that could be adapted for late twentieth century dancers and for late twentieth century audiences. This process of reinvention continues to this day.

Meanwhile, and bearing in mind there are still consultants to the Laban Conservatoire who trained and worked closely with Rudolph Laban, Brandt describes what she calls her 'adaptive teaching method'.

> I absorb Laban's core theory and practice; break down and analyse the component parts of his original doctrine; abandon redundant practices to the laws of natural selection; adopt and develop those qualities that are fittest for today's performing environment; embrace theory and practice that inform each other; seek inspiration from people and events beyond the disciplines of dance and performance; teach as a core skill the intense observation of innate human behaviour; [and imbue] students with a sense of how the union of movement/dance and music/sound lie at the heart of what it is to be a creative artist.

Perhaps to the 'revival', 'renaissance', 'awakening' and 'reinvention' theories of contemporary oral storytelling should be added the 'adaptive'.

Finally, there is an unspoken assumption amongst some storytellers that perpetual change, development and growth follows inevitably from current practices, developments and trends. Yet no one needs reminding how historical events, cultural fashions and evolutionary processes can also bring stasis, reversal and even the eclipse of an art form. Witness how the invention of the moveable type printing press eclipsed the lettering arts in Europe for five hundred years and how Brandt's interview reminds us of the changing fortunes of her own dance discipline. Rudolf Laban, born 1879 in Hungary, became a dancer, choreographer, theorist, inspiration for twenty-five Europe-wide dance schools, and by the 1930s, was acknowledged as one of the founders of European modern dance. He directed shows for, and was later rejected by, the Nazi authorities in Germany and so, in 1937, some of his followers moved to the USA, while he and others came to Britain to found the Art of Movement Studio in Manchester and develop what he called 'community dance' and 'dance education'. Since his death in 1958 Laban's followers have rebuilt his reputation, his workshop methods can now be found widely across Europe and the USA and the Laban Conservatoire in London is the largest dance academy in Europe.

Scientific methods

It came as no surprise to me to hear from our performing artists that science and technology are compelling sources of imagination and inspiration, since the concepts and methodology of the physical sciences (but not the mathematics) have been a primary companion and guide throughout my own creative career. If I may suggest a shortcut that leads us directly into this world and reflects back on the practices of storytelling it would be a slim volume of six lectures published as *The Origins of Knowledge and Imagination*[5] by one of the twentieth century's master communicators of scientific practice, Jacob Bronowski (1908-1974), mathematician, biologist, historian of science, author of both scientific and artistic works and best known for his 1973 BBC and Time-Life television series *The Ascent of Man*.

Something of the creative method of the scientist can be deduced from the subject matter of these six lectures. 1. Inferential imagination as an instrument for understanding. 2. Symbolic languages as communicators of knowledge and tools of analysis. 3. The paradoxical relationship between the laws of nature (e.g. gravitation) and the nature of scientific laws (e.g. mathematical formulae). 4. The incompleteness and provisional nature of the scientific enterprise. 5. How biological and scientific evolution is built on the exploitation of error and the connections between self-sustaining phenomena. 6. The causal trajectory that links the scientific personality, the role of the scientific community as a creative force and the social value of science as an ethical activity.

The first five lectures may find some common ground with storytellers as they clearly do with many performing artists; however, it is the final lecture in particular that seems to reflect well on the world of contemporary oral storytelling. As with the physical sciences Chapters One and Two of this study draw attention to the singular nature of the person who becomes a storyteller; Chapters Four and Five highlight the collective will of communities that drive and celebrate storytelling; and Chapters Three and Seven reflect on the principles and personal values that drive much storytelling practice in our society.

Just as our performing artists affirm that 'science is an intimate companion to art' so scientists affirm that art is an intimate companion to science. Bronowski famously wrote: 'Physics becomes [early in the twentieth century] the greatest collective work of science – no, more than that, the greatest collective work of art of the twentieth century. I say "work of art", because the notion that there is an underlying structure, a world within a world of the atom, captured the imagination of artists at once.'[6] One of the founding fathers of twentieth-century physics, Niels Bohr, once said to his colleague Werner Heisenberg, 'when it comes to atoms language can be used only as in poetry. The poet, too, is not nearly so concerned with describing facts as with creating images.'[7] Theoretical physicist and consultant in science communication, Graham Farmelo, says, 'The beauty of a fundamental theory in physics has several characteristics in common with a great work of art: fundamental simplicity, inevitability, power and grandeur. Like every great work of art, a beautiful theory in physics is always ambitious, never trifling.'[8] Albert Einstein remarked that Niels Bohr's theory of the atom exemplified 'the highest form of musicality in the sphere of thought'[9] (although, according to several accounts, Einstein played the violin execrably). And British physicist, Paul Dirac's 1927 breakthrough equation in the development of quantum mechanics – $i\gamma.\delta\psi = m\psi$ – was hailed by Frank Wilczek as 'achingly beautiful'.[10]

Science, like storytelling, has a long history of being staged as entertainment. An advertising poster from 1799 describes 'Mr Nicholson's Philosophical and Chemical Lectures [as] a course of entertaining and popular instruction'. The Royal Institution of Great Britain's lectures have been inspiring Londoners since 1825. Today, science as a performing art and as 'pop science' is commonplace. Audiences can become participants in and co-creators of both the science and the entertainment. For example, as someone who never learnt any science at school, it was a thrilling experience to attend, free of charge, London's Dana Centre recently and to assist a leading theoretical physicist with building a model of a conceptual time machine out of cups, saucers and cutlery. Science festivals abound. And for its entertainment value it is hard to beat another recent experience of joining other paying audience members to become a human guinea pig in an experiment about infrasound, especially when our contribution could then be scrutinised later on the researchers' website.

My personal introduction to the physical sciences has been largely though the rise of a genre of literature, 'popular science', that barely existed three decades ago. This emergent trend has been driven by scientists with an authoritative but accessible writing style and a broadening realisation in the scientific community that they have to reach out to a wider public and explain to a sometimes sceptical world the added value that science brings to our daily lives and to a wider society. Today bears witness to something of a golden age of popular science writing that feeds a widespread appetite for the big ideas that science has to offer.

Pictorial representation

The literature on the visual arts seems to have very little to offer on how the collective practices of individual artists can translate into a causative driver of change and development in the wider artistic movement. The best model I am familiar with comes from Austrian-born Ernst Gombrich (1909-2001), a formidable theorist and historian of the fine arts and author of *Art and Illusion: A Study in the Psychology of Pictorial Representation*. I am fearful of skipping dry shod, as it were, over the stepping stones of this densely argued, four-hundred-page magnum opus, particularly as Gombrich himself warns us in the introduction and with certain professorial menace that 'I am well aware that this lengthy approach through the quicksands of perceptual theory puts a considerable strain on the reader who is in a hurry to get to the emotional core of art'.[11]

However, Gombrich's theory is based on a psychological process that takes the form of an interpretative dialogue between an artist during the creation of a picture and the observer's interpretation of a completed picture which he calls 'making and matching'. The artist interprets the world they know to make pictorial schemata on the paper or canvas in their own pictorial style, which they then adjust by a process of trial and error and error correction, to match the way they experience the visible world. The observer interprets the artist's stylistic suggestions on the paper or canvas, again by a process of trial and error and error correction, to transform and match the marks on the picture with the visible world of their own personal experience. Central to this collaborative dialogue is the artist's skill of involving the observer in the creative process to allow them to experience something of the thrill of making or creating, which had once been the exclusive privilege of the artist. This trial and error experimental method, as Gombrich reminds us, is the method which all living organisms use to ensure their survival – as do human beings to a marvellous extent. He attributes a similar process to account for why the fine arts – by implication any creative enterprise including storytelling – have histories at all. In its most elemental form, Gombrich is proposing that change and development are driven by the sum total of all such individual, interpretative, trial-and-error experiments within a culture, whether influenced by external events, inspirational personalities, technical innovations or even passing fashions. His thesis seems to mirror precisely two phenomena that are widely discussed here in previous chapters: the idea of a dialogue between the creative artist and an observer, and the idea of change and development in an art form being the product of emergent properties.

Reflections

Detailed comparisons and contrasts between oral storytelling and other creative enterprises described in this chapter should be self-evident to those who have followed our journey through the preceding chapters. Beyond this, there are perhaps three ideas worth revisiting from this chapter's multiple detours.

First, the idea that storytelling stands, and perhaps should stand, apart from other performing arts and creative enterprises seems patently untenable. Whatever the personal feelings of some storytellers, linking pathways and parallel journeys can be found everywhere: in performance tools and other practices, the methods of organisation and co-ordination, the social and cultural roles played by creative communities, and in the many forms of complex network interactivity. The working lives of practising storytellers criss-cross many invisible boundaries, creative enterprises and professional disciplines. Perceptions and definitions of storytelling phenomena are diffuse and overlap with other performing arts. Examples abound of practitioners and participants who remain unaware they are involved in a creative process because their practices are so embedded in the very fabric of everyday life. What previous chapters show, and what this chapter attempts to validate, is how all creative enterprises, even the physical sciences, gain strength by the collective will of communities that are not, and can never be, an island, entire of themselves.

Second, for those who affirm that 'storytelling is an adolescent art form and we should look at other art forms and learn from them', this chapter shows us the many ways that the wider world of creative enterprise is already accomplishing this objective. As we find above, in the art form of character dance, it is not a matter of uprooting what remains of outmoded traditions and replanting them in a contemporary context, but of analysing and adapting what survives and inventing new techniques for today's audiences and other participants. The examples in this chapter demonstrate just how inspiration can be found in people and events far beyond the disciplines of the performing arts and even beyond the further reaches of all creative enterprise. I would suggest we are approaching here the views of the storyteller who said, 'We must create a new form of British storytelling for the twenty first century.'

Third, preceding chapters discuss how audiences experience a storytelling through the individual persona of the teller and how storytellers tend to take a very personal approach to their art. For those who follow Gombrich's reasoning this study offers us a vision of any human enterprise, whether in the arts, the sciences or even in the progress of history itself, where the efforts of the individual can play a significant role in driving change, development and growth.

Notes & References

1. *Messa di Voce*, created by Golan Levin and Zachary Lieberman, performed by poets Jaap Blonk and Joan La Barbara.

2. Lucy Bannerman, 'Poetry to his ears: how asylum seeker from Iran won school verse competition', *The Times*, London UK, 23 May 2009, p. 15.

3. From the board, 'Now is the time to get involved', *Storylines*, Society for Storytelling UK, Spring 2012, p. 3.

4. Richard Morrison, 'Edinburgh: bloated, over-priced – and unmissable', *The Times*, London UK, 30 July 2008, section Times 2, p. 7.

5. Jacob Bronowski, *The Origins of Knowledge and Imagination* (New Haven USA: Yale University Press, 1978).

6. J. Bronowski, *The Ascent of Man* (London UK: British Broadcasting Corporation, 1974), p. 330.

7. *Ascent of Man*, p. 340.

8. Graham Farmelo, *The Strangest Man* (London UK: Faber and Faber, 2009), p. 74.

9. *Strangest Man*, p. 71.

10. *Strangest Man*, p. 142.

11. E.H. Gombrich, *Art and Illusion: A Study in the Psychology of Pictorial Representation* (London UK: Phaidon Press, 1977), p. 25.

NINE

HOMECOMING

ഇറ

The Preface to this study outlines how early encounters and informal conversations with career storytellers reveal a number of common issues that
were uppermost in their minds at the time, and by process of distillation,
how they became the three research questions this study has sought to answer.
Inevitably, as this journey progressed, emphases have changed, evidence has
undermined early assumptions and conclusions have become ever more fugitive.
However, while acknowledging the inherent limitations of the research methodology employed in such a wide-ranging study, this final chapter presses forward
to grasp at some answers.

What are the principal drivers of change, development and growth in oral storytelling today?

The original question addressed only the drivers of growth in oral storytelling.
This proved to be too limiting a question, and with the unavoidable expansion of
this study's scope, the concepts of 'change' and 'development' were added at an
early stage to take account of the more complex dynamics of this emergent social
and cultural phenomenon.

But first it should not be assumed that 'change', 'development' and 'growth'
are uniform, on-going and inevitable or that these terms are synonymous. As we
find in the last chapter all cultural movements and creative enterprises are also
prone to regression, decline and extinction. That said there is manifest evidence
for progressive expansion in the world of oral storytelling. The number of those

describing themselves as practicing storytellers and storymakers, even during the four-year research period of this study, has shown a steady rise. The Storytelling Café's evaluation reports for the mid-2000s demonstrate growth of about 15 per cent per year. Of those mature storytelling festivals studied, all show a steady growth since they were founded. There are no historical records for the growth of local storytelling groups but a 2007 Society for Storytelling list for the UK and Northern Ireland refers to about 70 such groups. By 2012 the records of the Mythstories Museum show a figure of about 85, but this comparison may not be calculated by similar means. They also report their lists are subject to frequent amendment because new groups are established and old ones fade away, while even some high profile groups choose not to be included on such lists at all. Storytellers of Ireland's website lists 12 well-established local groups. Add to these figures informal and unregistered groups and the total number of local storytelling groups in Britain and Ireland may now be well over 100. This study has however kept a record of the numbers of storytelling events promoted by the Society for Storytelling in their London region for the years 2007-13. A snapshot sample for the months of March shows:

2007: 9 events at 4 venues.

2008: 6 events at 6 venues.

2009: 17 events and 1 conference at 13 venues.

2010: 10 events and 4 training workshops at 12 venues.

2011: 21 events and 5 training workshops at 20 venues.

2012: 24 events and 7 training workshops at 23 venues.

2013: 20 events and 2 training workshops at 21 venues.

Even with reduced events in March 2013, these figures show a doubling of events over a six year period. It seems unlikely that this rate of growth has been replicated elsewhere in Britain and Ireland, except perhaps in other major urban conurbations, or perhaps notable centres of storytelling such as Edinburgh, Cardiff and perhaps the English West Midlands.

Further anecdotal evidence for the growth of storytelling can be gained from Chapter Seven which describes 17 venues currently used for storytelling within a kilometre of my south London house. Of this total, 15 have come into use as storytelling venues in the last ten years. At 13 of these venues storytelling is incidental to the principal function of the venue and has been introduced to enhance, in some way or other, the experience of any visitor there. It might therefore be reasonable to claim this incidental application of the storyteller's art as a significant driver of change, development and growth in oral storytelling.

Joseph Daniel Sobol's *The Storytellers' Journey* contains a section titled Structure and Anti-Structure[1] which draws on the work of anthropologists and folklorists to discuss two innate but seemingly oppositional human impulses: to build organisational and social structures and to overthrow such structures in a bid for individual liberty and freedom of expression. Sobol goes on to affirm that both these impulses have a complementary role to play if a revival movement is to become established within a broader culture. He also alludes to the emergent qualities of revival movements.

> The storytelling world grew, as many such worlds do, through relationships and an intensity of interactive commitment that turns a job, a pastime, an idea, or a technique into what was once commonly called a "school" but now is more often dubbed a "movement".[2]

Evidence from this study also suggests that aspects of structure, anti-structure and emergence all form symbiotic relationships between individuals, communities and organisations, and all in their own ways, bring about change, development and growth. The anti-structure approach to storytelling is commonplace amongst career storytellers and is well articulated by the storyteller quoted in Chapter One who responded to my request for an interview with the words, 'I feel a little wary of the work you are doing. [...] Your message gives me the impression that you seem to want to intellectualise, sanitise and organise a folk art.' Accounts of the variously named revival, renaissance and re-awakening of oral storytelling in Britain and Ireland over the last three decades[3,4,5] rightly identify the initiatives of a small number of individuals who have driven the early years of this movement. The extended interviews for Chapter One reveal many career storytellers as individualists who navigate their own personal pathways through the brave new world that is today's oral storytelling. Audience interviews for Chapter Two also reveal how much of the personal experience of a storytelling event is bound up with the individual persona of the teller. Chapter Eight identifies similar characteristics amongst performance poets, stand-up comedians and even lettering artists. Chapter Six finds how emergent movements in the performing arts are often associated with the names of their pioneering founders – Stanislavski, Grotowski, Laban, Lecoq. And again in Chapter Eight Ernst Gombrich offers us a view of pictorial art in which an interpretative dialogue between many individual artists and many individual observers can ultimately determine why the fine arts have histories at all. We seem to have arrived at a point where an innate impulse towards an anti-structure approach amongst individual career storytellers can be seen as a potential driver of change, development and growth.

Sobol's allusions to the emergent properties of oral storytelling are also self-evident in nearly every chapter of this study. In its most elemental form, all storytelling events display such emergent properties, including audience members as self-assembling communities, the live performance itself as an emergent event and storytelling as a social art also displays qualities of emergent relationships. Many of the informally constituted local storytelling groups are quintessential communities; they display properties of self-sustaining emergence and they tend to effect change, development and growth through collaborative relationships and an interactive engagement with the group's practices. The many and varied genres of storytelling described in Chapter Three also tend to draw specialised practitioners into their spheres of interest and in turn become loosely associated and largely self-sustaining communities with the potential to drive change, development and growth.

It is in the nature of emergent processes that the drivers of change will be different for each type of community. In Chapter Eight, when Jacob Bronowski talks about 'the role of the scientific community as a creative force'[6] he is referring to the worldwide community of scientists working on a particular subject and embracing the accepted methodology developed for their specialised scientific discipline. In the same chapter, when our performing artists talk about how 'the language of management, organisation and governance is now imbued with concepts of team-working, community, participation and consensus' they are referring to the wholesale adoption of more emergent practices in the performing arts. And in all thirteen local storytelling groups and all eleven storytelling genres researched for this study, all reveal very different emergent properties with a potential to drive change, development and growth.

Structures also abound in the world of storytelling. Chapter Four describes the organisational structure of a range of local storytelling groups researched for this study. Any organisation that promotes and stages storytelling events needs some form of administrative framework to remain self-sustaining. Membership and representative bodies display a wide range of effective organisational structures, each adapted to their own particular needs and aspirations. Chapter Five describes in some detail the organisational models employed by five very different types of storytelling festival, and even to this scaly-eyed management consultant, the quality of management and leadership demonstrated is impressive by any standards. Clearly, structures are a primary driver of change, development and growth in contemporary oral storytelling.

In any form of cultural movement it is common for even primary drivers of change to remain completely hidden from public awareness. So in the last chapter we find the lettering arts can be ubiquitous in every commercial high street yet go completely unnoticed by Saturday morning shoppers. Storytellers are commonly unaware when they cross boundaries between structure and anti-structure practices. One of our most innately anti-structure storytellers I interviewed became visibly distressed when I reminded them of all the storytelling organisations and institutions they had founded over the last three decades. It is also in the nature of almost any kind of community activity that its participants are only infrequently aware of its emergent social properties. Community storytelling events are often so subsumed in the fabric of everyday life that neither the teller nor their audience members are fully aware they are co-creators of a highly structured social ritual. One example of a storytelling audience with a dawning awareness of their own social role is recounted by a storyteller engaged by the Royal Opera House to tell the stories of Wagner's Ring Cycle operas at a pre-performance talk. They described how even these mature and informed listeners took some time to realise they were experiencing a formal storytelling event, how therefore the social dynamics of the event was supposed to work, and consequently what their role in it was supposed to be. And the sublime example of the hidden qualities of structure, anti-structure and emergence as drivers of change comes from the middle-aged Norwegian couple we met in Chapter Two, who insisted they had never heard of storytelling as a formalised art form, yet by the end of my interview with them, had revealed themselves as experienced multi-genre storytellers of notable distinction.

Simon Heywood's *The New Storytelling* identifies eight cultural and historical precursors that, to a greater or lesser degree, were significant influences on the early years of the storytelling revival in England and Wales.[7] These include: the literature and scholarship of traditional stories, analytical psychology and psychotherapy, the 1960s counter-cultures and alternative spiritualities, professional and semi-professional theatre traditions, the cultural traditions of informal minority communities, the traditions of storytelling in schools and libraries, folk revivals since the middle of the last century, and the mass media. Interviews with career storytellers for Chapter One add to this list of factors significantly influencing today's storytellers, including: peer inspiration, particular styles of stagecraft, high standards of teaching practice, the social roles played by certain storytellers, other performing arts and cultural phenomena, and the personal inspiration of individuals unconnected with storytelling. I may be in danger of over-fishing the evidential pond here, but it is tempting to interpret all these significant influences on the careers of today's storytellers as on-going drivers of change, development and growth.

Some drivers of change are clearly not exclusive to oral storytelling but are the product of far-reaching social and cultural trends in our society. One such is the trend towards a more collaborative, participatory engagement with creative processes – the doing and making of culture as opposed to the observing and consuming of it. Ruth Finnegan's *The Hidden Musicians*, referred to in the Preface, is an early celebration of people-power as a driver of change, development and growth in the arts. Adult education in cultural subjects has seen explosive growth in recent decades. Five million Britons now attend weekly classes in contemporary dance.[8] Primetime television is currently featuring a choir of military wives and girlfriends. My local adult education college plays host to the celebrated Can't Sing Choir. Calligraphers and lettering artists attribute the growing popularity of their art form to two demonstrable factors: anyone can do it and get great pleasure from it, and the desktop computer, because anyone can exercise total control over the design and creation of text-based documents.

In Chapter Eight, we see how even the totally unlearned can now become participants in the making of scientific knowledge and co-creators of science as entertainment. Chapter Three outlines how the acquisition of storytelling skills is often undertaken as a means to self-revelation and personal development. Chapter Six shows how my own participation in performing arts workshops led directly to the acquisition of valuable life skills with practical applications in all human communication. Chapter One explores the idea of storytelling as a social art with a dialogic relationship of teller and listener at its heart. Chapter Two, which reveals qualities of co-creation in storytelling, also outlines how audience members bring with them a richly cultured hinterland of participatory experience, and how many then put lessons they have learnt during a storytelling to practical use in their vocational and/or social lives. Chapter Three describes the application of the storyteller's art in a broad range of professional and vocational contexts, in each example its success relies on collaborative participation in the processes of storytelling and storymaking. Chapters Four and Five may be read as a state-of-the-storytelling-nation and how storytelling practices have now reached out into some of our most inaccessible communities. It would be hard to imagine another emergent social and cultural movement that combines such diversity of aspiration with such singular collaborative and participatory intent. These qualities, I propose, should also be considered as strong drivers of change, development and growth.

There has never been much doubt from the outset of this study that complex network interconnection has the potential to become a powerful driver of change, development and growth. In this respect it seems the world of oral storytelling holds a very privileged position over other emergent cultural phenomena. An online ticket agent has only one mode of interconnection available to them: the internet. In complete contrast, the preface to this study recounts how, in a pre-internet age, my colleagues from the Somali Film Agency communicated with their families in rural Somalia by means of multiple modes of interconnection that typically involved about thirty hubs and at least five different communications media. From a review of all the preceding chapters it seems that almost anyone and almost any organisation in the world of storytelling, however informally constituted, has the potential to be an effective network hub with myriad forms of communications media available to them. The word 'potential' is used here because it is in the nature of all complex networks that some parts will be more active than others and some may be completely dormant. In very crude terms the emergent properties of any complex network of interaction are determined by the accumulative actions of all its users.

How is oral storytelling adding social value in our society?

Attempting any sort of answer to this question was always going to be ambitious. Its original form referred both to 'social value' and 'public good' but some storytellers felt the latter term had an institutional ring to it, so I took it out. And in case the term 'added social value' carries a specialised meaning in some academic discipline that I am unaware of, I am using dictionary definitions here to mean some incremental benefit or worth of some kind to individuals and communities in our wider society. Chapter Three explores some narrowly defined issues of the efficacy or utility of specialist applications of the storyteller's art. Here our pathway leads us into those borderlands where the multiform roles of oral storytelling reach out into society and interact with individuals and communities. Of course, many human endeavours add social value in society and certainly this is the case amongst our control group, the creative enterprises described in the last chapter. They all, in one way or another, serve the needs, wishes and aspirations of a wider public, and in particular, those most disadvantaged in society. Jacob Bronowski, whom we met in the last chapter, has said of the scientific community, that since the time of Isaac Newton 'what holds it together, how it works, and why it has had spectacular success […] has made it the largest single factor in our social life'.

There is a broad consensus amongst storytellers and storymakers that their art can be a valuable therapeutic tool to bring about some form of 'transformative process' or 'healing change' in individuals or groups. This process can be ameliorative or palliative and is widely employed in the practices of psychotherapy, dramatherapy, mediation, conflict resolution, restorative justice, psychiatric social work and as a pastoral skill for the relief of personal distress in many emotionally charged social situations. As one storyteller from an arts-based social project put it, storymaking 'changes people's personal stories in order to change their real lives'. In Chapter One, some career storytellers describe how the practices of storytelling, the act of making and telling stories itself, can be an effective form of self-therapy that allows them to come to terms with some physical or social trauma in their lives and helps them to create a new personal identity as a storyteller.

Examples of the pedagogical role of oral storytelling are found throughout this study. Educational storytellers talk of their skills as powerful tools, not only for delivering the national primary school curriculum, but also for 'teaching what a story is and why it matters' to people's lives, how 'storytelling can teach children social skills' and as an aid to 'playing with language'. In Chapter Three we find how the learning/teaching of storytelling itself can be a 'journey of self-revelation', how 'self-awareness is the foundation for making a difference in your personal life' and how all 'transformational learning requires a deep and holistic engagement in the learning process as well as in the content of learning'. The consultant we met in Chapter Three, who coaches senior executives in storytelling skills, talks about how a multidisciplinary approach leads to a deeper 'understanding of the psychological reasons why [organisational] change is needed, [how this] can be achieved through stories [and why] the power of story is undeniable'. Chapter Three refers to academic research that outlines how 'storytelling and narrative can provide a valuable tool for assisting learning about museum collections'[9], and by inference, for enriching a visitor's experience at art galleries, heritage sites and visitor attractions. And therapeutic storytellers also observe how young clients from disadvantaged communities often have no concept of narrative, no mental model for stories, so have grown up without recourse to this basic tool for life. In this example the therapist has to teach the skills of what they call 'oral literacy' before therapeutic storytelling can bring any form of healing change.

The added social value that storytelling practices can bring to communities and neighbourhoods hardly needs restating. Many local storytelling groups that are based in rural areas or the suburbs of large cities are the only organisations to offer live cultural events and a generous welcome, to all-comers, of any age, from any social background and at an affordable price. As we find in Chapter Four, these self-assembling communities engender a spirit of conviviality, openness, understanding and tolerance and they can be torch-bearers of fundamental human values in doubting and uncertain times. We have also seen how many local storytelling groups are engaged in outreach activities with other local communities, organisations and public institutions, so creating networks of communities that share similar social and cultural values. About 75 per cent of those career storytellers I have interviewed for Chapter One report they are engaged in community storytelling, in education, the criminal justice system, care homes, social projects, public institutions, places of worship, any community where people gather together to share common purpose. Many affirm the primacy of community storytelling over all other genres, as one puts it, 'Community storytelling is the core storytelling function, at its best in prisons, classrooms and as a pastoral skill.' This is not to suggest – and no storyteller has claimed – that the storytelling movement occupies a privileged position amongst all types of social outreach activity. However, the preceding chapters yield much evidence to suggest that oral storytelling can reach very deeply and very broadly into scattered communities and can add social value where it is often needed most.

While the self-therapeutic qualities of storytelling have been discussed above, here we weigh the evidence that storytelling practices themselves can add social value to the lives of individual participants. This idea rests on the notion that storytelling is an innate human skill. As one experienced storyteller puts it, 'storytelling is the ultimate act of shared humanity. It gives shape to what it is to be human.' Just as our calligraphers say that anyone with a pen, a piece of paper and a kitchen table can do it, and get great pleasure from it, so storytellers remind us that 'everyone is a storyteller'. In traditional and informal storytelling communities, at local storytelling groups, even around a workplace water cooler, people are steeling themselves to tell a story to a sympathetic audience; an appreciative response engenders confidence; added skills and experience bring incremental pleasure; the cycle repeats itself; a new storyteller is born.

Every chapter of this study reveals the act of storytelling to be an immensely powerful medium of self-expression. In Chapter One several career storytellers describe extreme storytelling experiences of cathartic self-revelation. Chapter Two notes how audience members treat a storytelling event as a learning experience and then apply the lessons learnt to their vocational and/or social lives. In Chapter Three one storyteller describes their experience as a student at the Emerson School of Storytelling as a journey of self-revelation. In a formal coaching environment, the same chapter reveals how storytelling can be a powerful tool for personal development and the learning of life-skills. And here is another example of how the practices of storytelling can add social value to individual lives as well as to communities.

> A woman of my acquaintance, blind since birth, discovers storytelling and thereby comes to terms with her physical disability, and in turn, the social disadvantages that often follow. Her storytelling, folk music and workshop coaching become widely acknowledged in the inner-city neighbourhood where she lives. Her perseverance creates a public persona that is greater than the sum of her disabilities. She has become something of a role model for the disabled, a public face and voice of oral storytelling and even something of a local hero.

Can and/or should ways be found to raise public awareness and attract greater recognition to oral storytelling?

In one sense these linked questions are simply answered: there are many ways that 'can' be found to raise public awareness of oral storytelling; however, from my storyteller interviews it seems the word 'should' tends to be used only in reference to others. There were three questions asked during these interviews that I hoped would yield positive responses, but in the event yielded little of interest. Twelve storytellers commented directly on this research question: Two suggested storytellers generally should improve their core skills. Two referred to initiatives they were already spearheading in their own regions. Several wanted higher fees for themselves and more funding for storytelling in schools and for national tours. One proposed there should be more storytelling competitions, stories recorded and sold on CD and added that libraries should be 'forced' to host storytelling. And one turned on me for raising the subject at all, saying: 'I am in abject opposition to any form of raising the profile of storytelling – we don't want to become Coca-Cola!'

Several attempts have been made during research to assess the wider public image of oral storytelling, but as noted above, very few people have a clear image of what it is. As one director of the Society for Storytelling wrote recently, 'Being an oral medium, it has always been a challenge for all of us to explain to friends just what exactly storytelling is – handing over a book or leaflet on the subject, or directing them to a website can only go part of the way to introducing them to an art that really needs to be experienced to be understood.'[10] And storytelling is also many things to many different people. The audience member at a festival, the refugee, the psychiatric social worker's client, the educational director at a visitor attraction, and so on, all have different images of this art form. Career storytellers also have contrary views. While one affirms that the image of storytelling today is 'the Armani suit – the folk and camping image now being redundant', another likens the storyteller's role to that of a shaman, another suggests that community storytelling is just 'feeding a spurious sense of public nostalgia' and another describes performance storytelling 'as an alternative night out [and] not much more than a form of light family entertainment'.

These widely divergent views also led to an e-debate with one storyteller who has experience of arts marketing about whether storytelling is better promoted as a profession or a business. I argued that storytellers are craft professionals offering a service. No business entrepreneur would recognise storytelling as 'a business'. And even the term 'business' can be intimidating to those predisposed to a humanistic approach to life. They argued that businesses attract more development funding; that storytellers should accept 'that they are selling themselves [which requires] a certain degree of business-mindedness [and that] the term 'professional' smacks […] of the old English class system'. We did agree, however, that both business-mindedness and professionalism seemed to fit the required image of all storytelling genres. Meanwhile, a former director of Apples and Snakes, the representative body for performance poetry, who does have a professional qualification in arts management, offered in interview the phrase 'professionalism without institutionalisation'.

But moving on from this semantic jousting, a review of all preceding chapters reveals the many ways and many means that storytellers and organisers of storytelling events are already raising public awareness and attracting greater recognition to oral storytelling, and it has to added, to great effect. Some are innate emergent processes that tend to pass unnoticed because they are subsumed in storytellers' everyday practices. Some are deliberative strategies to advertise, promote, market and brand individual storytellers, groups, organisations and oral storytelling as a whole. Some are the spontaneous product of complex network interactions in any or many media. And some are combinations of all of the above.

Chapter One describes those many storytellers who express an active distaste for any sort of personal marketing and how only a few build networks of interaction to get more work. Chapter Two attempts to draw up a demographic profile of a composite storytelling audience, and as an exercise in audience research, this may be of interest to those planning a storytelling event. The Norwegian couple who chanced on a festival poster and discovered themselves to be storytelling heroes is a good example of the random nature of all promotional initiatives. Chapter Three reveals how each storytelling genre has its own distinctive public image that in turn requires very different methods of attracting greater official recognition. And since many storytellers are also members of professional institutions, these too offer opportunities for promotion and greater public recognition of oral storytelling.

Chapter Four explores how the organisational models of local storytelling groups and other coordinating and organising bodies can be adapted to become powerful network hubs. It also explores how they can develop collaborative networks with partner organisations and raise their public profile through outreach activities. Many local storytelling groups now offer workshops on 'storytelling as a business'. At the time of writing the Society for Storytelling is seeking advice from its members with experience of change management, social marketing, arts promotion and knowledge of business methods. The Scottish Storytelling Centre employs a specialist Communications Officer. And also from the same chapter can be inferred the reason why marketing plans need to be as individually distinctive as the local groups and organisations they promote.

An outline of the organisational models adopted by the festivals described in Chapter Five refers to the promotional methods they employ and it is notable how many involve multiple forms of networking and multiple modes of communication media. Most of the larger festivals now cross-promote their core programmes, their outreach projects and other storytelling events that take place throughout the year. Chapter Six outlines a number of research and development initiatives taken within the world of storytelling but also notes how few of these are shared or communicated with a wider public. Interviews for this study with representatives of five cultural organisations that now host storytelling reveal they might be encouraged to stage more such events if there was a reliable and well publicised accreditation system in place. It is also clear from Chapter Seven that all venues that host storytelling, of whatever genre, are potential hubs for cross-promotion of storytelling events. And the same chapter corroborates evidence from other studies to show how the public image of an individual or organisation is often created, not by the activities they practice, but by the design quality of the print or electronic documents they distribute. Finally, Chapter Eight takes a sideways look at how other performing arts and creative enterprises reach out to a wider public. Of note here is how each develops its own unique promotional strategy and each its own forms of network interaction.

Sometimes a public endorsement can come from a wholly unexpected quarter. So, when Britain's Secretary of State for Children, Schools and Families commissions Sir Jim Rose to review the national primary school curriculum, the resulting 2009 report becomes a very public recognition by the state of the value of storytelling in schools today. Its print version is read by tens of thousands of people and its downloadable version remains freely available to anyone visiting www.education.gov.uk/publications/primary curriculum review.

Opening up this discussion on promotion, marketing and the public image of oral storytelling, the storyteller who said 'I am in abject opposition to any form of raising the profile of storytelling – we don't want to become Coca-Cola!' probably knows as little about these topics as I do. This situation has only been partially ameliorated by spending an afternoon trawling the bookshops of London's Charing Cross Road. To my great surprise many of the high profile books on selling, marketing, public relations and branding take an apparently contradictory position to the arrogant, mass media corporatism that I was expecting. For example word of mouth marketing, the method by which most people first discover storytelling, has become an essential component of what is now voguishly called 'social marketing'. It is a highly developed technique used by global corporations to boost revenue by generating informal discourse between individuals and social groups of current and potential customers or clients. The titles of many of the books surveyed that afternoon, and the terms used as chapter headings or topics for discussion, seem to bring echoes of the many promotional methods already used by storytellers and referred to above. My contemporaneous notes include the following:

> Book title: *Marketing to the Social Web* (building customer communities via social networks). 'Guerrilla marketing' (speaks for itself). Book title: *Word of Mouth Marketing* (how smart companies get people talking). 'Bottom-up marketing' (connecting directly with individuals in a market). Book title: *Can we do that?* (outrageous PR stunts that work). 'Brand community' (consumers become co-creators of, and advocates for, a product or service through community behaviour).

Book title: *Web Marketing for Dummies* (speaks for itself). 'Brand equity' (financial value of a brand built on consumers' behaviour). Book title: *Unmarketable* (emotion-based techniques such as folk-branding that appeal to a sense of mystery, sensuality and intimacy). 'Mocketing' (marketing by self-ridicule). Book title: *Beyond Buzz* (marketing by word of mouth and promoting conversations with and between customers). And so on.

To pursue this train of thought further I arranged an interview (it took ten months) with the Director of Relationships for one of Britain's most famous corporate brand names who is responsible for maintaining this company's worldwide public image. I asked them one question: Can lessons be learned from a global brand like yours that might help raise the public profile of storytelling in this country? A free interpretation of their brand-speak response and subsequent discussion is reproduced here: 1: Suggests assembling a representative group of leading storytellers. 2: Define the objectives. 3: Identify the 'real culture' of storytelling. 4: Select a well-focused 'catalyst for growth', probably 'event-led' like National Storytelling Week to create a 'corporate identity'. 5: Raise the profile of storytelling over other 'cultural movements' and 'national weeks' by recruiting 'volunteer experts' externally (assuming there are no suitably qualified storytellers). 6: First identify and appoint 'a national figurehead with gravitas and popular appeal' to become the initiative's 'public face' (best from the world of communications but broadcasting and publishing also mentioned). 7: Also appoint an external 'chair/coordinator' who helps recruit other expert volunteers in finance, fund raising, lobbying, creative marketing and mass-media (check Sunday Times Public Appointments pages for possible candidates). 8: The initiative is managed internally by regional representatives with appropriate time, skills and resources. 9: A lower-key option involves collaboration with an education, creative or media faculty of a high profile university. 10: Raise the credibility of storytelling by raising storytellers' 'professional standards'. 11: To attract large scale funding generally requires 'going big and going commercial' and creating 'established organisational structures'. 12: Large scale social marketing techniques generally work only with established brands that already have a national or international identity.

OK, OK, I just asked the question here; no storyteller is expected to associate with the answers! However, I just mention in passing, that in the physical sciences, negative results of an experiment can be as valuable as positive ones. (For example, Einstein's famous discovery that $E=mc^2$ was inferred, in part, from the negative results of the Michelson-Morley experiments a decade earlier.) But this interview did raise the question as to whether substantial fund-raising is a realistic prospect without 'going big and going commercial'. Some storytelling festivals do attract corporate sponsorship, often in kind, as National Storytelling Week has in the past. One Biggest Liar competition is sponsored by a local brewery. And one recent storytelling event, 40 Winks Bedtime Tales – 'we're going to seduce you with tales of love, lust and longing' – has attracted sponsorship from cult lingerie brand What Katie Did (products for sale at the venue) and Purely Roses (one free for every attender). Although most discussions I have held with storytellers about corporate sponsorship have however ended gloomily.

But to press forward on this theme and to try and get inside the thinking of corporate sponsorship, I arranged an interview (it took seven months) with the Head of Sponsorship, Europe, Middle East and Africa, for a global financial services firm, and my notes of this interview may offer some guidance. Global annual sponsorship budget runs to about US$ 10 million. A top tier, consuming most of this budget, goes to high profile sporting and cultural events in support of 'brand awareness' as part of their global marketing strategy. A middle tier supports the kind of prestigious cultural institutions their corporate and wealthy private clients like to associate themselves with. Notably, this form of sponsorship is not an all-or-nothing process – just funding an event on the basis of an application – but tends to evolve over years and often starts by establishing a personal relationship. Initial sponsorship often comes in the form of specialist advice which the recipient organisation often lacks, can involve research and analysis of greatest needs or long-term planning, and only later does financial sponsorship follow. This cyclical process of an extended relationship, specialist advice, and ultimately financial sponsorship, can then begin again. The bottom tier of sponsorship is managed by Community Affairs teams based at all their offices worldwide. This form of sponsorship supports needy local organisations like schools in deprived inner city areas, and as above, often starts with specialised advice in kind, and only then leads on to targeted funding. As a matter of policy, four days paid leave are allowed for every staff member worldwide to take part in community volunteering for selected organisations.

Subsequent enquiries suggest these middle and bottom tier forms of sponsorship are quite common amongst small businesses and even the wealthy retired, in particular when the sponsorship required is in kind. Continuing on the theme of personal relationships as a prelude to financial sponsorship, I interviewed a Relationship Manager for Literature (which includes oral storytelling) for one region of Arts Council England. What had surprised them most in the eight months since their appointment was that no storyteller or storytelling organisation had been in touch to establish such a relationship. This contrasts starkly with the many cultural organisations that had established relationships, even though they had no plans to apply for public funding, and included commercial companies that are ineligible for any form of Arts Council funding. The benefits that flow to those who establish such relationships lie with the Arts Council's role as a regional hub for complex network interactivity, a source for market research and a vehicle for raising public awareness and attracting wider institutional recognition.

In the same vein, museums, libraries, archives and heritage sites are prolific hosts of storytelling events, yet at the time of my interview with the Museums, Libraries and Archives Council (the MLA has subsequently been subsumed into the Arts Council) they reported only sparse contact from individual storytellers and none recorded at an institutional level, ever. They did however suggest that storytellers and storytelling organisations would be better advised to establish such relationships with the three individual professional bodies that represent museum curators, librarians and archivists.

History

This concluding chapter addresses, as directly as the evidence allows, the three research questions posed in the preface. It does not address, nor does any part of this wide-ranging study address, a historical account of oral storytelling in our own or in less familiar cultures. However, in addressing the here and now of contemporary oral storytelling, and in particular the working practices, social roles and complex network interactions of this emergent social and cultural phenomenon, it seems appropriate to take one further detour on our journey. It does not address the recording of historical events, their causes and their consequences, but rather some aspects of the infinitely complex processes which provide the raw materials of history.

Ernst Gombrich, whom we met in the last chapter, was a close associate of the philosopher-logician Karl Popper, best known for his contribution to the philosophy of science in *The Logic of Scientific Discovery* and to political philosophy in *The Open Society and its Enemies*. In the late 1980s Channel 4 Television issued me with a challenge: try and persuade Popper to come in front of my television cameras with an accessible summary of his life's work. On the face of it this was mission impossible. Popper was already in his late-80s, increasingly deaf and unwell, had never owned a television set and had bluntly dismissed all previous approaches by other programme-makers. I nearly abandoned all hope when his publisher addressed me at length in Latin. But thanks to Popper's ever-loyal assistant Melitta Mew a meeting was arranged when Popper greeted me with the words, 'they all want to film me before I die'. As protracted negotiations edged uneasily forward (top tip: never attempt to negotiate a legal contract with a philosopher-logician) he suffered three transient ischaemic attacks (minor strokes). Notwithstanding these early rites of passage, a three-part television series titled *Uncertain Truth*[11] was successfully completed and network broadcast in 1989.

The first programme takes the form of a debate between Popper and Gombrich which opened with a withering assault on deterministic theories which hold that history is somehow preordained by the spirit of its age. Evidence from history itself, they argue, shows us how such theories lead to populist ideologies and totalitarian states. Instead they propose an indeterministic theory in which history is driven by the collective will of society as a whole. As Popper says, 'Anything that happens: a bad night – not only of a very important and influential man, but of anybody – is part of the historical process.' For example in ancient Greece the advent of 'literacy had its consequences: Athens established a democracy, courts of justice and a place where people met and made decisions about war and peace. There are quite a number of examples of such historical explanations which explain things, of course only conjecturally, which at first seem almost inexplicable.'

Popper and Gombrich accept this more open-ended, emergent interpretation of history is psychologically counterintuitive because we all instinctively long for the shelter of the tribal certainties and simple doctrines and dogmas of a closed society. Instead they propose an interpretation of the historical process that looks to Popper's trial and error experimental method referred to in the last chapter. As Popper at his most impish puts it: 'One can say that from the amoeba to Einstein there is only one step: both learn by trial and error and the elimination of error. The main difference is that Einstein is intensely self-critical [EXTENDED THEATRICAL PAUSE] which the amoeba is not.'

He proposes instead that it is by the same process that society as a whole can acquire the mastery of all human competences: 'We obtain knowledge up to a certain level, and starting on this new level we have a new starting point and so on.' The importance of continuity in this collective learning process is raised at this point of the debate because history warns us of the consequences of trying to revert to an age and a time of natural innocence. As Popper adds: 'I have often formulated it by saying, if we start from Adam, start all afresh, wipe out everything, it leads only to the results which Adam achieved.' This more open-ended, indeterministic view of the historical process leads to Popper's concluding statement of this debate.

> It is impossible for anybody who has any interest in history, not to see that our world, the world in which we now live in the Western countries, is really the best and most beautiful world which has so far existed. About the future we know nothing, but that it is open, that it is not predetermined and that it will depend on our own efforts whether it is better or worse than it is now. It is we who are really making the future.

Much evidence gathered for this study on the working practices of individual storytellers and the collective social and cultural behaviours of storytelling participants seems to support this more open-ended, indeterministic vision of history and the historical progress. It seems a fitting conclusion to this book that two intellectual titans of our age should propose such a humanistic theory that makes the individual, quite literally, the driver of the historical process.

Postscript

My journey is done. I have come home. The final interview was held in March 2011. My diary/log records 249 storytelling-related entries. All these have been followed up, researched, analysed and now form the central narrative of this study. No way of encapsulating this experience occurs to me. Paradoxes still lurk at every pass and every crossroads on our route. Emergent processes tread hidden pathways to unknown, perhaps unknowable, destinations. Indistinct waymarks hint suggestively at future lines of more focused enquiry. The thrill of this journey has been the exploration of a human landscape that was completely unknown to me. For this I thank all those who have accompanied and sustained me.

Notes & References

1. Joseph Daniel Sobol, *The Storytellers' Journey: An American Revival* (Urbana USA: University of Illinois Press, 1999), pp. 224-26.

2. *Storytellers' Journey*, p. 88.

3. Simon Heywood, *The New Storytelling* (Society for Storytelling UK, Papyrus Series No.2, 1998).

4. Donald Smith, *Storytelling Scotland: A Nation in Narrative* (Edinburgh UK: Polygon, Edinburgh University Press, 2001).

5. Patrick Ryan, *Storytelling in Ireland: A Re-awakening* (Derry/Londonderry UK: Verbal Arts Centre, 1995).

6. Jacob Bronowski, *The Origins of Knowledge and Imagination* (New Haven USA: Yale University Press, 1978), p. 117.

7. *New Storytelling*, pp. 7-17.

8. Jane Mulkerrins, 'Dance Nation', *The Times*, London UK, 12 January 2010, section Times 2, p. 4.

9. Maureen James, 'What can investment in narrative contribute to museum education? (unpublished master's thesis, Institute of Education, London UK, 2002), p. 20.

10. From the board, 'Now is the time to get involved', *Storylines*, Society for Storytelling UK, Spring 2012, p. 3.

11. *Uncertain Truth*, director/producer: Michael Howes (Channel Four Television Company, 1989). Quotations from Popper are from the unpublished transcripts of these programmes.